The Jagged Years
of Ruthie J.

Chestnut Lodge, Rockville, Maryland

The Jagged Years of Ruthie J.

Ruth Simkin

Ekstasis Editions

Published in 2010 by:
Ekstasis Editions Canada Ltd.
Box 8474, Main Postal Outlet
Victoria, B.C. V8W 3S1

Ekstasis Editions
Box 571
Banff, Alberta T1L 1E3

LIBRARY AND ARCHIVES CANADA CATALOGUING IN PUBLICATION

Simkin, Ruth, 1944-
    The jagged years of Ruthie J / Ruth Simkin.

ISBN 978-1-897430-54-5

    1. Simkin, Ruth, 1944-. 2. Psychotherapy patients--Abuse
of--Maryland. 3. Psychotherapy patients--Canada--Biography.
4. Epileptics--Canada--Biography. 5. Physicians--Canada--
Biography. I. Title.

RC464.S55A3 2010   610.92   C2010-901108-2

Canada Council   Conseil des Arts
for the Arts   du Canada

BRITISH COLUMBIA
ARTS COUNCIL
Supported by the Province of British Columbia

Canadian   Patrimoine
Heritage   canadien

The Jagged Years of Ruthie J has been published with the assistance of grants from the Canada Council for the Arts and the British Columbia Arts Council administered by the Cultural Services Branch of British Columbia. We also acknowledge the financial support of the government of Canada through the Book Publishing Industry Development Program (BPIDP) for our publishing activities.

Printed and bound in Canada.

This book is dedicated to

My parents

Jean and Blackie Simkin

Who gave me life

And

Dr. Frances Brennecke

Who taught me how to live it

Authors Note

Memory is a tricky matter. This memoir is my recollection of events to the best of my ability to recall them accurately. Some characters are composites, some names have been fictionalized, many not. It has never been my intention to cause any discomfort to people I write about. However, I recognize that events are remembered differently by those who live them. This is my story.

Chapter One

Winnipeg, Manitoba; August 1963

"Get the hell out of my car!" The two guys in the back looked at each other.

"I said get the hell out of my car!" I turned and screamed at them.

The slamming of the back door synchronized with the sound of screeching tires as the car lurched out of the parking lot.

"What the hell did you do that for?" Massey faced me. "Those guys were the best dates we had in a long time. Our date lasted all of three seconds. You ruined everything." The tone in Massey's voice changed from annoyance to fear. "Ruthie J., why are you driving like this?"

"I am trying to kill us," I calmly answered, speeding on. I had no idea what I was doing or why. I assumed I would figure it all out later.

Massey sat in stiffened silence, petrified. A moan came from her lips as we turned the wrong way onto a one-way street and began to pick up speed. Suddenly, there was a loud crash, windows and cars shattering, and screams filled the air.

In slow motion, shards of sharp glass wafted down upon us and the car. Everything was snail-paced until I opened the car door. I bounded out of the car, leaving a stunned and confused Massey examining her knee.

"Well for Christ's sake, Massey, we hit Zeke! Imagine our luck, half a million people in the city and we smash into Zeke! Hi Zeke, how's it going?"

Zeke eased out of his car, blood pouring down his face. Massey limped up to him.

"Oh my God, Ruthie J., what have you done?"

I noticed it didn't take very long for 'you know who' to get here. Massey was sitting in what was left of the car, crying. Zeke was moaning, pools of his blood accumulating on the concrete. Massey watched the blood drip, horror on her face. To me the red seemed a pretty colour one could use for finger-painting. I was bouncing around, trying to cheer everyone up. Massey and Zeke were really getting to be a drag. They couldn't understand why I wanted to play. I, on the other hand, could not understand why I was acting this way.

"Hi cop," I flicked the visor on his cap down over his eyes.

"Guess what, street," I shouted, "I hit Zeke! What a coincidence! To know the guy you hit!"

"Get your friend to shut up," a stocky policeman ordered Massey.

Massey walked over to me and pulled me off the street. "Ruthie J., we're in so much trouble already, please, what's happened to you? Why are you acting like this?"

I shrugged my shoulders and watched the street – hopping from one leg onto the other, then back again. How could I begin to explain that I had no idea what was happening; that my behaviour confused me as much as anyone else. It was coming from my head and body, but I had no way to control or censor anything, as if on automatic pilot – a grotesque automatic. A flicker of fright passed through me.

"I wrecked the car, didn't I, Mass? But you're okay, eh? I mean, look at that car – the front fender is almost touching the steering wheel. Heh, heh. Do you believe in miracles, Mass?" I continued jumping from one leg to the other.

"Whose car is the Pontiac?" bellowed the stocky policeman. His tall partner stayed with Zeke, preparing him for the ambulance.

"What's it to you, twirpy?" I jumped, one foot to the other, one foot, the other, my eyes alert, my head looking around and around. It seemed almost like I was watching the entire scene from up above, or someplace removed.

"Is this her car?" he faced Massey.

Massey gulped, nodded her head, and tried to hold me still.

"Open the trunk," he ordered.

"Ruthie J., they need to open the trunk."

"So? I don't have the stupid keys. Look in the car, dopey!" I spit out.

I was fascinated by my own behaviour – I had never acted like this before. It was like watching an unbelievable movie and I could hardly believe what was emanating from me. I couldn't understand where it was coming from, but chose not to think about it at that moment.

The stocky police officer was definitely getting riled. First, he opened the trunk of my car. There, in the back, was half a case of Jordan's Crackling Rosé wine.

"Ach, you drunk kids," he muttered.

"I beg your pardon, sir?" I lurched up to him, "but I am not in-eeb-re-ated." I said this very slowly and it had the desired effect of further angering the officer.

He sneered at me. Making a sign of utter distaste, with scrinched eyes and pursed lips, he stuck a gloved hand through the passenger window to unlock the glove compartment. He pulled out my boda, the light tan wineskin that my friend Susan had given me as a present the year before. Trimmed with a red and yellow braided string, if it was not in my glove compartment it was over my shoulder where I often uncorked the lid and took deep swigs of the Rosé wine with which I kept it full. I loved the feel of the soft leather combined with the pungent taste of the cheap wine.

The policeman looked at my boda, holding it at arm's length as though it were contaminated with the most virulent of pathogens. Really, it just contained my emergency supply of Jordan's Crackling Rose. I loved this boda; it came everywhere with me.

"Massey, the bugger's into our emergency supply. Theft! Theft!" I could not believe that hollering was coming from my mouth. I resumed my hopping, while somewhere in the back of my head, part of me again puzzled over my behaviour.

"How much did she drink?" he asked Massey.

"Nothing," Massey answered. "I've been with her since seven o'clock tonight and all she's had to drink is Coke."

"You mean to tell me that from seven o'clock tonight until one o'clock in the morning, this pissed friend of yours has only drunk Coca Cola?"

Massey gulped and nodded.

"Well, you must be drunk too then." The officer dismissed her and went to attend to the newly arrived police cars and ambulance.

Massey whispered, "Ruthie J., what is going on? Why are you acting like this? What's happening?"

"Massey, you know I'm not drunk, don't you? That idiot thinks I'm drunk. Well, I'm not, am I, Massey?"

Massey nodded and rubbed her sore knee.

The ambulance left, carrying Zeke on a stretcher, head wrapped in bloody bandages. Both the stocky and tall police officers approached the two of us. Massey was swallowing hard and trying to hold me down, while I was happily hopping away.

"We're going to have to take you down to the station for booking," the tall policeman said. "You're both drunk." Massey's head turned quickly towards the officer, tears squeezing from her eyes and travelling down a freckled path on her ashen face.

"Fine." I agreed. "We can't go anywhere in that wreck anyway."

I looked over at the pink and charcoal 1960 Pontiac sedan. This car was really my mom's and Auntie Fan's car. People were always amazed at how two sisters-in-law, who lived beside each other, could actually share a vehicle successfully, but share it successfully they definitely did. The car first arrived in Winnipeg in 1960. At the time it was one of the first cars in the city to have electric windows, ordered to accommodate my aunt's severe arthritis. About two weeks after the car had arrived, my mother was stopped by a police car. A careful driver, she couldn't understand why she had been pulled over.

"What's the problem, officer?" she asked anxiously.

"Nothing at all, ma'am. I just heard about this car. It's the one with the electric power windows, right? I wondered," he cleared his throat and lowered his eyes, "if you would mind showing me how they work?"

My mom happily obliged and after he'd tried the windows a good while, the officer left and she continued on her way.

Now, not even four years later, the two-toned Pontiac looked like a modernistic pink and charcoal metal sculpture of a, of a, well, of a car crash. I felt more than a little sad about that. I liked that car, but even more importantly, so did my mother and my aunt. Their sharing the car symbolized the ease of their whole relationship; indeed, that of my whole family. Everyone seemed to get along, to share things and to enjoy each other. And now, for reasons that were still completely unclear to me, I had added them to the growing list of people I had aggrieved this evening.

The two officers secured us with handcuffs, which made me burst out laughing, much to their dismay. They locked Massey and me in the back seat of the police car, then went around to the front and started driving to the station.

"Vroom, vroom, hey, speed it up there, will ya? Old MacDonald had a farm, ee ay ee ay oh! Vroom! Vroom!"

"Keep it down back there."

"Oh yeah, what're you going to do about it? Vroom, Vroom!"

"Well," I said to Massey on the way down to the main station, "I've always wanted to experience everything, so now I can cross being handcuffed off the list."

Massey soothed my hand, then my face. "Shh, Ruthie J. Shhh. We're in so much trouble already. Shhh."

I looked over at Massey, my poor basketball buddy – always somehow managing to get into trouble through no fault of her own. We had played on the same University of Manitoba basketball team for three years now, travelling across Western Canada in the process. My best friend Susan and I were always pulling pranks and Massey always seemed to get caught for them. Now, in the glow of flashing red police lights, seeing her pale freckled face, straw blonde hair askew, thick glasses far down her nose, I thought – poor Massey, in trouble again, and just *wanting to go home and go to bed. Now she was going to be booked for under-age drinking in a public place, which would get her into severe trouble with her strict parents. I sat quietly until we arrived at the police station, thinking about the police and their archaic laws (to my way of thinking) and of Massey's parents, who would be upset with her and especially angry at me, for once more leading their daughter astray.*

Entering the building, I decided I would act like a lady. I sashayed through the door, slid into a chair beside a desk, crossed my legs, placed my hands in my lap, smiled reassuringly at Massey and very softly asked the befuddled officer, "Now then, sir, what can I do for you this evening?"

"We would like some information."

"Why surely, sir, whatever you request."

"Name?"

"Ruthie J. Simkin."

"Address?"

"5 Seven Oaks Place."

"Age?"

"Nineteen."

The entire form was filled out in this polite manner, me smiling sweetly after each question and answer. It really was an intriguing movie I was watching. I still didn't get what was happening.

I cocked my head and asked, "If you would be so kind, sir, what are the charges against me?"

"Driving the wrong way down a one-way street."

I nodded.

"Illegal possession of liquor."

I nodded.

"Drunk driving."

"Drunk driving!" I exploded. "Are you crazy?? I was not drinking! How dare you accuse me of that!"

I jumped up onto the desktop. "You assholes, you just try to lay it on us! I was not drinking!" I screeched. Somewhere in the back of my head came the realization that I was now acting a little crazy. I continued to watch from the ceiling.

"Dumb cops," I muttered as I jumped from desk to desk, scattering papers and books all around. "Ha, ha, you can't catch me."

The two officers tried to catch me, but had to run around the desks while I merely leapt from one to another. I knocked over the stapler from one desk, the telephone off another, while the police knocked over chairs in their clumsy chase. It

11

reminded me of when I was twelve and we had moved into our new house. There was a circular path between the dining room, kitchen, family room, hall and back to the dining room. When my parents tried to catch me I would just run in circles, them following. Mostly we would dissolve in laughter at the absurdity of it all.

Massey sat in a corner with her mouth open, following the action. I reached the cloak rack, put a police hat on my head and then slipped on a police jacket, its sleeves coming well below my fingertips. I waved my arms, flinging the sleeves in the air. Fascinated with the sleeves, I stopped to watch them dangle and the officers finally caught me.

By now, I was starting to come down – I didn't know from what – and was confused and frightened. I wondered what had become of Massey. Led through the station between Mr. Tall and Mr. Stocky, as I had christened them, I was un-hand-cuffed and shoved roughly into a large room. Eight policemen sat at desks, drinking coffee.

"Well, well, and what have we here?"

"Another drunken kid," Mr. Stocky replied. I gritted my teeth.

A policewoman came up to me and began examining me.

"Hey, what are you doing?"

"Take it easy, kid, just frisking you," she replied as her hands started to get more personal.

"Can you please stop it?" I asked politely and more than a little urgently. I was terrified she would reveal my most hidden secret to the world. No one knew, and I didn't want anyone finding out now. I would die of mortification if they knew.

The policemen all began hooting. "What's the matter, kid, you modest?" laughed one.

"Hey, Jane," another officer called, "frisk her up good."

"What's the matter, kid, this bother you?" sneered another.

I whispered to Jane, "Could we please go somewhere private?" If I had to reveal the secret, at least I wanted to do it in private with just one woman, not in front of a hostile collection of male cops.

Jane just continued amidst the hoots and laughter.

Once again, I asked, this time quite desperately, "Please stop." My voice caught as a tear slid down my throat.

Jane undid my belt and was unzipping my jeans and laughing.

She had now unbuttoned my shirt, and was getting ready to stick her hand in my bra. My heart was pounding, my mouth was dry. Tears blurred my vision and the hoots and laughter of the men pounded in my ears.

I took her hands in mine. "Please," I begged softly, "can't we just go somewhere privately?"

"What's the matter, kid, too much for you? Don't get drunk next time."

"Hey kid, how do you like being frisked?"

"Hey Jane, do a real good job on her."

I knew that I could not allow this to happen. My dignity couldn't survive this. I didn't want to hurt anyone, but I could not bear the derisive scoffing of the police if my secret was revealed to them.

I looked at Jane, shrugged my shoulders, pulled back my arm and bopped her right in the face. Jane flew over a chair, bounced off a desk towards the policemen and was caught just as she and the floor were about to make contact. Then all hell broke loose.

Within seconds, they had my belt whipped off, and my shoes and jacket were thrown on the floor. My arms felt as if they would break as they were pinned high up behind my back – only released after I was thrown into a room four paces by four paces, which I very quickly realized was a prison cell.

Clank! Clunk! Oh shit, here I am. What have I gotten myself into now?

Milking the situation for all it was worth, I huddled in a corner, knees pulled up to my chin. Wasn't that the way jailbirds did it? I looked around at the four grey concrete walls, the almost invisible door set into one side. A single naked light bulb hung about fifteen feet in the air and one small drain gurgled in the corner.

Tears filled my eyes as I realized I hadn't peed for a long time and would have to deal with the drain.

I wanted my parents. I was beginning to feel very upset and lonely. I wondered what happened to Massey.

After several hours, the door opened and a policeman stuck his head in.

"It's past four a.m. – is there anyone you would like to send a message to?"

"Go to hell!"

"Are you sure there is no one who might be worried about you?"

"I said, go to hell!"

"Okay. Suit yourself."

Clang. Clunk. The tears started flowing down my face. What had I done? What was going on anyway? I sat and quietly sobbed. I was too young to be locked up in prison, alone. Though my tough girl image was more or less working for the police, I was really a very scared little girl – acting in ways incomprehensible even to myself. I wanted my parents to come and hold me. But I knew that if by some miracle they did appear, they would not hold me. They would most certainly disapprove of everything I had done.

But I was still their little girl and I really needed my parents' arms around me right now.

Chapter Two

Memories of those events months ago faded in my mind as I was jolted back to reality when Mrs. Jackley, my constant guard, awoke with a start and almost fell off her chair. Her ample body, covered in nurses' whites, spilled precariously over the seat of a wooden chair. Gathering the covers around me, I turned towards the wall as my warder in white made herself comfortable again. It took me a minute or two to remember where I was. I had not even been here for twenty-four hours yet. Where was I? I remembered arriving on the ward just this morning. Oh yeah, I was a patient at Chestnut Lodge, a mental hospital in Rockville, Maryland, USA.

The elevator door had closed with a clunk in front of me, criss-crossing bars locking me into it along with a strange woman in white. We jerked to a sudden stop on the fourth floor, both of us bending our knees and shuffling our feet to stay upright. Mrs. Lohmer, the Head Nurse of Main Four, had been called down to the business offices to come to get me, the new patient. She smiled at my parents as the doctor suggested that I go get adjusted to my new home while they completed the paperwork.

"I'll take her right along now up to the ward to settle in," she drawled. "You two can come up once't you are all finished with Dr. Tatelman."

In the elevator, Mrs. Lohmer pushed aside the bars, and leaned against the heavy door. It opened on to a large sunroom.

"This room is like the 'living room' of the ward," she drawled in a heavy

Southern accent. "Our patients sit here, play cards, listen to music or just socialize. We're very proud of it."

I looked around the spacious, bright room, filled with windows. At the far end of the room, a card table with four chairs stood in front of a large record player. Two ratty mustard yellow sofas leaned against opposing walls. Three brown and orange patterned armchairs were scattered about and a wooden rocking chair creaked beside a small table. It looked pleasant enough. Around the corner was an alcove, its folding door pushed open. Inside a long, dark brown, wooden conference table and chairs filled all available space.

"Come right on down here now, I'll show you around," said Mrs. Lohmer. Her Southern accent intrigued me. "This here's the kitchen," she said, indicating a small room right beside the elevator. "You can make tea or coffee here or have juice, and there is bread for toast. You can use it whenever you like. And over here," she said, pointing to the room beside it, "is the nursing office."

I looked through the glass window. The room was narrow and enclosed. The glass window could be slid open only from the inside. The windows of the far wall had solid steel bars through which the trees outside could be seen. Two long walls were lined with locked cupboards. Under the sliding window was a built-in desk, covered with papers and a telephone. Behind it stood a trolley full of blue charts. A mouse of a woman bustled about, moving things from one side of the counter to the other. Like Mrs. Lohmer, she also wore a nurse's uniform, complete with matching hat. "Hmm," I thought after watching her for a few seconds, "that uniform is going to help me tell who's on whose side around here."

"Mrs. Jackson," called out Mrs. Lohmer, "come meet the new girl."

The tiny Mrs. Jackson mouse-walked out to the hall, cocking her head and twitching her upper lip. My gut did not like her one bit.

"This is Ruthie, our new patient. Ruthie is from Canada and will be staying with us for a while."

Mrs. Jackson nodded her head and stared at me.

A sharp, squeaky voice from across the hall interrupted Mrs. Jackson's stare. "I'm not left here. I tell you, I'm not *left* here. Don't believe anything they tell you. I'm not left here, you know."

On my right, standing behind the closed bottom half of a Dutch door, was an elderly woman, yelling and shaking her finger, "IIIIIII'mmmmmm not left here." She had white hair and a sweet face, not unlike a small beaver.

"Now, Miz Swarts," crooned Mrs. Lohmer, "don't frighten the new girl. This is Ruthie, from Canada."

"From Canada, you say?" Mrs. Schwartz inclined her head and her jowls flapped. "Oh, oh, oh, an important girl." She grasped Mrs. Lohmer's arm across her barrier, and pulled her closer to whisper conspiratorially, "Mrs. Lohmer, who is it? A new one? Who is this?"

"She's a new patient, Miz Swarts. Her name is Ruthie."

"Ah," nodded Mrs. Schwartz. She studied me carefully, then started howling again, "I'm not left here. Nooooo, I'm not *left* here. Only crazy people are left here." Mrs. Jackson went into the room with Mrs. Schwartz, led her over to a chair and began to speak quietly to her.

I was delighted with Mrs. Lohmer's pronunciation of Mrs. Schwartz' name: 'Miz Swarts'. I had rarely heard true Southern accents before and found Mrs. Lohmer's musical intonation very pleasing to my ear, as well as somewhat humourous.

"This is the hall, obviously," laughed Mrs. Lohmer, as our tour continued down a long hall. "Over here on the left are the bathrooms and the showers. And all down the hall are patients' rooms, except for the TV room, over here," she said, leading me into a small room with a TV in one corner. Behind it was a second, even smaller room filled with chairs.

"You're getting the last bed. We're full up after you."

"Well, where is everybody?" I asked, gesturing to the empty ward.

"Oh, they're all off having lunch or out on the grounds. You'll meet them soon enough. Your room is the last on the right. You'll be sharing with Lenore. I'm sure you girls will get along right fine." She ushered me into a double room with two beds, two dressers, a chair and a closet. I looked at the bars on the window and the large trees waving their leaves tauntingly on the other side of them.

"You can leave your things here."

"I don't really have very much," I said, pointing to my square blue Samsonite overnight bag. I only packed for a few days."

"I'm sure you'll get your things soon enough. Come to the kitchen and we'll see if we can rustle you up some lunch."

As we started down the hall, a slight woman whom I judged to be in her thirties came towards us. Blonde curls fell about her ashen face and her clothing was as disheveled as her hair. She walked slowly, thin hands up in front of her, gesticulating in the air. She walked right up to us, but seemed oblivious.

"Oh Quentin," she sighed in a low voice, "fuck me, Quentin, fuck me now." A deep maniacal laugh issued forth from her beautiful, angelic face.

"Now Janie," Mrs. Lohmer remonstrated, "no language like that."

Janie laughed again, another deeply deranged laugh, and carried right on down the hall, "Oh Quentin, fuck me, Quentin. Aaaaaahhhh."

"Don't let her bother you," said Mrs. Lohmer. "She's like that part of the time, but not always. She can be a very nice girl." We walked into the little kitchen with "I'm not left here, oh no, I'm not *left* here," following us into the room.

By four o'clock that afternoon, I had met many of the patients of Main Four. I did not want to be with any of them. Janie carried on about Quentin. Mrs. Kane, a short woman in her fifties with drab brown hair cut straight across at the neck, sat on a bench in the hall, relentlessly swinging her right leg up and back under a flowered print dress. She didn't speak. Mrs. Schwartz kept up her harangue. I met Mrs. Richmond, who was Mrs. Schwartz' roommate. In her eighties, she was all propped up in a chair with pillows. She didn't talk at all, but smiled a lot and moved her hands in the air. I liked her the best.

Max seemed to be an okay man – a balding, absent-minded professor type in a tweed jacket. Looking me over, he asked, "Do you play bridge?"

"I play a little," I answered, "but I would really like to learn how to play well."

Max grinned, clearly pleased with my answer. I was about to sit down to talk when one of the aides took me aside.

"Listen, you need to watch it. Max has a tendency to be violent," the aide explained and abruptly left the room, leaving the two of us alone. I quickly found an excuse to go to my room. I still had not met Lenore, my roommate.

"What did I get myself into?" I wondered, sitting down on my bed. I was frightened. Perhaps this whole venture was a very bad mistake. I needed to get out. Would I be able to do that?

Seated on the big, yellow-patterned armchair, I studied the bars on the windows of my room. I felt numb. I sat there without moving for about an hour, replaying the last few days that had taken me from being a fourth-year student at the University of Manitoba in Winnipeg to being a mental patient in a hospital called Chestnut Lodge in Rockville, Maryland. I remembered how just last week my mom told me we were going to Kansas.

Winnipeg, Manitoba; December 1963

"Kansas! Mom, why?"

"Because that is where the Menninger Clinic is, and they have agreed to see you there and give us a second opinion."

"A second opinion? What for?"

"Because they say you have epilepsy and we want to know more about that."

"But mom, I have a good doctor here. I'm fine."

"I know dear, but your father and I really want a second opinion."

"How long will we be gone?"

"We leave next Thursday evening, two days after New Year's Eve. Our appointment with the doctor is Friday and Saturday if necessary. We'll come back Saturday night."

"Okay mom. If you really think that this is needed." I was feeling guilty, because I had managed to cancel two of the last four appointments with Dr. Doupe. It was the Christmas holidays and I was feeling pressure from Dr. Doupe and also from Donna and Locky. I didn't know how much to talk about or to whom.

On Thursday, I kissed Locky and Donna goodbye and said I'd see them in two days. I went home to pack my overnight bag with a change of underwear, toothpaste and a copy of Vonnegut's Cat's Cradle, and went off with my parents to Kansas.

In the 1960's epilepsy was considered the worst kind of mental illness. I understood my parents' concern, although I did not share it. I knew I was not mentally ill. Now that I had a diagnosis of epilepsy, I hoped I could get some treatment and get better – which meant to me, to stop acting in ways I did not understand. I was pleased with my Winnipeg doctor. But my parents were not. They so did not want the diagnosis to be true that they were willing to traipse all over to find someone to negate it, this slur upon the family name. Epilepsy.

Topeka, Kansas; January 1964

Kansas was a big blur. Menninger's Clinic was a large sprawling place of low white buildings. There were lawn chairs on the grass even though it was winter, and people were out and about. Friday morning, my parents and I reported in, and I talked at length to an elderly woman psychiatrist who was very tiny and seemed highly intelligent. I liked her. She spoke with a heavy German accent and seemed caring and relatively harmless, so I told her about living with Locky, about doing some hooking with Donna, about going to university, about fighting with my dad and all the machinations of my Winnipeg life. Then she spoke alone to my parents for a long time as I waited outside her office on a white wicker chair. I couldn't imagine what they had to say that would exclude me and I became angry that they would keep secrets from me. Soon Dr. German-accent called me in.

"I have just been telling your parents about our little talk," she informed me.

Strike one. Actually, strike two, too, because I did not think it was so little.

"I feel it would be very bad for you to go back to Winnipeg at this time."

Strike three.

"We (when did we switch to 'we'?) feel you should receive help with your problems, but we do not have a bed available here. There is a very good hospital in Maryland. Would you consider going?"

Strike four.

"Of course, doctor, she'll do whatever you advise," answered my dad.

"Is that so, Ruthie?"

"Yes, doctor, whatever is best for her."

"But dad, I don't want to go away. I want to go back home. Besides, what has this got to do with epilepsy?"

"It will only be for a short time, and then you can come home," my mom offered.

Dr. German-accent jumped in, "It will give the doctors a chance to study your epilepsy. And you can deal with some of the psychological problems we spoke about."

We did? Psychological problems? Wait a minute, now. We talked. I talked. I said what I felt. I didn't think I had psychological problems.

"Ruthie, we think it would be a good idea." My dad looked sad but resolved.

"Good," said Dr. German-accent. She picked up the phone and asked for long distance to Maryland.

"Martin? Hello, Martin, how are you? Oh, good. Listen Martin, I have a young woman and her parents here from Canada. She needs a bed and we don't have one. How are you fixed over there? Uh huh. Oh good. Okay, then, I'll send them over to you. Her name is…"

Wait a minute. My mind was racing. What is happening? I am going to Maryland? I don't even know where Maryland is! In what seemed far off in the distance, I could hear my parents and Dr. German-accent making the arrangements. I sat there, wondering what Locky would say. I was going to miss him. Well, okay, Ruth, think of it as another experience. Maybe it will be interesting. Maybe I will be able to get some insight into some of my problems. After all, I am in fourth year university, studying psychology. It couldn't hurt me to go to a mental institution for a short while. Think of it as an elective. I'll be back before midterms, and move into Locky's and graduate from school, and live happily ever after.

"Okay," I concurred. "I'm ready to go to Maryland."

Dulles Airport, Virginia; Rockville, Maryland; January, 1964

We landed that night at Dulles Airport in Virginia. I thought we got on the wrong plane. I still didn't know where Maryland was exactly. I knew the name of the hospital to which I was going – Chestnut Lodge. That name made me laugh. It was ludicrous. We had hotel reservations near the hospital and an appointment with Dr. Martin Tatelman the next morning.

As we pulled off the freeway and drove along a smaller road lined with enormous trees, the cab driver jerked his head to his right and said, "See that place over there? It's a resort for rich nuts." He laughed.

"Oh really," I smiled, "what's it called?"

"Chestnut Lodge. Yep, Chestnut Lodge."

I burst out laughing. I felt my mother, sitting beside me, cringe. My dad, sitting in the front seat, straightened himself up and cleared his throat.

"A resort for rich nuts," I chuckled. I peered down the long driveway lined with large, leafy trees, past the ominous metal gate, seeing nothing but blackness. "That's funny."

The next morning, our cab drove down the long driveway and pulled up around the circular drive in front of a large white house. Behind it, or attached, I couldn't quite tell, was an imposing red brick building, four stories high. To the right, on the grounds, was a broad expanse of green and trees, and some other low white buildings off in the distance. So this was Maryland.

Chapter Three

Rockville, Maryland; January 1964

The three of us walked up the stairs to the big white house. Inside the door to the right was a receptionist behind a glass window. My dad gave her our names as I wandered to the left into a sitting room. It was old and refined with doilies on the arms of the sofas, straight-backed chairs and a fireplace that looked as if it was never used. My mom and dad came in and sat down with me. In a few minutes a woman came to get us. We followed her down a long, dark hall with doors, all of them closed, dotting the hall. At the end of the corridor, we turned left to the offices. I noticed on the right there was an elevator with a lock in front of a steel door with bars on it. It struck me as being a very strange elevator. I was beginning to feel this might be an interesting adventure.

We walked through a section of medical offices and were ushered into Dr. Tatelman's office.

"Come in, come in," motioned Dr. Tatelman. I liked him at once. Of medium height, with glasses and thin sandy hair combed over to the side, he had a twinkle in his eye and a friendly expression. I felt comfortable with him, as if he could be one of my relatives, like my Uncle Abe, smiling, warm, intelligent and loving.

We spent all morning in his office, it seemed, though I don't really remember much beyond his warm office and his laughing eyes. I remember my parents talking with him. My body was there, but I seemed to have left. It was decided that I would stay, though he carefully explained it would cost at least $2,000 a month. This was indeed a resort for rich nuts. He made sure to tell my parents, while I was there, that I would likely beg them to take me home, but if they really loved me and *cared about me, they would leave me there to finish therapy. It would be difficult for us all. He suggested my parents go away for a few days to let me settle in, and come back to see me before returning to Canada. So my parents went off to New York for a few days, and I went off to Main Four with Mrs. Lohmer.*

She wore a starchy white uniform and a matching hat with a pouf of lace on the top. That frivolous pouf of lace on her brown curly hair made me smile. It was so not Mrs. Lohmer, who was a no-nonsense get down to business nurse. The head nurse on Main Four, she was kind and considerate, but a strict follower of rules. Leading me to an elevator, she turned a key and the elevator clunked to our level. Pushing back a steel grill, Mrs. Lohmer nodded me in. She then put the key in a panel in the elevator, the gate of steel bars clanked closed and we lifted off to the fourth floor. I remember looking up at her and thinking how tall, overbearing and overpowering she was.

It amused me when I remembered how, when she was showing me around the ward an hour ago, I had realized that Mrs. Lohmer was actually a tiny snippet of a woman, barely five feet and probably not one hundred pounds.

Suddenly, walking into my memories and the room was a young woman. She was wearing a plaid skirt and a white short-sleeved shirt, with long brown hair falling soft and straight down her back to the waist. Her right arm was badly scarred and deformed.

"Hi, you must be the new patient, Ruthie. I'm Lenore, your roommate."

"Hi, Lenore. Have you been here long?"

"Oh, a few years, but in and out. I lived in Rockville, that's the little town, but then had to come back." She plopped down on her bed and smiled at me. I liked her at once.

"Lenore, you seem so normal. There sure are some weird people around here."

"Yeah, this is Main Four, where the sickest patients go. Normally, people like you and me would go to Hilltop, the house at the other end of the grounds, but these were the only beds left, I guess. I hear the hospital is now full up."

"So tell me about this place."

"Well, let's see. This building is Main and there are three wards in it – Main Two, which is all women; Main Three, which is all men, most of them violent and Main Four, which is for the real sickies. Then there's Upper Cottage and Lower Cottage. They are sort of open wards, but lots of the people there are totally out of it. That's where most of the manic-depressives live. And there's Hilltop, where most of the young people are. And we are on the most famous ward, you know. It's the ward written about in the book *I Never Promised You a Rose Garden.* The doctor in that book was really Dr. Freda Fromm-Reichman, who worked here for ages. There was also another movie made about this place – "Lillith" with Warren Beatty. The whole crew was filming in town just this past year. And sometimes famous people come to stay here. It's very expensive and I guess they are also pretty exclusive and keep quiet about their patients."

"How did you end up here on this ward?"

"Same as you I guess, shortage of beds anywhere else."

"What do you do all day?"

"On Monday there is the ward meeting. That's when Dr. Stepford, the administrator, comes up and we all meet in the sunroom and talk for a while. Then he goes into the TV room with Mrs. Lohmer and sees each patient alone for a few minutes. That's when you get to ask for privileges."

"Privileges?"

"Yeah, like walking on the grounds escorted or unescorted, town privileges, you know, things like that."

"What kind of privileges do you have?"

"Oh, now I have unescorted grounds. That means I can go out alone when I want, but I have to stay on the grounds."

"Hmmm. I wonder what kind I have?"

"You probably don't have any yet, until you see your therapist. Do you know who you have yet?"

"Gee, Lenore, no one's told me anything."

"Well, you'll find out soon enough. Do you want to come downstairs to eat?"

"Sure, I'm hungry."

We walked over to the nursing office. Lenore asked Mrs. Decker, a mountain of a woman, in white, if I could go to the cafeteria for dinner. Mrs. Decker nodded, but insisted, "She needs an escort. No one here now. You'll have to wait." It was clear Mrs. Decker was not overly loquacious.

Lenore and I walked into the sitting room to wait for someone to take us down to the dining room.

"Mrs. Decker is a pretty nice person," Lenore explained. "She's the charge nurse on evenings. She has a sister who works here too – Mrs. Jackley. I think she's on tonight as well. They sure look alike, those two."

I thought about not one, but two large, silent mountains, who were now in charge of my fate. Lenore and I chatted about the hospital for another fifteen minutes until a small, lean man with thick wavy jet-black hair came up to us.

"Come on, ladies," he said in a heavy Puerto Rican accent, "chow time."

"Hey, Jorge," Lenore pointed to me, "meet Ruthie."

"*Mucho gusto*," answered Jorge. He put the key in the elevator door and it swung open for us.

"Thanks for waiting for me, Lenore."

"Well, we roomies have to stick together," she smiled.

"What did you say his name was?"

"Jorge. It's pronounced 'Hor-hay.' He's Puerto-Rican."

"Okay, thanks," I practised under my breath, "Jor-ge, Jor-ge."

I followed Lenore through the dining room, filling my tray as she did and walking behind her to a table.

"Hey George," she said to a young man sitting and rocking at the table. I sat down beside Lenore and totally forgot about my food. George sat across from us, rocking vigorously up and back on his chair, his fork in his hand with the prongs up. He had a sweet, angelic face framed by beautiful, slate black curls. He was muttering phrases I didn't quite understand as he rocked and rocked.

"George lives on Main Three. He is autistic," Lenore explained. "He won't hurt you. Sometimes the others tease him and he throws things, but I like to sit with him." Lenore then started to cut George's food, encouraging him to eat.

"Here, George, take some meat."

"Meat." Rock. "Some." Rock. "Meat." Rock. "Some." Rock. "Meat." Rock. "Some."

George smiled at me. I smiled back and gulped.

I looked down at my tray. "Hey Lenore, what's this?" I indicated the brown flat pieces of thin somethings surrounded by mashed potatoes.

"Those are pork chops," she grinned. "Can't you recognize pork chops?"

"Can't say as I've ever seen them before," I grinned back.

"What? How could you not know pork chops, Ruthie?"

"I'm Jewish," I explained. "I grew up in a kosher home because my grand-mothers lived with us. Do you know what that means?"

Lenore shrugged her shoulders.

"Well, no pork. Pork is not allowed in the house. This is my first time see-ing pork chops."

"Really? Not allowed in the house at all?" Lenore shook her head.

I looked down at the overcooked slab of brown leather and ground my knife through it, cutting off a small piece which I gingerly placed in my mouth.

"Well?" asked Lenore who had been following my every movement, "what do you think? Do you like it?"

The piece of pork stuck in my throat. Besides being a forbidden food, it tasted exactly as I imagined a piece of burnt leather might. "Not really," I responded. "It seems pretty overcooked."

"Yeah, but I'm hungry," Lenore dug in and bit off large pieces of pork chop, licking her lips as the pork-cum-leather slipped down her throat. My piece remained undisturbed, after that first cut.

"So this is the first time you've ever had non-kosher food?" she queried.

"Oh no, we eat Chinese food and spare ribs – they're not kosher – but we just don't eat them at home or at least not on our dishes. You see, we have plates for milk stuff and plates for meat stuff and we're not supposed to mix them up."

"Really? Why not?" Lenore seemed genuinely interested.

"Cause the Bible says you shouldn't cook a lamb in its mother's milk or something like that. So we have our milk dishes and meat dishes and paper plates for anything else."

"Is that legal?" Lenore asked.

"No, of course not. It's just a way of getting around a rule some Jews don't really want to follow. But see, both my grandmothers are really religious kosher, so we have to respect them and keep all the dishes just right. Once I wanted a cheeseburger and I put cheese and the hamburger on a meat plate and my grandmother flipped out. She was so upset, she broke the plate and threw it in the garbage."

"No way!" Lenore's eyes opened wide in surprise.

"Yeah, really. Just because a little bit of cheese touched a meat plate. I sort of felt badly that I hurt her, but I like cheeseburgers! The worst thing I ever did in terms of kosher was about five years ago on Yom Kippur. It's the holiest day of the year and you are supposed to fast all day and atone for all your sins. I was pissed off at my folks and wanted to do the worst thing I could think of, so I broke the fast with a ham sandwich, definitely not kosher, and washed it down with a glass a milk, mixing the two forbidden things, meat and milk."

Lenore and I both burst out laughing at the silliness of it all. Our laughter was interrupted by a loud disturbance two tables away.

"I'm not eating this shit!" I heard, as a tray banged against the table. A very tall man stood up and three male orderlies rushed to grab him. He easily dislodged them and started banging on the table. Bells went off and suddenly ten people descended upon him and carried him, screaming, from the room.

"That's Big John," explained Lenore. "He's from Main Three. He can be very violent. But he's a brilliant pianist, plays only Grieg."

"Hi, Lenore, who's your friend?"

A short, fat man resembling an oversized peach sat down across from me and began appraising me through and over his glasses. His dull brown hair, parted limply to the left side, hung over his forehead, obstructing the large brown eyeglasses.

"Hi, Ambrose, this is Ruthie. Ruthie, Ambrose. She is the new patient on Main Four."

"Well, welcome to our little home," Ambrose chuckled. "Lenore is my best friend, you know. We go back a long way, don't we, Lenore?"

"Yes, Ambrose, we sure do."

"Say, John was quite upset, wasn't he? Probably in a cold pack right now. Yep, a nice cold pack."

"What's a cold pack?" I asked.

"What's a cold pack?" Ambrose mimicked. "You'll see for yourself soon enough. When they want to keep you down, they keep sheets in a cooler on ice and put the sheets on your bed, throw you on them and wrap you up so tight you can't move. You have to lie on the freezing sheets for two to three hours, all tied up. The more you struggle, the tighter they get. But don't worry, the sheets turn warm. It's supposed to have a calming effect," Ambrose chuckled. He then looked over at Lenore's plate, which was empty and at my plate, which was relatively untouched except for a few missing blobs of mashed potatoes. "Hey, can I have your meat?" Ambrose asked.

"Knock yourself out," I pushed the plate towards him. The peach smiled. The peach emptied the plate.

Jorge came over. "Okay, that's enough, time to go up now."

"See you soon, Lenore. Nice meeting you, Ruthie." Ambrose waddled away. Lenore and I slowly followed Jorge into the elevator.

I went back to my room. Lenore had gone out. People were sitting in the sunroom, but I needed to be alone to absorb the experiences of the day. After just a few minutes, a large woman in white walked into the room, carrying a small chair. Her sensible shoes were polished white and her white stockings bagged at the ankles. Her grey hair was pulled back into a bun at the nape of her neck, little wisps doing far better at escaping the situation than I. Setting the chair in the middle of the room, and slowly sighing, she lowered her prodigious self heavily into it and looked over at me.

"Can I help you?" I asked.

She laughed. "I'm Mrs. Jackley. Being a new patient and all, you are on observation and I need to watch you." Watch me she did. I sat in my chair; she sat in her chair. When I got up to go to the bathroom, she followed me. Instructing me not to fully close the curtain, she stood outside the bathroom until I was done. I walked to the sunroom and she walked to the sunroom. I sat down on the sofa, she sat down on the sofa. Starting to freak out and feeling more than a little trapped, I tried to concentrate on the bridge game happening in the sunroom. Two women and two men were playing. One of the men was Max and one of the women was Janie.

I was introduced to the other two by Max. "Uh, here comes the new girl. This is Matt and Betty. Two spades."

Matt was an extremely handsome middle-aged man, with beautiful white hair, horn-rimmed glasses and a pipe sticking out of his mouth. He appeared very distinguished. He smiled at me. "Howdy. Welcome to our little home."

Betty asked, "What was your name again? I'm Betty. I live in Upper Cottage. Where did you come from? Pass."

I liked Betty immediately. She was also middle-aged, round and soft with blonde hair and a beautiful smile.

"Uh, Ruthie, and I'm from Canada."

"Oh, Canada, you've come a long way then," said Matt. "If there is anything I can do to help, just let me know. Three spades."

"Janie, your bid. Come on now, be a good girl. Sit down and bid." Max was getting exasperated. Janie, on the other hand, had begun to talk with Quentin, and was laughing in a very deep voice.

"Janie," Matt said firmly, "sit down and play."

"Yes, Matt," she answered in a little girl's voice. "Four clubs." Then she folded her cards up, put them down in front of her, got up and began slowly moving her arms in the air. She clearly was not involved in the bridge game.

"Hey, girlie, did you say you play bridge?" bellowed Max.

"Uh, just a little. I'm not very good," I answered.

"Well, do you want to play?"

"Not tonight, thank you very much."

"Max, leave her alone," chastised Betty. "She just got here. You take it easy, honey. It takes a while to get used to this place."

I agreed. "I'm feeling a little tired now. Goodnight everyone."

I walked back to my room with the white shadow right behind me. The nurse stared at me as I unpacked my nightgown and followed me to the sink when I went to brush my teeth. She followed me into the toilet. She followed me right back down to my room. As I got into bed, feeling overwhelmed and terrified, I heard her sigh as she sat her prodigious weight down on the chair in the middle of the room to stare at me while I tried to sleep.

Instead of sleeping, I thought about my situation now and remembered where I was a week ago with Locky and Donna. In the darkness, tears slid down my cheeks. I heard Mrs. Jackley begin to snore and tried to remember the very beginning of what was now, not an adventure, but a nightmare.

Chapter Four

Rockville, Maryland; January 1964

The sun's rays, shining through the bars and glinting off Glass, clutched tight against my chest, was the first thing to hit my eyes the next morning. I looked around to find myself alone in the room. I could hear footsteps down the corridor, the shower running in the bathroom and voices in the hallway.

Lenore was not there, but her clothes across the bed told me she had come and gone. I got up and checked Glass, still clenched in my hand. I brought Glass with me from the hospital in Winnipeg. It was my small, plastic glass with "Made in Canada" stamped on the bottom. Glass was my friend. Last night, I snuck it from my bag and cuddled up with it in bed. It was the only familiar object I had. I always found it easier to relate to inanimate objects – they didn't hurt me. Glass was an entity to whom I could pour out all my love and fears and whom, I was sure, as much as one could be sure about such things, would never hurt or betray me. I gently placed Glass on the dresser, put on my housecoat and walked out the door. As soon as I left the room, a tall and extremely thin, young black man jumped up from a chair outside the doorway.

"Good morning," he smiled. "I am Hector," a West Indian accented voice informed me. "I am your watchdog today." He grinned.

"Do you have to watchdog me while I have a shower?" I asked.

"No," he smiled, "when you are ready for a shower, we will have one of the ladies watchdog you. Come now, get washed up and dressed. You have to see the doctor this morning."

"Oh, who is my doctor? Do you know?"

28

Hector smiled again while he put his hand on my back and gently pushed me towards the bathroom.

Ten minutes later, Hector ushered me to the doorway of the TV room. I never did understand why it was called the TV room, as it was mainly used for small meetings and people rarely watched the small TV which sat apart in a corner.

"Hello, Miss Simkin. How do you do? My name is Dr. Stepford." A portly gentleman held a pudgy hand out to me. He was tall, with sandy hair parted on the right and neatly combed. His dark blue suit looked elegantly out of place on Main Four. A blue patterned tie lay meticulously over a starched white shirt. Out of his smiling mouth, a Southern drawl declared warmly, "Welcome to Main Four."

Mrs. Lohmer was at his side. "Dr. Stepford is our administrator," she explained. "We normally meet with him on Mondays, but since you missed him yesterday, he came up to see you today."

"We hope you will abide by the rules here, Miss Simkin. We feel sure we can help you. This is an excellent hospital.

"Come into the TV room for a few minutes." Dr. Stepford led the way and Mrs. Lohmer brought up the rear as the three of us marched into the small room. He sat down in an armchair and indicated I sit in the chair beside him.

"How are you doing here? Is everything going well for you so far?"

"Oh, she's settling in real nice, real nice," said Mrs. Lohmer.

"Do you have everything you need?"

"Oh, her parents are bringing her some clothes after the weekend," Mrs. Lohmer responded.

I realized with an internal smile that I had yet to participate in this conversation.

"They tell me you're a university student," Dr. Stepford stated. He raised his eyebrows and looked steadily at me. I decided to be a part of this interview.

"Yes sir, I'm in fourth year university and due to graduate in the spring, so I think I'd better be going home soon so I don't miss too much school." It was worth a try.

"Well, we'll try to get you home just as soon as we can. In the meantime, you will be starting psychotherapy. We expect you to attend all scheduled appointments. That is the reason for your stay here. We also expect you to attend all ward meetings. Is that understood?"

"Yes sir."

"Good. For now, you are on observation until your therapist has a chance to assess you. Then we will see what your privileges are. You have an appointment to see your therapist later this afternoon. Do you have any questions?"

I nodded. "Do you have any idea how long I will have to be here?"

"No, I don't. Not at the present time. I wouldn't hold out any hope of finishing school this semester, however." With that, he put his hands on his knees, pushed himself up with a small grunt and strode towards the nursing office, Mrs. Lohmer always one step behind him, clipboard at the ready.

I couldn't figure out why he would say that. Was he trying to frighten me or let me know that he was indeed the boss around here? Of course I would be home before the end of semester. Anything else was truly unthinkable. I wandered into the hall – Hector, as always, within arm's reach of me. I knew now why it was called arm-to-arm specialing.

Still puzzled by Dr. Stepford's remark, I walked into the sunroom and almost bumped into Matt.

"Oh hi," he removed his pipe from his mouth. "How're you doing? Settling in okay?"

I shrugged my shoulders and looked over at Hector with a frown.

Matt put his hand on my arm and led me over to the sofa. Hector followed.

"Now then," he puffed on his pipe, "don't let this place get you down. There are some amazing people here. You can learn things."

So far I hadn't been too impressed.

"Take Max, for instance," Matt offered.

"Oh yes, he's dangerous, right?"

"No, he gets a little riled up now and then, but I wouldn't worry about him. Now he is a well-known mathematician, you know. When he first came here, the army was in trouble and had spent six months trying to solve a problem. Then, in desperation, the Pentagon sent someone here to see Max." Matt puffed on his pipe, pausing for effect. "Max solved the problem over the weekend. So now they bring him math problems all the time." He puffed away.

"Hey, great. How long have you been here?"

"Oh, about six months. I'll be going home soon, back to my medical practice." He smiled at me.

"You a doctor?"

"Sure am. A psychiatrist. Have a busy practice too." He puffed away. "I used to do cardiology, but then I switched to psychiatry. I know a lot about the physical heart and the human soul, but I developed some problems of my own." He puffed on his pipe slowly, then knocked its bowl into an ashtray, dislodging the embers.

"I got very depressed," he explained. I'm sure he was leaving out some details because I didn't think one would be locked up here for depression. Yet he didn't have a shadow trailing him and he seemed to have full privileges. He came and went as he pleased and when he was around, the sunroom looked like a comfy porch with Matt filling his corncob pipe. A comfy porch, though only until the hallucinatory Janie arrived or Max stomped in screaming in paranoia that "they" were going to kill him or Mrs. Schwartz yelled for all to hear that she was not left here.

I looked at Matt carefully. He seemed perfectly normal. Dressed in a clean, pressed blue and white striped shirt and a pale blue cardigan over neat navy corduroys, he was casually fashionable. His lush white mane was one of the most attractive heads of hair I'd ever seen. He spoke appropriately. Yet there was something almost sinister about him – like a beautiful poisonous snake slithering across the floor, circling his prey. I couldn't quite put my finger on it, but I knew I could never trust him.

Mrs. Lohmer brought a breakfast tray into the room and set it down on the table. Hector pulled out a chair for me and sat down in another to watch me eat the watered-down porridge and cold, burnt toast.

After my breakfast with Hector, I sat in the sunroom trying to contain my panic. I heard keys and locks and crying. I heard Mrs. Schwartz yelling, "Nooo, I'm not left here. *I'm* not left here." I walked into her room and sat down besides Mrs. Richmond. Mrs. Richmond smiled. I smiled back. She lifted her hands up and slowly rotated them. I lifted my hands up and slowly rotated them. Then she smiled. Then I smiled. And only ninety seconds had passed.

I slipped into a rocking chair and began to rock in silence. I smiled to think that while my friends were into rock and roll, I was into rock and remember.

Winnipeg, Manitoba; August 1963

About eight-thirty the next morning, the door to the prison cell opened. Two police-men entered and handed me my shoes to put on, then silently and roughly picked me up. Dragging me between them, we walked down long hollow corridors, up an elevator and into a bustling room.

"Massey! Where were you?"

"Oh, they kept me in the big cell, with about thirty other women." Massey winked. "All night long, I had them all yelling, 'Ruthie J., Ruthie J.' Even the men's lock-up was yelling for you. Didn't you hear us? Are you okay? What did they do to you?"

A haze came over my eyes, and engulfed by anger, I put my head down and butted a very official looking man in the chest.

"You had no right to keep Massey!" I screamed. "She didn't do anything wrong."

The butted man flew backwards against an open window and almost disappeared through it.

I picked up a jacket and started flinging it about, snapping it on chairs, on desks, and in his face.

"Who is this youngster?" he asked as he pulled the jacket out of my hands while four policemen helped me sit on a chair.

"Ruthie," Massey whispered, "that's the commissioner. He's trying to help us."

"Well, he had no right to keep you, Massey."

I looked around the room. Ten, I counted; ten women, apart from me and Massey, sat on benches waiting – for something. Massey pulled up a chair beside me and put her hand on my shoulder. The four policemen eased away. I sat straight, my eyes darting around the room, feeling very agitated. Off of this large room were three tiny offices, big enough only for a desk with a chair on either side of it.

"Donna Taggart."

A slight, attractive looking woman with brown, wavy hair looked around, got up and disappeared into one of the offices.

"Rosa Nicky."

I looked around the room.

"Is Rosa Nicky here?"

"Ya cop, I'm here."

"Would you step this way please?"

Rosa Nicky stood up, a sneer almost covering her face. She slowly made her way to the officer, put her right hand on her hip, hiked her short, dark, very tight green skirt up even shorter, looked him up and down twice, shrugged her shoulders, and slid into the office. The police officer rolled his eyes, raised his eyebrows and stepped in, closing the door after them.

"Margaret Dobbin."

Massey and I exchanged puzzled glances as Massey started to walk toward the office.

I sat in the chair, my right arm slung over the back of it, my legs straight out ahead of me, set apart from the other women who were coming and going.

"Ruth Simkin."

I turned around quickly. Behind me, in front of an office, stood a short policeman, looking about the room. I leisurely pushed off the chair, and turned around to face him, a mixture of annoyance and scowl on my face, the best I could do to buoy up my own courage.

"This way please." He held the door open for me. I entered the office and sat down as he closed the door.

"So, Ruth Simkin?" A question, but I took defiant position No. 2 and stared at

the leg on the desk.

"You are charged with illegal possession of alcohol, are you aware of that?"

More attention was paid to the desk leg.

"You seem to have a problem with alcohol, is that so?"

"Look," *I quickly slapped both palms on top of the desk as I partly stood,* "I was not drinking!" *I then resumed defiant position No. 2 and refused to speak or answer any more questions.*

"Wait outside." *The officer was annoyed.*

I quickly opened the door and sulked into the waiting room.

Not long after that I heard, "Ruth Simkin."

I looked to my left to see a smiling, young officer holding another office door open for me. He had dark black, curly hair and I thought he was extremely good-looking, his well-built body accenting his handsome face. I went in and sat down.

"Hello Ruth. I am Officer McCharles. Ruth, do you know what VD is?"

The question took me by surprise. I quickly jerked my head up and sneered.

"Have you ever been tested for VD?" *the dashing Officer McCharles continued.*

"Ruth, I have to stress the importance of this. We have doctors here who will gladly check you. Or if you want to wait a week or two, go to this place to be checked." *He handed me a slip of paper.*

In the 60's, VD was the bad boy of sexual promiscuity. No one had ever heard of AIDS – it simply didn't exist – and the expression STDs was not yet used.

I slipped out before Officer McCharles noticed my tears. Soon Massey joined me and all twelve of us women were marched into the elevator.

"They thought I was a whore," *I turned to Massey.*

"Naw, the girls say this is routine for everyone, Ruthie."

We marched past the men's lock-up. The sound of heels on the concrete signaled the men before we reached the cell area and I heard catcalls shouted at us.

In an effort to cheer me, Massey yelled, "Hey fellas, Ruthie J.'s back with us."

"It's Ruthie J., Ruthie J." *the men chanted.*

"Yep, here I am fellows, it's Ruthie J. herself." *I was starting to perk up.* "How've you been guys, you miss me?" *I left the scared little girl in the interrogation room and became a leader of rebels once more.*

"Ruthie J., Ruthie J.," *they laughed.*

More hollow corridors lined with chipped green paint followed, with many more turns on concrete floors, before we arrived at a large cell with about twenty other women locked inside. The matron opened the door and shoved us, not very gently, into the crowded space.

"Are you Ruthie J.?" *a young woman came up to me.* "Massey had everyone calling for you all night."

"Yep, I'm Ruthie J. Thank you all for calling for me." *I swaggered into the cell like a conquering hero.*

"Hey, how come you call your friend Massey?"

"Yeah, what kind of a name is that?" asked another woman.

"Well," I drawled, "once our basketball team was on the road and we were eating and I wanted to say 'Margie, pass the milk please' but instead by mistake I said 'Massey, parg the milk please' and she's been Massey ever since." There were scattered chuckles. I was enjoying the attention.

"Okay, breakfast," the matron called out as she wheeled up a cart. She was short and stocky, her brown hair streaked with grey. She wore a white, dirty uniform, somewhat akin to a nurse, but there was no TLC emanating from her being whatsoever.

"Jesus, I'm hungry, Mass, are you?"

Massey nodded. "But Ruthie, let's try to get out of here, okay?"

I hung onto the bars awaiting my turn.

"Coffee?" was spit out at me.

"Yes, please, black," I answered.

The matron laughed and poured me a mug of coffee. It had cream and sugar in it. All the coffee had cream and sugar in it.

"Here." I was handed a bowl with a gruel-like grey substance in it and a piece of soggy toast on top. I sat down in a corner and looked around. There were eight bunk beds in the room. I counted twenty-nine women. On one side of the room, against the wall, were three toilets, in the open, with only low partitions between them and one sink off to the side. The women were eating and chatting and smoking, three or more sitting on a bed and a few, like myself, sitting on the floor.

"Hey, Ruthie J.," called a young blonde woman sitting beside the attractive woman I remembered as Donna. "Come over here and tell us what you did to get solitary."

I looked around and stood up. I walked over and crawled onto the lower bunk with the young woman and Donna, lit a cigarette and groaned.

"What's the matter?" Donna asked.

"Oh, my head is really starting to hurt." I rubbed my head, feeling the large bump that had come up during the night. "I think I got a concussion from the car accident last night."

The blonde woman whose name was Fran went up to the bars. "Hey, matron. Matron! Get your ass over here. We have an injury. Matron!"

The matron looked through the bars.

"It's Ruthie J. She bashed her head good last night. Look at the bump!"

The matron looked at me rubbing my head. "Oh, you're the kid that smashed Jane, eh? Suffer, kid." She turned and walked away.

"Hey Fran, find another seat. Come here, Ruthie J." Donna sat at one end of the bed. "Lie down here, put your head on my lap. I'll fix it for you."

I lay down on the bed, feeling the exhaustion of the past two days wash over me. Donna began to massage my head ever so gently. The rest of the room disappeared.

"What're you in for?" I asked.

"Fran and I escaped from the psych ward at the hospital. A cab driver turned us in."

"You ever been in jail before?"

"No," Donna answered, "have you?"

I shook my head which was beginning to feel much better. I just wanted to burrow into Donna and be held and comforted. Not a large woman, Donna seemed frail and vulnerable, with a gaunt, pale face and sunken cheeks that made her look somewhat sickly. Still, through it all, I felt such a warmth from this woman, a warmth that was new but not at all unpleasant to me. I felt she really liked me and somehow that made me feel not only safe, but incredibly strong.

"Don't worry, Donna. I'll take care of you here. Looks like there's some pretty rough women around."

Donna smiled and continued stroking my hair, then my face. For a long while she soothed my head, while I rested and was comforted.

In the meantime, Fran had been going around to everyone in the cell, talking it up. Every once in a while, someone would get called out, and Fran would shout out after the echoing foot steps down the corridor, "Don't you forget now."

"Donna Taggart. Frances Wilson." The big iron gate swung open.

"At last. That's us, kid." Donna lifted my head up and swung off the bed. "Quick, kid, want to send a message to anyone? Hurry it up."

"Uh, yeah, tell my friend Patty where we are – here." I quickly scribbled down a number on the paper Donna held out to me.

"Okay kid, see ya." Donna bent over and softly caressed my cheek, then bounded out of the cell. I was uneasy and felt lonely inside. I had truly been comforted by this woman.

"Bye, everyone," Fran waved as she followed Donna down the hall.

Massey came over to sit beside me on the bunk. For a long time, we sat there smoking heavily, speaking minimally.

"Hey, gimme those matches please, Massey."

"Shit, we better get out of here soon or we'll run out of cigarettes."

"Lunch," called the matron.

More coffee with cream and sugar. Stale bologna sandwiches. That was it.

Well, I thought, cross jail meals off my list of 'always wanted to experience.'

"Margaret Dobbin and Ruth Simkin."

"Ooh," I jumped up. "Are we discharged?"

"No," sneered the matron, "just some visitors."

"Visitors? You're kidding." Massey and I hopped off the bunk and ran to the door. We were led, yet again, through corridors to an open door.

"Three minutes, you understand? That's all you get," we were told.

Massey and I looked about. There were six enclosed desks, each with a chair, and presumably a chair on the other side. I went to the first chair and looked through the screen separating the two sides. There was Carol, pointing to her sister, saying, "Patty's next door."

I sat down across from Patty, while Massey slid in across from Carol.

"Well," Patty asked, "what did you want? Some girl named Donna called and said you were here, but she wouldn't say anything else. There must be quite a story to this one." Patty chuckled. "Do your parents know yet?"

I shook my head in the negative.

"So how come you wanted us to come down?" Patty asked. "Your bail is set at fifty thousand dollars. There's no way we can get you out."

"Fifty thousand dollars! My God, what did I do?" I winced.

"You mean you don't know?" asked Patty incredulously.

"Three minutes are up."

"Bye Ruth, see you around," smiled Patty as she got up and walked off.

I turned just in time to see Massey waving to Carol.

"What'd she tell you?" I asked.

"Later," replied Massey as we fell in line to march back to the lock-up.

Back in the cell, Massey explained, "They really set your bail high. Apparently, they want to keep you. You have a lot of charges against you. Mine's pretty low. Carol was going to call my parents…"

"Your parents! Jesus Christ, Mass!"

"Well Ruthie, I got to get out of here. I have classes tomorrow. So do you, for that matter."

"I'm not telling my parents," I sulked. "They can bloody well find out for themselves."

An hour and a half passed and the matron again approached the gate.

"Margaret Dobbin."

"Here I go, Ruthie. Are you sure I can't call your parents?"

"Yes, I'm sure. Let them worry," I spat out.

"Well, what are you going to do?"

"Stay here, I guess. Gimme your cigarettes – you can buy more. Thanks. Bye, Mass."

I stretched out on the bottom bunk and turned my face to the wall. I felt Massey touch my shoulder and then she was gone.

My head was really beginning to hurt, just over my right eye. I felt tears welling up in my eyes, surely from the pain in my head as I lay listening to Massey's retreating footsteps.

I lay there for a long time, stretched out facing the concrete wall. I became very aware of my senses – the smell of the dusty mattress, the stale cigarette smoke, the cold of the concrete, the soft chattering of the women, the occasional flush of a toilet. I dozed, tumbling in and out of consciousness, never waking up enough to question my environs.

"Ruth Simkin."

I was startled up to a sitting position, bumping my head against the upper bunk.

"Shit," I rubbed my head and looked up at the cell door.

"Simkin. You're busted out. Get up here."

I turned around to face the cell's occupants. I gave a half wave, grinned a sickly grin, turned around and walked out of the cell.

"Who's here?" I asked the matron as we traversed the corridors once more.

"How should I know? That's not my job."

Jesus, I thought, these matrons must have to pass mean school to work here. That thought cheered me up a bit and I felt an added spring enter my saunter. I could feel a slight smile on my lips when we passed though a door into a cavernous room.

I left the spring and the smile in the doorway. There, in front of a large counter, were my parents. I stopped short and stared at the point where floor met counter while my father concluded the arrangements. He spoke softly to the officer behind the counter, something that was very unusual for him. My father was a large man, over six feet tall, well over two hundred pounds, well-muscled from physical work and sports, crowned by a head of thick, black hair – yet somehow, in this room, he seemed much smaller. He wore his brown overcoat, which was unbuttoned showing brown slacks and shirt. Beside him was my mother, also looking very small. She was only six inches shorter than my dad, but now she looked tiny. Her light blue overcoat was also unbuttoned. I wanted to run over to them and button their coats and cover them up. They shouldn't be here. It was as if they were deflated – all life and air gone. They both seemed so vulnerable I felt I needed to protect them. I wanted to rush to them, to run into their arms. But something inside me prevented that and I stood up straight, tall and defiant. I didn't understand why I was so angry at them – for it was I who got us all here in the first place. I pushed away any tears welling up inside, squared my shoulders and waited in the doorway.

When my father was done, my parents came up on either side of me and, without a word or a touch, the three of us left the police station. Both of them seemed so tired I could feel their exhaustion enter my own body. I wished we could touch, *and could not understand why we didn't. But I knew I would never make the first move.*

Crossing the street, I looked at my mother on my right and my father on my left. Looking straight ahead, I muttered, "This is the best one yet, eh?"

There was no response. We all got into the front seat of my father's dark blue Buick, with me in the middle.

"How did you find me?"

My mother answered in a tired monotone, "When you didn't come home last night, we started to worry. This morning, when none of your friends knew where you were, we called all the hospitals and police stations until we found you."

I heard the pain, the worry and fatigue, the entire sleepless night in the voice of my mother, who stared straight ahead at nothing. I saw my dad's hands gripped so tightly on the steering wheel they were white. His unusual silence roared in my ears.

Only then could I understand, ever so slightly, just how badly I had frightened and hurt my parents.

Chapter Five

Rockville, Maryland; January 1964

At lunch, no aide was available to take me to the dining room so the kitchen sent up a tray. Mrs. Lohmer set it on the table in the sunroom and I sat in front of it, but hardly ate. I wasn't very hungry. About a quarter to three, a black man who looked like a football linebacker, with muscles bulging under the sleeves of a yellow polo shirt, came up out of the elevator. I was still sitting in front of the untouched tray.

"Who's the new girl?" he bellowed. "I've come for the new girl." He walked over to the office. "Howdy girls. How are all of you lovely ladies today? Where is the new one? I've come to take her to her therapy."

Mrs. Lohmer came over to me. "Ruthie, this is Alvin. He is going to take you to see your therapist now. He will pick you up and bring you back here when you're finished."

"Come on, little lady. We have a walk ahead of us," said Alvin as he turned to Mrs. Lohmer and smiled.

"So," Alvin asked as I inhaled the first fresh air to hit my lungs in several days, "what are you in for?"

"In for?" I echoed.

"Yeah. In for. What did you do?"

"Do? I didn't do anything." I was genuinely puzzled.

"Suit yourself," said Alvin. We walked along a tree-lined road which curved gently to the left revealing a long, low building over on the right. Horizontal slats of wood showed peeling white paint even from a distance. Around the building were bushes and small trees, with wooden benches interspersed among them. It looked like a warm, welcoming place, unlike the looming four-story brick building in which I was housed.

"This here's the Center," said Alvin, pointing to the building. "It's where they have activities – arts and crafts, movies, dances, things like that." Outside a group of young people about my age stood talking. "That there group is the gang from Hilltop. Don't rightly know why you didn't go there. It's where the young'uns go. No beds, I guess. You're on a doozy of a ward, you know."

"I noticed," I commented as Alvin kept up with his tour.

"And this here over on the left is the Kiosk," Alvin continued, pointing to a small, square yellow building in a field of grass. "That's where you can buy cigarettes, candy and the like. There's a juke box in there too. You'll like going over there when you have privileges." Beside a sliding door were picnic tables and benches and a few people seated with pop bottles in front of them.

We walked about half a mile on a blacktop road until we came to a small brick building. "Your doctor is in here. I'll be waiting for you. Don't leave without me."

Alvin walked down a hall with many doors, knocked on the one which had a name plate announcing 'Dr. Evanson' and stood tapping his foot until the door opened.

A man in his late thirties sporting a brown crew cut opened the door. He was tall and slight and wore a dark blue suit over a white shirt with a knit tie, loosely knotted around his neck. He glanced at me, turned to Alvin and said, "Alvin, wait outside, will you? We never know how it will be with these new patients." I thought he was kind of creepy.

"Sure doc. I'll be right out here. Just holler if you need me." Alvin leaned back against the wall outside the room.

"Come in." He turned to me, and with his arm, indicated a chair across from his desk. I dutifully sat down in it. He walked around to the other side of the desk, and started to shuffle some papers in front of him.

"Name?"

"I beg your pardon?"

"What is your name?" He asked this slowly, articulating very carefully. I thought it very strange that he would ask me this question; surely he knew the name of his new patient. But I wanted to be cooperative and tried to be as pleasant as possible.

"Ruthie Simkin."

"How old are you?"

"I'm nineteen; I'll be twenty in March."

"Good. Where are you from?"

"Uh, Canada. Winnipeg, Manitoba."

He wrote this down. Then he shuffled his papers some more. His dull brown eyes flitted about the room and would not meet mine. They certainly lacked any of the warmth I had seen in Dr. Stepford.

"I understand that you have been having some problems." This he said as a statement.

"Well, I guess so. I'm here, so I suppose so."

"Don't get smart with me, young lady!" he snapped, slamming his papers down on his desk. This outburst took me by surprise. I didn't think I was being smart. I was scared – first just being in this hospital, but now even more, frightened of this strange man.

"Tell me about yourself. Where were you living before you came here?"

"Well, I was living with my friends, Locky, Donna and Curley. In Winnipeg. In a house."

"What do your friends do? Do they go to university?"

"No, actually, they are bootleggers."

"What do you mean, bootleggers?"

"Well, they sell alcohol after hours."

"Is that legal in Canada?"

"No, it isn't."

Dr. Evanson got up, walked to the door, opened it, nodded to Alvin, closed the door and sat down again behind his desk. I wondered if he was frightened of me, now that he knew I had criminal proclivities.

"I thought you were a university student," he challenged. He did not seem to believe anything I said. He glanced at me momentarily before his eyes quickly darted away.

"I am, at least I was, before I came here. I'm to graduate this spring with a BA."

"You're kidding. What are you studying?"

"Psychology," I mumbled, embarrassed that a psychology student would find herself in such a predicament. "And English and Philosophy as minors."

"Hmph." He sat straight up in his chair and squared off the scattered papers in front of him. He folded his thin hands and placed them on the desk, then turned his left hand to look at his watch. "Well, and now you're here. What do you think of the place?" His voice was quiet, calm, but had an undertone of threat. I tried to be as nice as possible so as not to upset him.

"Well, I would rather be home."

"Home with your bootlegging friends?"

"Yes, and with my family."

"But with your friends too?"

"Yes, they are my friends. I like them."

"Well, that settles that," he snapped curtly. "You are anti-social. We'll have to do something about you." He spoke calmly, an icy edge to his voice. I felt my skin crawl.

My heart started pounding quickly and I felt frightened. This was the person who was in charge of my immediate future. I was willing to try psychotherapy, but I didn't think this was it. This man was truly bizarre. I knew from previous experience and through studying psychology in university that this was not how good psychiatrists were supposed to behave. Could this be some sort of test the hospital had devised for me – to see how I reacted to craziness or something? Surely, they couldn't be serious about this man?

I looked around his office for clues. It looked normal enough, whatever that meant – a desk with papers and files, some photographs which faced him so I could only see the back of the frames, a low bookshelf not quite full and a few pleasant, pastoral paintings on the walls. Everything looked as I would expect, yet the words coming from this weird man did not belong in this picture.

"You have to cooperate with me, you know. I could have you locked up for life."

This remark so startled me that I automatically stood up. Why would he even want to do that? What had I done or said to make him say that? I stood rigidly fixed by my chair, terrified to say anything or even to move.

"Where are you going?" he yelled. "What are you doing? Alvin, Alvin, come here."

The door burst open and Alvin ran in to see me standing beside my chair, my arms down at my sides and Dr. Evanson sitting in his chair across the desk from me.

"What is it, doc? What is she doing?" Alvin grabbed my arms and pulled them tightly behind my back.

"Nothing, she's just acting out. Take her back, Alvin. That's all for today."

I couldn't understand what the problem was or why the doctor was so upset. It seemed as though this kind of situation kept repeating in my life. I remembered feeling like this often with my parents, not understanding what the problem really was.

Winnipeg, Manitoba; May 1957

"We're invited out for dinner tonight, kids. We're going to the Shores for dinner."

Great, I thought. I liked going to the Shores. They had two kids, one of whom was my age. They were good friends of my parents and everyone laughed a lot when we were together. I put on my best jeans, a clean and ironed shirt, combed my hair and presented myself at the appointed time.

"Ruthie, you are not going out for dinner like that!" my mother yelled at me.

"Like what?" I thought I had taken care to dress neatly and cleanly.

"You are not wearing pants for dinner. Go upstairs and put on a skirt right away."

"Mom, the Shores don't care if I have on pants or a skirt and I'm much more comfortable in pants. I hate wearing skirts!"

"I don't care what you like or don't like. I am not going out with you dressed like that! You are thirteen years old and no longer a child."

"Dear," my dad interjected, "let her come. She looks okay."

"No," my mother insisted, "if she wants to come with the rest of the family, she has to wear a skirt. I will not go out with my daughter dressed like that!"

"I'm not wearing a skirt to dinner!" I dug in.

"Then you are not going with us," my mother insisted.

"Fine. Then I won't go. I am not wearing a skirt when there is no reason to wear a skirt."

"You can stay home alone and cut off your nose to spite your face. The rest of us are going. Come on, kids."

They walked out the door.

I run upstairs to my parents' room to watch them from the window. My father had my baby brother Sam, not yet two, in his left arm while his right hand held onto my eight year old brother Jack. Jack's right hand clasped my mother's, whose other hand held onto my sister Judi, not quite three years younger than my thirteen years. The five of them formed a beautiful family unit; a stranger could not even tell I was missing. They all walked down the street the three blocks to the Shores' house.

Tears rolled down my face. I might have put on a skirt and run down to join them. I even liked my new plaid skirt with the big safety pin on the side. But I just couldn't. I could not understand how wearing a skirt would make me any more appropriate for having dinner at friends. It just didn't make sense to me. My tears soaked my clean blouse and I thought my heart would explode with pain. I loved my family and so wanted to be a part of them. Life just didn't make any sense.

Rockville, Maryland; January 1964

Back on the ward at Chestnut Lodge after the disturbing session with Dr. Evanson, I sat down in the sunroom. I really wanted to be in my room, but since I couldn't be alone anyway, I felt I had more space in the sunroom. I could hear Mrs. Schwartz crying, "Take me away. I'm not left here. Noooohohoho, not left here."

Janie wafted in and out of the room whispering to Quentin sotto voce.

Max was storming up and down the hall, his voice rising louder in anger with each word, "They're all trying to murder me, yes sirree. I know what they want, they want to murder me. Yes sirree, they do!"

Into the room walked a very tall, skinny woman with a large woven basket over her arm. She wore a heavy brown sweater with blue trim over a tweed skirt and white cotton blouse. Her gray hair was wrapped in a neat bun and her eyes were covered by thick glasses. On her legs were lisle stockings and brown oxfords with dark brown laces, evenly tied.

"How do you do. I am Margaret Bullard. What, may I ask, is your name, and who are you?"

"My name is Ruthie," I sighed. "I'm new here."

Margaret Bullard leaned over to me and whispered conspiratorially, "You have to watch them you know. Don't eat any food here. I carry all my own." She nodded toward her basket. "Don't believe them about anything," she continued, "they will only try to confuse you. Don't tell them anything."

I believed Margaret Bullard. Wise words were spoken by her. She then flipped up a small blanket and pulled a portable typewriter out of her basket, put it on the table and very efficiently, with considerable flair, put a piece of paper in the carriage and began typing.

I watched this tall, elderly woman with amused curiosity.

To my left sat Mrs. Jackley, her nurse's uniform straining the buttons at her ample bosom, wisps of grey hair escaping from her nurse's cap. Her scuffed white shoes sat flat on the floor while both hands were laid on her thighs. Every once in a while she would sigh deeply. She was my guard, the one who needed to be within arms reach of me every second of every day, at the bequest of Dr. Evanson. I was still on arm to arm special and after my appointment with him today, it did not look as though I would be released from this accompaniment any time soon. I thought of these guards as my shadows. I had only been here less than a week, but the presence of another person right beside me twenty-four hours a day was starting to get to me. I felt like an egg that they were trying to crack.

I sat listening to the clacking of Margaret's typewriter, the cacophony of

Mrs. Schwartz, Max and Janie and, not for the first time, felt tears come to my eyes. Then I felt them running down my face.

I rocked in the rocking chair I had chosen, not only because I liked rocking chairs, but because at least I had my own chair while the white shadow had to sit on the sofa. My parents were coming back from New York tomorrow and I knew I had to convince them to take me home. This was indeed a madhouse.

I rocked forward and back thinking about being alone in the midst of these people. I remembered how alone I felt at the trial – how alone I felt so often in my life.

Chapter Six

I went to the trial alone. I did not want my parents there and, to make sure of this, had not given them the trial date. I had decided not to use a lawyer to help ensure that my parents would not find out the details of my latest escapade. Massey showed up with her parents. I thought that was kind of wimpy. I sat alone in the back row through most of the docket, feeling confident and a little arrogant.

"Ruth J. Simkin."

"Ooh, that's me," I thought as I jumped up with a smile. "Good luck me."

"Ruth J. Simkin, raise your right hand. Do you solemnly swear to tell the truth, the whole truth and nothing but the truth, so help you God?"

Jesus, what an idiot this guy is, I thought. I could never figure out why they asked that question, since if someone was going to lie, they would obviously lie about telling the truth as well.

"I do," I said.

I turned to face Judge Dubienski.

"Your Honour, before we begin…"

I turned to my left. There was a tall, skinny, blond, mean-looking, vaguely familiar man. I couldn't quite place him.

"Your Honour, I had the pleasure…" he accented the word 'pleasure' to sound super-sarcastic, "I had the pleasure to prosecute this young lady in provincial court just last month…"

Oh shit, all of a sudden I remembered – the prosecuting attorney. I had never even told my parents about that one. I remembered with amusement the incident that got us caught. We were playing Judah Maccabee, *Bobby, Annie and me. We had to leave Annie's house very quickly because her mother was getting apoplectic. We threw our case of beer into the back seat of my open convertible and headed out to the university to sit beside the river and drink our beer in peace.*

As we were driving along, I was telling them about Judah Maccabee *and how he used to pick his men. To get into his army, a soldier had to gallop by on a horse and pull a tree up out of the ground as he was passing. And just then, there happened to be on the road those yellow conical road markers. Well, they were just right there. Bobby and I looked at each other and I began zigging and zagging in and out of the lanes while he leaned over the side of the car and heaved the pylons into the back seat. Yehaw! We're in* Judah Maccabee's *army! Yahoo! Thunk. Thunk. Bobby was a master; he missed very few until – oh shit – the cops! We were charged with theft of government property. Theft! I couldn't believe it. We were just playing. And, of course, we were charged with drinking in an unlicensed premise – my car. So it cost us ninety bucks each. And the very prosecutor who scared the shit out of me last month was back again in full force.*

"Last month, if I'm not mistaken, Miss Simkin was convicted of an offense involving alcohol. Your Honour, it is my opinion that this young lady has a serious drinking problem."

Filled with rage, I fought to hold the tears back. I could feel my face turning red as I stood and stared at Judge Dubienski.

"Is this true, Miss Simkin?"

"Yes, it is, your Honour, and we should throw the book at her," bellowed the blond bullock.

"Quiet, Mr. Answeg. Miss Simkin, do you have a drinking problem?"

How could I begin to talk? The courtroom was full. The interchange had already insured silence in the room as everyone focused on the little triad of drama. What could I do but stare? I felt I had already lost. I stared right into Judge Dubienski's eyes.

"Miss Simkin, can you tell us in your own words what happened the night of August 17, 1963?"

I could, I thought, but asshole over here wouldn't believe me; probably no one would believe me. So I just stared.

The judge asked again. More stares. Finally, he got a little exasperated. "Miss Simkin, you are a university student. Surely you can articulate!"

I could have won a staring contest. The blond bullock was stomping away in his corner, shuffling papers like a bull misplaces tufts of grass.

Bang! went the gavel. "This trial is postponed until the court can get some more information. Ruth J. Simkin, you are to be put in the custody of a probation officer." Bang again.

I was still staring as the bailiff led me away, out through the murmuring court-room into a small waiting room. "Wait here," he said, leaving and closing the door behind him.

I didn't even have time to get comfortable. A woman, about thirty, came in and said, "Hi. My name is Glenda. Judge Dubienski asked me to see you. Would you like to come into my office?" She led the way across the waiting room into her office.

I loved her office. It felt human. On one wall was a poster of a lake with weep-ing willows, the blues and greens and golds, contrasting with the marble and dark wood of the courtroom. The desk was piled high with books and files. Over a book-shelf was a small poster: "Out of chaos comes order – Nietzsche." Behind her chair was a cork bulletin board loaded with messages and jokes and cartoons.

Glenda had brown hair and laughing eyes. She looked intelligent, certainly a distinction from the rest of the people in the police and judicial system encountered so far, I thought.

I opened my mouth to say something flippant, but somehow Glenda's deep brown eyes made me take the situation seriously.

"You had some trouble in court today, I hear."

I waited. I still wasn't sure about the idea of having a probation officer.

"Would you like to tell me about it?"

"Look, I was not drinking."

"I believe you," Glenda said. "Tell me what happened."

"I was with Massey. We were at Patty's house, horsing around, watching TV. Patty's whole family was home. Massey and I had dates with these two bartenders. They didn't get off work until twelve-thirty. At twelve o'clock, we left Patty's and parked the car in the lot by the pub. We talked about what neat guys our dates were and about where we might go. The guys came out to the car. They got in the back. I don't know what happened. All of a sudden, I went crazy. I don't remember a lot of it, but Massey told me. I don't know why I acted the way I did. But I was not drunk."

With Glenda's face urging encouragement, and the weeping willows facing us, I felt a dam break.

"When I was twelve years old, I told my parents I thought I was crazy. I told them I needed help, that something was wrong with me. First, they took me to the family doctor. He told them there was nothing wrong with me. How the hell would he know?" I could hear the bitterness in my voice.

"Then in high school, I started fainting. They took me to another doctor. He spent an hour with my parents while I waited in the waiting room. Then he called me in and said, "All sixteen year old girls faint." And that was it.

Then I went to a psychiatrist. He used to tell me to do things I couldn't do and to feel ways I couldn't feel. And when I couldn't do what he asked, he told me I was a big failure. Then I didn't see anyone anymore. But I'm so confused. I just don't understand what's happening to me. Sometimes I'm driving and I get lost. Sometimes I don't remember several hours. And with no drinking, Glenda, honest!" I looked up at her. "Well, I drink lots of times with my friends. We drink wine. I think I drink because I get confused about how I am feeling, about fainting and about not remembering things. But not that night."

"I believe you," she said softly. "How're things at home?"

"Okay, I guess. I fight with my dad sometimes."

"What do you fight about?"

"Mostly my friends. He doesn't like my friends and the things I do. He thinks I should hang around with Jewish kids and I think the Jewish kids are a drag."

"Why?"

"They are so boring. They tee-hee when a boy looks at them. They can't have intelligent conversations or talk about their feelings. They're snobs. I hate them. I feel like a big dumb hulk around them. I like my friends. I feel normal with my friends."

"What about school? Are you happy in university?"

"Oh yeah, I love it. I fool around a lot, but I still manage to get okay marks. And I'm in my last year now, you know."

We talked for over two hours. I felt so much lighter when I left and happy that I was to come back in two days to talk with Glenda some more.

Just prior to the second attempt at a trial in Judge Dubienski's courtroom, Glenda met me outside the court house.

"The Judge wants to talk to you before your hearing. Do you agree?"

"What do you think, Glenda?"

"I think it's a good idea."

"Okay."

Glenda and I went into the courtroom and sat together. Just after a case was finished, Glenda caught the Judge's eye and signaled him with her finger.

"Court recessed for fifteen minutes," boomed the Judge and disappeared through a door behind his bench.

"C'mon," Glenda said and took me gently by the arm down a hall to a frosted glass pane announcing 'Judge Dubienski.' She knocked.

"Come in, come in," the judge called. He was sitting behind his desk, a glass of water in his hand. "Sit down, sit down."

"Thank you," I murmured.

"Oh, it's nice to hear you do have a voice after all."

I looked up quickly. He smiled warmly. "Sit down. Glenda has told me a few things about you. I can understand why you were so angry when Mr. Answeg kept talking about your alcohol problem, so to speak. I understand you don't recall what happened that night, is that so?"

"Well, your Honour, I recall some, and was told some, but I was not drinking."

"Yes, I do believe you. However, you have committed many infractions of the law. Would you agree to obtain voluntary psychiatric help?"

"Oh yes, your Honour."

"If so, then I will give you only a suspended sentence. But you will have to plead guilty to the charges. And, of course, I will have to suspend your driver's license. It is the minimum penalty for these offenses. Oh, and Miss Simkin, if you ever need any help, please don't hesitate to call."

"Yes, your Honour, thank you, sir."

"Now," he stood up, black gown billowing out behind him, "let's finish up this case."

The blond bullock was there again. When, as had been pre-arranged, I pleaded guilty as charged and the judge gave me a suspended sentence on the grounds that I receive immediate psychiatric help, the prosecutor got up and started pounding his book on the table.

"Your Honour, I protest. This young lady has proven to be a problem. She appeared in provincial court only last month and presently is in magistrate's court. The prosecution feels she should get the maximum sentence, not the minimum."

"The court has considered this case well, including the report from the probation officer. Overruled, Mr. Answeg." The Judge winked at me and I smiled at the blond bullock who sat down on his chair, deflated, as if someone had pulled a cork from his behind.

Glenda walked with me to the front door of the courthouse. "The hospital will call you in a few days. Good luck, Ruth."

"Thanks, Glenda."

I ran down the stairs and across the street, my head swimming in happiness and confusion.

Rockville, Maryland; January 1964

"Ruthie, hi." I looked up to see Lenore standing in front of me.

"You seemed so lost in thought," she smiled.

"Oh yeah, I was remembering, Lenore, just remembering things."

"Well, any privileges yet?"

"No. You know, Lenore, that Dr. Evanson is weird. What do you know about him?"

"Well, not much. Only that he's pretty new here. He came last year. He's young, just finished his residency. Sort of strange, because most of the doctors here are older. I don't exactly know how he managed to get here. This is quite a prestigious hospital, you know. Harry Stack Sullivan worked here and Freda Fromm-Reichmann."

I nodded, recognizing those well-known psychiatric figures from my psychology studies.

"I know Dr. Evanson has six patients now – you, David and Petey from Hilltop, Judy from Main Two and Maury and Luther from Lower Cottage. All of them except you are really sick. David doesn't talk at all, ever, to anyone. At least, not that we know of. And Maury and Luther are on that new drug. I think it's called thorazine. Judy is new, but I hear she had too many shock treatments. It's hard to find normal people around here, isn't it?" We both laughed.

Lenore turned to the clacking typewriter.

"Margaret," she asked, "who are you writing to today?"

Margaret stopped typing, sat up straight, pursed her lips, straightened her eyeglasses and informed us, "I am writing to the manufacturers of Colgate toothpaste. Do you know that Colgate toothpaste gives you sexual dreams at night?"

"Don't I wish," I smiled, glad that I used Colgate toothpaste in the hopes that something exciting might happen.

"There is nothing to smile at," Margaret continued. "This is serious business and they must change the formula." She turned back to the typewriter as Lenore and I shook our heads.

"Margaret, here's your mail." Mrs. Jackson dropped a huge pile of mail on the table.

"Holy shit, Lenore, look at that mail! How come she gets so much?"

Lenore smiled. "Margaret is always writing letters. She writes to everyone all over the world. A lot of them answer back. Watch."

She turned to Margaret. "So Margaret, who did you hear from today?"

Margaret looked up from her sorting. "Well, here's one from the consulate in Ethiopia. Here's one from Portugal. A lot from this country." She opened one and began to read. "'Dear Miss Bullard, Thank you for your inquiry as to what chemicals are in our product. We would like to reassure you that there is no danger, either mental or physical, in using our products. Enclosed are some scientific papers supporting this. We hope you continue to enjoy Boynton's Tuna.' Hmph." Margaret slammed the letter down. "Don't believe them. They're all liars."

Lenore said, "Margaret doesn't eat the food here. She carries canned goods in her basket, right Margaret?"

"Of course. I won't be poisoned here. You should be careful too." She returned to her mail.

I studied Margaret for a while. Her thin arms were strong from carrying the basket everywhere with her. She wouldn't even go to the bathroom without the basket. At night the basket was linked over her arm, like a cherished lover, as she dozed.

Lenore later told me that Margaret was from a very wealthy family – it seemed that everyone here was from a very wealthy family. Margaret had been a patient here for nine years. Although she was totally paranoid, she was quite pleasant in a prudish way. I liked Margaret. There was something very compelling about her.

Chapter Seven

The day after I had arrived at Chestnut Lodge, my parents went to New York City for a few days. The doctors told them it would be a good idea for me to "settle in." It was also an opportunity for them to process what had happened in the last few days. Besides, they needed to get me some clothes. I had arrived with only my little overnight bag, expecting to be back at Locky's house long before I was introduced to my new room at the hospital. I anxiously awaited my parents' return as I was sure they would understand that we had all made a terrible mistake and take me home.

They were at the hospital early the day after they returned from New York, but went straight into meetings before seeing me. I knew from telephone conversations with them that the doctors had asked them to leave almost immediately upon my admission. This was all "for my own good."

It amazed me that men who had just met me could profess to know me better than myself or my own parents. And it astounded me even more that my parents believed them and so completely deferred to them. I imagined it was because the doctors were thought of as being "educated" and since my father hadn't finished high school, he looked up to men who had university degrees. My mother did finish high school and did not hold the same inherent belief in strangers, educated or not. However, my mother was a woman of the fifties and sixties. Although her thinking was a lot clearer, she was not recognized as being a person who could contribute to the situation. Her role was one of peacemaker in the family, but she was not allowed much authority. I'm sure my father

53

would have denied that had someone confronted him about it. I'm sure he thought they were equal partners.

"We've just come from a meeting with the doctors," my dad greeted me.

"Hi dad. Hi mom. How was your trip to New York? Which doctors?"

"Oh, I don't know their names. Your mother will know. Dear, which doctors, do you remember?"

My mom looked very tired as she answered in a monotone, "Dr. Tatelman, Dr. Stepford and Dr. Evanson. We brought you some things, some clothes and some books. Shall we go to your room?"

My mom seemed to be flat, showing no emotion at all. She moved as though she were a robot, automatically – almost involuntarily, as though some unseen force were jerkily pulling her strings. Her brown eyes, usually sparkling and full of life, were dull and blank. The beige blouse, brown skirt and cardigan sweater she wore just seemed to hang on her body. My heart ached to see her, especially since I was the cause of this physical and emotional change. It brought tears to my eyes as we walked down the hall to my room in silence.

Back in my room, with my mom unpacking clothes, my dad looking very uncomfortably around him and with Hector guarding in the hall, I took a deep breath and began. "Mom, I don't think I should be here. They're crazy here. It's a real nuthouse." I smiled weakly.

"Ruthie, don't joke, this isn't funny."

"Mom, I know it's not funny. Please, take me home. I promise I'll be good. I'll do whatever you want, but please don't leave me here."

My dad intervened as tears prevented my mother from speaking. "Now Ruthie, you'll be home soon. The doctors think you won't be here that long, and that they could help you."

"But dad, there is nothing wrong with me."

"Now Ruthie, you had all that trouble a while back." I'm not sure if he was referring to jail or, even more likely, the fact that I was diagnosed with epilepsy, a scourge on the family name. "You just stay here a little while and then you can come home. The doctors tell us it's normal for you to want to go home. They say it's normal for you to feel like this."

Right. Those assholes really have it made. They tell you how to be, tell you how to feel, put the keys in their pockets and collect the cash.

My mother was visibly upset, the tears falling freely down her face. It seemed as though she didn't even have the strength to wipe them away. My father kept looking over his shoulder; he was afraid to be on the ward, a fact I found somewhat incongruous as I thought of him as being so strong and capable. How he could leave me in a place where he was so clearly frightened, was beyond me.

"Dear, let's get back to the hotel now," my mother managed. "We have to pack."

"The doctors told us you would be better off if we left you to get used to the place. We'll come back whenever they let us. They said we could come back in three months to see you. But we could talk to you on the phone every week, and write to you." My dad was trying to lighten the situation, but the more he talked, the heavier it got. Both my mom and I were now sobbing.

"Three months! No, dad….three months……"

My dad gently put his arm around my shoulder and urged me to the door and down the hall. The three of us walked down the hall from my room to the elevator, Hector right behind us. It seemed like a death walk for me. I was in the last room at the end of the long hall and we slowly walked the empty distance to the elevator in silence, leaving only tears in our wake.

We had a tearful goodbye. I didn't want to let go of my mother. "No, please don't leave me here," I whispered. She loosened my grasp on her and walked into the elevator, not looking at me. "No, dad, please, wait, don't go…." I held on to him. He peeled my hands off his shoulders and followed my mother in silence. "No, wait…please…don't go…no…. no……." My arms reached out towards them and then fell limply to my sides. I watched the barred elevator doors close on them as an aide turned the elevator key and they descended, leaving me behind.

"Oh, they're leaving," yelled Mrs. Schwartz. "But I'm not left here. Oh no, IIIIIII'mmm not left here."

I was allowed one phone call to my friends. I called Locky's house late one afternoon.

"Where the fuck are you?"

"Oh Locky, I'm locked up in a nuthouse in Maryland!"

"What?! How the hell did that happen? We'll come bust you out."

"No, Locky. I think I'll be out soon. I miss you."

"I miss you too. So's the morals squad. The day after you left, they came looking for you."

I started to cry. For a few weeks before I left for Kansas, I had lived with Locky as his lover. Donna, who was lovers with Locky's roommate Curley, had introduced us. Once Locky and I met, I never left.

It seemed inconceivable (and extremely pleasing) to me that Donna kept appearing in my life. She was Curley's lover; this was the third place in the past few months that I had encountered her: first in jail, secondly at the Winnipeg psych ward and thirdly, at Locky's and Curley's house.

Curley was Locky's "business partner" in bootlegging and other forms of illicit divertissements. For the short time I had lived with them, I had gotten used to the "raids" every morning, when the vice squad, the morals squad, every conceivable police squad, would bang down our door at seven a.m. – almost immediately after we had gone to bed after a long night bootlegging and entertaining. The raids made me feel older, especially since I had to lie about my age as I was under twenty-one, the age of majority. I actually felt important, being a person of interest to the police.

"Listen Ruthie, we'll come down and bust you out. Where are you?"

"Wait a week or two. Maybe I'll be home by then. Write to me, okay?"

"Sure thing, sugar. I'm not much of a writer, but you got it. Don't let them get to you."

"Okay Locky. Thanks. Let me say hello to Donna now."

After briefly speaking with Donna and Curley, Locky came back on the line to whisper little obscenities in my ear. Then we said goodbye.

Rockville, Maryland; February 1964

"Do you like to drink?" Lenore whispered.

I glanced over to the door where Hector was sitting in the hall.

"Sure, why? Do you have anything?"

"All you want," Lenore smiled as she went over to the closet and, from under a laundry bag, produced a bottle of vodka.

"Here, let me put some in your glass. That way it will look like water if anyone comes in." Lenore poured us both large glasses of vodka.

"Lenore, how did you get this? You only have ground privileges."

"Well, you know...." She pointed to the door. "He really likes me. Once in a while, I kiss him or let him touch my breasts. He giggles and brings me presents. Sometimes, I give him a blow job, to keep him coming back."

"Oooh, that's good," I smiled, as the warmth from the large swallow of straight vodka spread throughout my body. "Well Lenore, I'm glad, because I sure like your present." We giggled. I looked over at Lenore. Her very long chestnut brown hair was combed straight down her back, coming to a neat edge just below her waist. She was beautiful. I looked at her mangled right arm.

"What happened to your arm?"

"A bear mauled me."

"A bear! Where were you?"

"In a zoo. I know it's weird. I was in a zoo in Belgium, and the bear reached through the bars and before I knew it, he was chewing on my arm. Then I lost consciousness and woke up in the hospital. For a while, they thought they were going to cut my arm off, but I kept it. It's pretty gross, isn't it?"

"No, it's not too gross," I reassured both of us.

We sat and talked and drank and exchanged life stories for most of the night.

Lenore had been born in Europe, in Belgium, but when she was two years old her family moved back to the US. She grew up in New York City and then, when she was twelve, the family went back to Belgium. Her dad was a diplomat and her mom was a housewife, her father coming from royalty in Belgium. Lenore was an only child. She spent a lot of time in boarding schools in Europe and I was impressed that she spoke several languages. She seemed so sophisticated and elegant; I had never been to Europe – it seemed so intriguing. When she was a teenager in boarding school some friends introduced her to alcohol, which she took to like a fish to water. She spent the next five years drunk. It was only after she was arrested in Brussels for "disorderly conduct" that her parents decided she was an embarrassment to the family and shipped her off to Chestnut Lodge which had been her home for the past several years.

I thought she was the most interesting person I had ever met.

"Tell you what," Lenore said a few days later, after I had been moaning about Dr. Evanson's not letting me go off the ward. "It looks like you're not getting privileges anytime soon, so why don't you let me cheer you up. I'll keep your glass full of vodka so you can stand it around here a bit more."

"Oh really? Lenore, that would be great! Sometimes I think I'm going crazy from boredom. I don't know how people can stay here for so long."

"Well, they need this place. It's very expensive, you know, and sort of a status symbol in some families."

"Get out! How can being locked up in a nuthouse be a status symbol?"

"Well, it is. You have to have a lot of money to be here. It costs two thousand dollars a month to be here. Not like St. E."

"St. E, what's that?"

"That's the state mental hospital, Saint Elizabeth, whoever she is. Some of the people here have come from there. That's where people from here go when they run out of the money to stay here. It's a nightmare. I was there once. I'm glad I got out alive."

The days passed slowly. My single activity occurred twice a week when I was escorted to Dr. Evanson's office. He had told Dr. Stepford that I was anti-social and should not be let off the ward except for therapy. Most of the time I would sit in the rocking chair and watch Main Four happen. There was almost always a bridge game going, usually with Max and Matt and whomever they invited. Mrs. Schwartz would alternately yell and sleep. Mrs. Richmond moved her hands through the air and smiled. Janie verbally fucked Quentin. If there was enough staff I got escorted to the cafeteria, but most of the time I ate alone off a tray in the sunroom. All but the very sickest people could go to the cafeteria and since it was in the same building, I didn't see why I couldn't go.

"Look, Dr. Stepford," I pleaded one day after rounds, "please just let me eat with other people. I won't do anything. I'm going nuts sitting around here."

"I'm sorry, Miss Simkin, but your therapist has advised us that would not be in your best interest."

"Dr. Stepford, sir, my therapist is crazy. Please sir, if I must stay here, please get me another therapist."

"You understand, Miss Simkin, that it's normal to have negative feelings towards your therapist. It's what we call negative transference."

"Yeah, I know all about that, Dr. Stepford, but please, can I have a new therapist? Please can I eat with the other people?"

"Maybe soon. I'll talk with Dr. Evanson again about it." He smiled and was gone.

A few days later, I was in Dr. Evanson's office.

"But *why* can't I eat with everyone else?"

"Because you are anti-social. You have a personality disorder. I don't want to talk about it again."

"When you say I'm anti-social, what do you mean?"

"Look, Miss Simkin, you still want to go back to your friends, the bootleggers, don't you?"

"Well, yeah, but…"

"So there you are. Tell me about your childhood."

I sat in silence. Dr. Evanson wrote on his pile of papers. Ten minutes elapsed. He picked up his papers and tapped them on the desk to straighten them, something he did repeatedly. He glanced up at me, I looked at him, he put his papers back down on his desk and started writing on them again. Another ten minutes went by. Again he straightened his pile of papers and again he started writing. This time, he didn't even bother to glance over at me.

I spent a good deal of my therapy sessions in silence. Dr. Evanson didn't seem to mind. He just did paperwork and when the time was up, summoned the aide to take me back. If I didn't initiate the conversation he would just continue writing and shuffling papers on his desk, sometimes even grunting at me if I did talk. There was not much point in talking to him – he didn't listen to me anyway.

I had developed the habit of going over and over in my mind all the events that led me to Chestnut Lodge – in the hope of finding a clue to what might get me out. I sat on the daybed with my back leaning against the wall and remembered how just a few months ago I had walked into my first psych ward.

Winnipeg, Manitoba; November 1963

I walked through the big glass door into the psychiatric ward of the Winnipeg General Hospital, after Judge Dubienski's order at my trial ten days before. A nurse closed the door and locked it behind her.

"Your room is just down the hall."

I followed the nurse into a small narrow room. At the far end was a large window with bars, and over the bars, a heavy screen. To the right was a single bed with a plain white bedspread, blue and white striped pajamas neatly folded by the pillow. Beside the bed was a round night table holding a small, metal ashtray and a plastic glass, and at its foot, a wooden chair. Across from the bed was a painting of a winter scene, the cool frost and snow in the painting matching the white of the walls in the room. A large heavy door to the room was now pushed open against the wall. I noticed the glass window in the door and the heavy lock in the handle.

"If there's anything you need, you call," the nurse said over her shoulder as she walked out of the room.

I walked to the doorway, feeling too intimidated by my surroundings to venture much further.

Suddenly someone rushed past me. A large woman walked by so quickly it was almost a run. She made me think of the roadrunner. She wore a gaudy purple print dress that was very tight over her large posterior. Her long, light brown hair was braided and wound about her head like pretzels. I immediately christened her Brunhilda. Brunhilda came to an abrupt stop at the doorway of the room next to mine. There she faced the side of the doorway, put her hands on the wooden frame and bumped the other side with her bum, twice. Then, she turned around and repeated that on the other side. She then faced the inside of the room, clapped her hands twice, slapped her thighs twice and disappeared into the room. I stood at my door, transfixed by the ritual. Brunhilda re-emerged and performed exactly the same ritual leaving the room: bump bump, bump bump, clap clap, slap slap. I moved inside my room as Brunhilda, without even a glance, churned down the hall right to my door and prepared to enter. Bump bump, bump bump, clap clap, slap slap. I pressed myself up against a wall, barely breathing. The large woman walked briskly around the room twice, not slowing her pace even for turns; then, without a glimmer of recognition that there was even another human being in the room, made her preparations to exit, bump bump, bump bump, clap clap, slap slap, and carried on her rigid way.

I felt my knees become a little shaky and slowly lowered myself onto the chair. "That lady would be hysterically funny if she weren't so scary," I mumbled softly as I released a long, slow breath.

"Would you like to join us for tea, dear?"

I looked up. There, in the doorway, stood a petite, elderly woman. Her curly hair was neatly combed, her face appropriately rouged and lipsticked. She wore a smart black and white print dress with a black leather belt and carried a small, black handbag. She smiled at me. "My name is Mrs. Snell, dear. Come join us for afternoon tea."

I immediately liked Mrs. Snell. She seemed so kindly and genteel, especially after Brunhilda's recent invasion.

I got up. "I'd be delighted to have tea with you, Mrs. Snell." I walked down the hall with this elegant, diminutive woman.

"Here we are, dear. Now, you sit over here." Mrs. Snell indicated a chair at the end of a semi-circle of about eight empty chairs.

I felt my smile turn to a puzzled expression, then I became amused, as I watched Mrs. Snell greet each invisible guest.

"How do you do, Mrs. Galley.

"Oh, you are so gallant, Sir Rodney."

She then went over to the table and began preparing pretend tea. I leaned back in my chair and watched with delighted fascination as Mrs. Snell poured tea for everyone, asked how they wished their tea and then complied with their requests, unheard by all except Mrs. Snell. She handed me an invisible cup and saucer, which I took. After the appropriate questions, she added two invisible sugar cubes.

"Do have some cucumber sandwiches, dear. They are lovely, but too many cause the nauseation in me. But do help yourself."

As Mrs. Snell turned back to Sir Rodney, I excused myself, hoping I could find some real food.

I walked down the hall, lined with a dozen chairs against the wall. Most of them were filled with women patients, interspersed with nurses and aides. I felt lost and afraid. I wanted to talk to someone – someone who did not have a glaringly obvious psychiatric problem. I reminded myself that I was locked here only until my evaluation, scheduled to begin tomorrow, was complete. Then maybe I would be put somewhere where I would feel more normal. I sat down beside an elderly woman who was fidgeting with her shoelaces. I tried to get used to the passage of time.

There was a large clock on the white wall across from the chairs where we sat. It was unusually loud, tick tock, tick tock, as though put there to ensure that if one were not already unbalanced, one certainly would be after minutes and hours and days of its stentorious tick tock tick tock tick tock tick tock.

"Dinner time," yelled one of the nurses as she wheeled a large, metal hospital meal cart down the hall. Very slowly, as if by electromagnetic force, the women drew themselves silently up out of their chairs to follow the noisy steel cart. Like sheep, I thought.

"Mrs. Garvey, come for dinner." I realized the nurse was addressing the elderly woman beside me. I looked over at the woman and then back at the nurse.

"She can't go," I said, "she's tied her shoelaces to her garters."

I smiled as the nurse roughly bent over to release Mrs. Garvey from her permanent crouch and Mrs. Garvey straightened out her left arm and cuffed the nurse over the ear. The nurse sputtered and stepped back.

"I'll bring her," I smiled.

"Now Mrs. Garvey, what's a nice lady like you doing in a place like this?" I crooned as I gently undid Mrs. Garvey's shoelaces from her garter belt. "Now, let's fasten up your stockings and go eat our dinner." Mrs. Garvey allowed me to dress her and the two of us, smiling and winking, walked arm in arm into the dining room, much to the amazement and chagrin of the rejected nurse, who stood aside rubbing her reddening ear.

I sat down at a long table with Mrs. Garvey on my left and Mrs. Snell on my right. Across the table was Brunhilda's plate. She did not sit, just strode to the table, and without losing a beat of her stride, took food off her plate and plunged it into her mouth as she turned and walked to the window, then the length of the room, and then back to the plate. This continued until her plate was empty, and then with a bump bump, bump bump, clap clap, slap slap, she was out of the room.

I looked around the room. There were nineteen women, counting myself, eighteen of whom looked as though their present abode was most appropriate. Further down the table a nurse was feeding two different women in tandem, one of whom let her scalloped potatoes dribble down her chin as she stared into her own private world. The other woman was carrying on a rapid conversation with anyone who might be listening. The nurse just waited until her mouth was wide open, and then she would pop a spoonful of food in her gaping mouth as the woman continued speaking.

I cut Mrs. Garvey's chicken for her and turned to look at the delicate Mrs.

Snell. *After every tiny mouthful, she dabbed at her lips with her napkin, carefully replacing the napkin on her lap.*

"Oh, this is ever so lovely, so fine," she turned to me, as though she were being entertained at the Queen's garden party.

My own plate sat untouched. "Would you like some more dinner, Mrs. Snell?"

"Oh, no thank you, dear. It's very lovely, but my sufficiency has been suffancified."

"Ruthie J!" I turned. There, standing behind me, was Donna, the very woman who had offered me such comfort when I was in jail.

"Why are you sitting here with these old dodos? C'mon, let's grab a hamburger at the cafeteria."

"Donna! Why, how come, are you…?" I sputtered.

"C'mon kid. I'll explain all over dinner."

I followed Donna down the hall to the big glass door and stood quietly while she arranged some passes to the hospital cafeteria.

As soon as we were on the elevator, Donna began, "My lawyer got me out of jail, alright. Right back into this dump. My room is next to yours. Stick with me and I'll show you the ropes. It's not so bad here once you know how to get around."

Standing in the cafeteria line I began to feel hungry again. We both loaded our trays and sat down in a corner of the large, clattering room. I began to tell Donna about the court trials and my arrival at the ward that afternoon.

"May I join you?"

I looked up to see a tall, handsome man in hospital pajamas and housecoat, with a cast on his left foot.

"Hi, Don. Don, this is Ruthie. Ruthie, Don," Donna concluded the introductions.

"Hi Ruthie."

I nodded a shy hello.

"Listen, Donna," Don turned to her, "are we still on for tonight?"

Donna winked and nodded.

"How about your friend here, can I bring my roommate?" Don asked.

"Hey, Ruthie J., want to go to a party tonight?" Donna asked. I nodded uncertainly.

"Donna, aren't we supposed to go back?"

"Oh, we got lots of time, kid. Okay Don, same place, in about fifteen minutes."

Don got up and smiled broadly. "See you soon," he limped off.

Fifteen minutes later Donna and I could be found tiptoeing though the deserted physiotherapy department.

"Donna, maybe I ought to go back. I mean, it's my first day here. I really don't want to get into trouble," I whispered.

"Stick with me, kid, you won't get into trouble. We won't be long. We'll be back before nine. They won't even miss us. What do you want to hang around with those weirdos for anyway? Now shhh."

Donna quietly eased into the treatment room of the physiotherapy department. There were ten treatment cubicles, all with large hard beds in them. They all had curtains pushed open but one. Donna peeked in and signaled for me to follow her past the curtains.

Don was sitting up on the bed, a bottle of Seagram's Whiskey in his hand, pouring a shot into each of four plastic medicine containers lined up on the cot beside him.

"Welcome," he whispered. "Meet Frank. Frank, this is Donna, and uh, ah…"

"Ruthie," I supplied, suddenly wishing I had said Phoebe or anything but my real name. I looked over at Frank. He was about thirty-five, dressed also in pajamas and a hospital housecoat. He had a cast on his right arm. His brown hair was shaped in a crew cut. He must have spent a lot of time in the gym, I thought, looking at his bulging biceps and his full chest muscles showing through his unbuttoned top. He leaned against the bed, busily knocking back several shots of whiskey.

"Okay, shall we go?" he pushed away from the bed and looked at me.

I was frightened. I looked at Donna, who already had made Don the sole focus of her attention. She rubbed his chest and let her hands drop down to his waist, where she began undoing his pajamas.

Frank had slipped through the curtain and had already drawn the curtains of the next cubicle.

I thought of Brunhilda, Mrs. Snell and Mrs. Garvey and then remembered the soothing presence of Donna when we were together in jail. With dread in my eyes, and my recently eaten meal an uncomfortable lump in my stomach, I left Donna and Don and walked into Frank's waiting arms. I could feel his hard-on pushing against me. I could hear Donna and Don in the next cubicle.

Under Frank's weight, I closed my eyes tightly, gritted my teeth and wished I could be back in my own room in my parents' house.

Chapter Eight

"You have some mail," said Mrs. Jackson, handing me a letter. I unfolded the dirty piece of foolscap.

"Dear Ruthie J.," I read to myself, "I miss your body in my bed." That from Locky in his shaky handwriting.

Then, in a neater, straight up and down script, the letter continued, "Donna here. We had a busy night last night. About eighty people all together (but not at the same time – ha, ha). We almost ran out of booze. I got back from my john's in time to help serve. We made good money. Then just after we went to bed, the vice squad knocked the door off again and busted into our room. What assholes. Hope you are fine. Miss you. Love, Donna."

Locky continued, "I want to fuck your sweet cunt and put it into you…"

Initially, Locky was true to his word. The letters started arriving as promised. At first, I would get two a week. They were all the same – he would write one sentence, then Donna would write about the latest raids by the cops or other adventures. Then Locky would write one or two inspired pages about what he would do to and with my body as soon as he got his hands and other parts on it. These letters gave new definition to dirty writing. I had never seen some of these words written on paper before, and in fact, had never even heard of others. The letters amused me and made me feel grown-up in a perverse way. But after the first few weeks, there was only one letter a week, then one every ten days, then two weeks, then no more.

Rockville, Maryland; March 1964

Weeks stretched into months. I had been at Chestnut Lodge for two months and two weeks. I was counting weeks now, not days, but realized I might need to switch to months. I still was not allowed outside; I went to my therapy sessions and that was it. In the interim, Max had taught me how to play bridge, and I was getting to be a good player. So now I added playing bridge to my sitting and rocking and watching. One morning in particular remains so vivid in my memory, I still see and feel it.

I get up in the morning, feeling good. Outside the window the sky is blue in the spring air. I see buds on the tree beside my barred window, a beautiful tree with sparrows flitting in and out of the branches. I hum to myself while I take a shower. I still don't understand why I have to be on "arm-to-arm" special; why they think me so strange or sick or dangerous that someone, an aide, a nurse, anyone from 'their side' has to be within arms' reach of me twenty-four hours a day. I try to ignore Jorge's hostility veiled as friendly chatter. Virtually all the patients in the hospital are despised or at least envied by the staff, because it was so costly to be a patient at Chestnut Lodge and the employees were often poor or students who needed the money. So Jorge is chattering away about how nice it is to have money and how lucky I am and how he wishes he could have just a bit of what some of us have and so forth. I don't really listen because I know that just after breakfast are the rounds, where the ward administrator sees each of us individually to decide on our privileges. I have been "good" this week, following along with the others, keeping to myself, reading, listening to music, playing a little bridge. I just know he will let me be outside – I can think of no reason why not to let me enjoy the spring.

I quickly dress. By now, I am used to dressing and undressing with the male aides pretending not to look and acting casual. I know they are watching me carefully, mentally assessing my body, perhaps for some future use.

"Good morning, Mrs. Lohmer," I cheerfully chirp to the head nurse while I make a cup of coffee. I don't risk going to the cafeteria with the others lest I miss my turn with Dr. Stepford, the administrator. Then I would have to wait another whole week to talk with him.

I nervously glance out the window and then relax when I see that the sun is still shining, the sky is still a clear blue and the freshness of the day is calling me. I sit in the sunroom with my back to the windows so I can see both the elevator and stair doors. I want to know as soon as Dr. Stepford arrives. I sit prim and proper, my hands in my lap and I wait. I wait and wait. For a while I relax and sling an arm over the back of the chair, my foot up on the chair. But I change back to prim and proper when I realize they might mistake this for a rebellious attitude. I wait. I think. I hurt from trying to sit still without fidgeting too much – then they will think I am hyperactive. They like it when you sit still and don't bother them. I am being a good girl. Of course they will let me go outside today.

I hear the heavy hum of the old elevator as it strains to bring itself up to the fourth floor. It is always amazing to me that with all its creaking and groaning, it works. I hear the grid door pulled back and the heavy steel door is pushed out, disgorging Dr. Stepford. He glances around him and briskly walks into the nurses' office, closing the door behind him.

I can wait no longer; the spring warmth is calling. I stand up and walk past the office. I see through the window that he is speaking with Mrs. Lohmer as she gathers up the charts, but I cannot hear through the thick glass. I walk down the hall slowly and back again.

Dr. Stepford comes out with Mrs. Lohmer and heads for the TV room where he meets each of the patients.

"Time for rounds now?" I raise my eyebrows.

"Yes, Miss Simkin, but you'll have to wait your turn." He brushes past me into the room.

I sit down in a chair along the wall, where Mrs. Schwartz, Janie and Mrs. Kane are spending their lives. They are not waiting for Dr. Stepford. They are waiting for their own things – Mrs. Schwartz to be rescued, Janie for Quentin, and Mrs. Kane for eternity.

I smile at them. Both Janie and Mrs. Schwartz are engrossed in their own private conversations with themselves.

Mrs. Lohmer comes out into the hallway. She takes Mrs. Schwartz's arm. "Come on now, Miz Swarts, doctor wants to see you."

"Oh, no, I'm not going, IIIIIII'mm not left here!" bellows Mrs. Schwartz.

"I'll go, Mrs. Lohmer," I jump up.

"You just sit down and wait your turn, missy. Now come on, Miz Swarts, you don't want to hold up the doctor."

"Oh no, not me, I'm not left here, oh nooo." Mrs. Lohmer gets behind her and pushes her into the room. I watch my right foot move up and down as it sits crossed over my knee.

Mrs. Schwartz comes out. "Ooooh, that man is a doctor. He knows I'm not left here." She sits back in her chair.

"Okay, Miz Kane, your turn." Mrs. Lohmer turns back to the slight woman sitting motionless, staring straight ahead.

"Miz Kane? Miz Kane, can you hear me? Come with me now." Mrs.

Lohmer gently puts her hand under the woman's elbow and lifts her up slowly. By now, more of the patients are gathering in the hallway. The noise and energy levels are getting higher. It seems I must wait until almost last, which doesn't seem fair to me, because the others don't appear in a hurry to get outside under the sun or to do much of anything.

"Okay, Ruthie, you can come see the doctor now."

I walk as slowly as I can without bursting into a lope.

"Hello, Miss Simkin, how are you? Sit down please."

I look around the small room. The stand with the charts takes up a good portion of the space. Dr. Stepford sits at a tiny table, Mrs. Lohmer by his side with a clipboard on which she takes notes. She hands him my chart and he glances through it.

"Dr. Stepford, sir, please, may I have privileges to go outside, sir?"

"Why do you want these privileges?" he looks up at me.

"Please, sir, it is so nice outside, maybe I can go for a walk."

"You understand, Miss Simkin, that we don't have staff to take you for a walk. Going for a walk is not getting better."

"Sir, I can go by myself, just on the grounds. Or else, not even a walk, just sit outside. I'll come back, I promise. I'll be good, honest."

"Hmmm. Let's see how your therapy is going." He glances through my chart and stops to read some notes.

"It seems that you are still resisting your therapy. I see some notes here that you persistently ask for a change of therapist."

"Dr. Stepford, I don't get along well with Dr. Evanson. Maybe it's my fault. But I really do feel I could do better with another therapist." I remember the fear I have experienced lately with Dr. Evanson, his threats that if I didn't cooperate with him, I would never breathe fresh air again.

"Dr. Stepford," I try again, "you know, it's really not fair. I am trying, but Dr. Evanson is always angry at me. Please just let me go outside."

"I'm afraid it's quite clear from these notes that Dr. Evanson feels you are not cooperating with him. You know, we have your best interests in mind here. I suggest you start working in your therapy sessions with him and then we can talk about off-ward privileges."

He turns to look at his watch, pushes back his chair and partially gets up to dismiss me. Tears well up in my eyes as I put out my hand to stay him.

"Please, please, just let me go outside for a few minutes. Dr. Evanson hates me, really he does. I am trying to get better." It crosses my mind that I have no idea what that means.

"We'll talk about it again next week. Bring in the next patient, Mrs. Lohmer."

"But it's not fair!" I slam my hand down on the table. Dr. Stepford jumps back.

"Watch yourself, young lady," Mrs. Lohmer warns. "Jorge," she calls, "come here and get this one. She wanted to go for a walk. Walk her up and down the hall a few times." She and Dr. Stepford grin at each other. Jorge comes into the room and grabs my arm. I fling him off with my shoulder. He grabs me tight this time.

"Need any help, Jorge?" Mrs. Lohmer asks.

"No, ma'am, we'll be just fine." He tightens his grip on my right upper arm and propels me into the hallway. I feel as though I do not even have the inner strength to shrug him off.

"Well, walk!" he says as he pushes me forward.

"I don't want to walk. Not here."

"You heard what Mrs. Lohmer said. Now walk!" He pushes me down the hall. My feet move one in front of the other. My eyes are blurry with tears, muting the beautiful day glimpsed now through bars in the window. I try not to hear Jorge talking, to me, to the other patients, to the walls. Sometimes I think he is crazier than many of us.

Inside of me grows a pain and an agony I can hardly bear. My feet march on automatically, my eyes tearing. But thundering inside me, belying the quiet exterior, a volcano is brewing.

After a time, Jorge has to look after two of us for a while so we go to sit in the sunroom. It is almost time for lunch. I have not eaten yet, but feel too dismal to be hungry. I wonder what forces bring me here to this place of insanity; how I got myself into this situation. I realize that, at least for the time being, there is not much I can do. I look out the window into the eyes of a little tree sparrow. It seems for a second that our eyes meet. I feel an anger build up in me.

Mrs. Lohmer comes into the room. "Jorge, go down and help them on Main Three – they just called for you."

Then she turns to me. "I'm sorry, but I have no one to take you to the dining room. I'll have a tray ordered up for you."

"But Mrs. Lohmer, I can go by myself. It's in the same building – I don't even have to go outside."

"Now you know that orders are orders and you can't be alone. I'll trust you a little out here while I work in the office, but I can't let you off the ward. Sit down and be good."

I sit. I wait. Soon someone comes into the room with a tray of food and puts it on the table. Interesting, I think as I sit at the table, that the tray is placed so that I face a blank wall with my back to the beautiful trees outdoors. I sit alone in the large room. I know Mrs. Lohmer is "trusting" me to be good. I look at the tray, with the wilted salad, dirty white soup and tomato sauce something. Off to the side, sits a little cup of canned fruit salad. I think that is what does it – that fruit salad, multi-coloured in its little cup.

"Noooo!" I scream, as I hurl the soup against the wall.

"I'm not crazy!" the salad splats onto the blank gray.

"You want crazy, I'll show you crazy!" The tomato entrée follows suit, splashing colour on the drab wall. By now I hear the alarm bells and footsteps rushing up the stairs.

With a wistful glance at the fruit salad, I pick up the tray and hurl the whole thing against the wall. I manage to throw two large flower pots before I feel my arms pinned behind me and my knees are kicked out from under me.

"Pack her!" I hear a voice say.

"Sure, pack me, I'm Crrraaaaazy!!!!!!"

I can hear the screaming and I know I am doing it, but the noise does not seem to come from me. I start struggling with the men who are holding me. I kick an aide in the stomach and quickly feel a fist in mine. An "ooemph!" expels all my air.

"Get me out of this madhouse!" I scream.

Five aides are holding me – one on each limb and one grabbing me around my torso. Although it looks as if it should hurt, I feel no pain. In fact, I feel curiously strong as I thrash against them. Alvin, the black linebacker aide, puts his arms right around my middle and lifts me up off the floor. Jorge holds my left arm pinned back up against my shoulder. My right arm is held out to the side by George. Brad and Ronnie each have a kicking leg. In this manner am I carried to my room.

"Well, we're ready for you now, missy. Yes, we sure are. Put her down here, boys." Mrs. Lohmer had put the ice sheets on my bed.

My feet hit the floor with a thud as someone yanks off my sweater and pulls my shirt up. I feel someone fumbling with my pants buttons.

"Leave her clothes on! Now get her in here."

The five aides hold me down on the cold sheets. The four limb holders each proceed to wrap an arm or leg in freezing ice cold sheets. My clothes, my clean clothes that I had hoped to sit outside in the sun in, are wet and freezing. They are covered up with more freezing sheets as the aides and Mrs. Lohmer roll me to the right and to the left and to the right, tighter and tighter in an ice cocoon. My arms are wrapped tightly to my sides, my legs wrapped individually and then my whole stiff body covered over and over and round and round with freezing wet ice sheets right up to my chin. I am yet to learn that, once packed, the more one struggles, the tighter the sheets become. I thrash and try to unwind myself out of this freezing nightmare. The cold soaks into my clothes, then my skin, my muscles, my bones, and even my bone marrow. My bones are ice. My feelings are ice. I am ice.

"It's cold, it's fucking cold. Get me outta here. Help. Help!!!"

I stop screaming when I realize I am totally confined. I cannot move.

"Wait!" I panic. "What if there's a fire? How will I get out of here?"

Mrs. Jackson, who has been watching the proceedings, replies, "We can take care of that if that happens." I am petrified. I lay staring at the ceiling, feeling the freeze enwrap my body.

"It gets warm after a while," Mrs. Jackson says. "At least, that's what they say," she smiles as she leaves for her observation post in the hall.

Once I am packed, four of the five aides leave. Mrs. Lohmer turns to Jorge. "Stay here with her. A few hours like this and she ought to cool down a bit." Then she turns to me, "And I thought I could trust you!" With a harrumph, she pivots and flounces out of the room.

I lay in that cold pack for two hours, looking at the ceiling. Mrs. Lohmer comes in. She is still angry.

"Okay, young lady. We're going to get you out of here. You have a lot of cleaning to do."

I am slowly unwrapped; I examine my wrinkled skin. Mrs. Lohmer grabs me by the scruff of my neck and marches me down the hall into the sunroom. I am not even given a chance to get out of my cold, wet clothes.

"Now clean," she orders, pointing to a bucket and sponge. All the glass and pottery shards have been cleared away, but the wall is a technicolor delight. I take the sponge and slowly start cleaning the wall.

The next morning, I was so depressed, I just shuffled right over Janie without missing a beat as she lay on the hall floor masturbating with Quentin. Usually the aides pulled her away, but no one was around right now except my ubiquitous guard. I plunked myself down heavily in the rocker.

All of a sudden, I had a strange feeling in my head, sort of fuzzy with indistinct lights. And I smelled tar and oil. I was going to get up to go to the window to see if they were tarring a road when I noticed my left hand jerking on the arm rest of the rocking chair. My head felt as though it were leaving me.

"Hey, what's going on here?" I heard my voice echo in my ears. "Hey, help!"

I woke up in bed, covered with blankets up to my chin. I tried moving my limbs; they felt stiff, but could move. I wasn't packed.

I looked into the face of Mrs. Wexler, the assistant head nurse from Main

Two. She was a large, soft, gentle woman and I liked her.

"Feeling better now?"

"What happened? Why are you here? Why am I in bed?" I tried to get up.

"No, stay down for a while. You had a seizure."

"A what? A seizure? You mean a grand mal epileptic seizure?"

"Yes, I'm afraid so. You've been asleep now for two hours. We moved you to your bed after the convulsion. I'm here because I'm an R.N. and we wanted a medical person to be with you."

Convulsion. This was too much. A cold wet pack one day, a convulsion the next. I was afraid to contemplate what the following day might have in store.

"Will this happen again?"

"It could. We're going to start you on some medicine and of course, the doctors will see you and order more tests. This was your first grand mal, right?"

"Right. Before they told me I was having psycho-motor temporal lobe seizures, like throwing things, but I never had convulsions before. I feel so tired."

"Try to sleep some more. Seizures are usually exhausting." She put a cold wet cloth on my forehead and I drifted off to sleep.

Late that night, Lenore and I were sitting on my bed looking through the bars at the big tree.

"What do you want to do when you get out of here?" she asked.

"Oh, Lenore, I don't even feel that I will ever get out of here. I don't know. Why? What about you?"

"I want my own apartment and I want to go to school and oh, I don't know, I want to eat when I want to and do what I want to." Lenore looked over at me. "You're so beautiful with that moonlight shining on you."

I could feel my face getting red. She reached over and touched my cheek. Her hand lingered on my face and then held up my chin. She slowly leaned over and softly, gently, kissed me on the lips. I kissed her back.

"Lenore," I whispered, "what if we get caught?" I indicated the door. My heart was pounding, but not from the fear of being caught as much as from the feeling of her lips on mine.

"Oh, Hector, he doesn't care." She leaned over and kissed me again. Her left hand went up to my head and pulled me nearer to her. "Ruthie," she whispered, "come into my bed with me. I want to be with you."

"Lenore, I have never done this before." I didn't think my voice was audible over the pounding of my heart and the mixed excitement I was feeling.

"Come," she crooned against my ear and took me by the hand. "Put your nightgown on," she whispered, as she started taking off her clothes.

We both quickly undressed and then she got into her bed and pulled the covers back for me. I crawled in beside her and she enfolded me in her arms. She started kissing my face and neck and then I could feel her hand on my back, then over my breast.

I was overwhelmed. I melted into her warm body.

Chapter Nine

In March, two and a half months after I was admitted to Chestnut Lodge, my parents came back to be with me on my twentieth birthday. I was not allowed to go out with them alone, but because my parents insisted they take me out for dinner, Jorge accompanied us.

Jorge always liked accompanying patients when their visitors came; it meant he got a nice meal out of it. Jorge was Puerto Rican, with curly black hair. Although just under five foot six, he acted as if he were over six and a half feet tall. He had a big personality and was very overbearing and imperious. I could never quite make up my mind if I liked him or hated him. He could be funny or kind and gentle and then I enjoyed his company. At other times, he was cruel and mean. More than other aides, he was very clear about the "sides" we were on – he had the keys and we did not. He never let us forget that.

I still had trouble understanding why I was not permitted to go out alone with my parents – or without them, for that matter. However, Dr. Evanson remained adamant in his assessment that I was "anti-social" and a "threat to society." What was worse, Dr. Stepford, the nurses and the aides all believed him. This was so puzzling to me. I thought it totally obvious to anyone who cared to look at me realistically that I was a gentle, intelligent, calm, non-anti-social type of person. I couldn't believe that everyone would agree with Dr. Evanson instead of just opening up their eyes and getting to know me. Yet, I remained loyal to Locky and Donna, refusing to say that they weren't my friends. And as long as I called them my friends, Dr. Evanson deemed me anti-social. I had considered lying to Dr. Evanson just so that he would grant me privileges, but felt uncomfortable doing that. I didn't want to denounce my friends, and I didn't want to lie. But I certainly didn't want to be locked up, so lying started to look like a real alternative.

The conversation at dinner mostly turned around family events and stories from home. My mother talked with pride about my brother Sam's wonderful ability to play the piano and a recent concert he gave. My dad told me about my sister Judi's latest bout with asthma, but that she was now recovered and doing well. My brother Jack was having trouble in school, but boy, could he play football! My little poodle, Peppy, was thriving with the family. I hungrily lapped up these family stories. I missed my siblings so much I could barely think about them for fear of the visceral pain of longing I would experience throughout my entire body.

I was on my best behaviour during dinner, reluctant to talk to my parents about the hospital with Jorge there. I knew he had to report everything that occurred. When we got back to the hospital I asked my parents to come up to the ward for a few minutes. Once on the fourth floor, we walked down the hall to the TV room. I asked Jorge to wait outside and give me a few minutes alone with my parents.

"Now Ruthie, you know that I am not allowed to let you out of my sight," Jorge grinned. This was one of the times I most definitely did not like him.

"Jorge, it's okay," my dad put his large hand on Jorge's shoulder, "I'll watch her. Give us a few minutes." I was never so grateful to my father.

"Well, Mr. Simkin, I'm not sure....I'm really not allowed to leave her alone for even a minute."

"Jorge, we'll just be in this room. No one is doing anything or going anywhere. Please."

"Please, Jorge, just give us a few minutes alone with our daughter," my mother looked at him with tears in her eyes. Her right hand reached out to brush some brown curls off my glasses and put them back behind my ear.

Jorge nodded solemnly and leaned against the wall immediately beside the door frame. My parents and I eased past him into the TV room. I felt embarrassed and ashamed that my mother and father had to beg to get a few minutes privacy with me.

"Mom, Dad, you've got to get me out of this place," I whispered. "It's a madhouse!"

"Now Ruthie, don't get smart." My mother was clearly upset with this conversation and it had barely begun.

"No, mom, you don't understand. They're crazy here. My therapist is a crazy man. They don't believe me, but it's true. Please, you've got to help me.

They won't even let me leave this ward."

My dad put his hands on my shoulders and said, "Tomorrow we're meeting with the doctors, so we will talk to them about when you can come home."

"Dad, just tell them you are taking me. You can do that."

"We'll see. It's been a long day for us. We will see you tomorrow, okay?"

"Okay," I sighed. "Thanks very much for dinner. Have a good night, see you tomorrow."

With drooped shoulders, I slowly walked to my room, Jorge right behind me, my ears full of the clanging of the steel as Mrs. Decker took my parents down the locked elevator.

The next morning, my parents came to have breakfast with me. We were allowed to go down to the cafeteria – with my escort, of course.

We entered the large rectangular room and walked through a gap in the tables to stand in the food line, which started on the far side opposite the door. I went ahead of my parents, confident in my actions, although, truth be told, most of my meals to date had been eaten in solitary on the fourth floor and not in the basement cafeteria. I picked up a brown tray and then put a glass of orange juice on it. I indicated that my parents should do the same.

People were seated at most of the twenty tables in the room. The soft murmur of voices filled the air, accented by the clinking and chinking of cups and dishes as the patients and aides ate breakfast. As far as I could tell, my parents were the only "non-Chestnut Lodge" people in the room. Mattie, one of the main kitchen workers, explained to them what the choices were for breakfast and asked what they wanted. I had only met Mattie a few times, but I liked her immediately. She was about my height, five four, but likely three times my age. A black woman with white hair, she had a strong Southern accent and an infectious smile. Taking a bowl of steaming porridge from Mattie, I placed it on my tray and headed out into the room. I chose a long table, where Lenore and George were sitting with ten empty chairs.

"Ruthie, do you think we should sit here?" My dad indicated George with a nod, as his plate and mug wobbled on his tray.

"Sure dad, this is George. He won't hurt you. Good morning, George."

"Morning." Rock. "Good." Rock. "Morning." Rock. "George." Rock. "Good." Rock rock rock rock rock. My father was not impressed and picked a seat as far away from George as he could.

"You know, Dad, George is a musical genius. He knows every piece of classical music. If you play a piece for him, he can usually identify it in about two notes. Isn't that right, George?"

"Music." Rock. "George." Rock.

"Now, Ruthie, leave George alone. I'm sure he wants to eat his breakfast."

My dad turned away to face my mother and myself. Lenore and I smiled at each other. Last night we had laughed over my father's discomfort in the hospital; it was definitely not subtle. I had done a little imitation of my father meeting some of the sicker patients and both Lenore and I were reduced to hysterical laughter. Hector had to come into the room to ask us to quiet down as we were disturbing the sleep of the other patients. Of course, this just made us laugh more.

My father devoured his eggs and bacon. He ate quickly, even for my dad who was normally a fast eater. He was clearly frightened of being in the dining room and was particularly uncomfortable sitting at the same table as George. He kept glancing at him or looking over his own shoulder all the time. He simply could not sit still. He could hardly wait to get out of there and had returned his tray with his dishes to the tray stand and was pacing up and down the room nervously before I had barely begun to eat. I was glad that my dad was so uncomfortable – maybe now he would take me more seriously and get me out of here. I was hoping Big John or someone really scary would "act out" in front of my dad. Maybe then he could see what I was talking about. My mother, on the other hand, seemed oblivious to her surroundings, and did not touch her meal.

After breakfast, my parents went to meet with Dr. Tatelman and I went back to my ward. Two hours later, they came back up and we went into the TV room, just my mom, my dad, and me. Mrs. Lohmer, being the head nurse, was a bit more lax with the rules. She whispered that she would keep an eye on me from the nurses' office while I visited with my folks.

"Ruthie," my dad started, "we had a good visit with the doctors. We met with that Tatelman and he's pleased with you."

"Dad, what does that mean? They won't even let me off this unit. And I haven't even seen Dr. Tatelman since I first arrived here!"

"He says it's normal for patients to want to go home. Your behaviour is not unexpected. Then he called in two other doctors, dear, what were their names?"

"Dr. Stepford and Dr. Evanson," my mother replied numbly.

"Yeah, those were the two. They said they had some trouble with you before but you seem to be settling down. I guess you broke some things. They want to get your seizures under control."

"Dad, they are under control. I've only had one big one and I'm on medication. I never had any before I came here. Epilepsy is no big thing. But I'm going crazy here."

My dad looked at me with kind eyes. "Ruthie, epilepsy is a big thing. We don't know how to deal with it at home. You have to get help here. The doctors seem very nice and they want to help you."

"Look, Dad," my voice rose, "epilepsy is not the end of the world. Just because all of you think it is this terrible thing, doesn't mean that I have to be punished by being locked up here. A lot of people live normal lives with epilepsy. You're just frightened of it, that's all," I spat out bitterly.

"Now Ruthie...." my dad put his arm out towards me. But he did not contradict me.

I tried again.

"Dad, Dr. Evanson is crazy. He hates me. He doesn't want to help me."

"Oh Ruthie, don't be silly, of course he wants to help you. He's a doctor. He's a very nice man."

I felt tears of frustration run down my face and my mother came over to hug me. She had been unusually silent this trip and I wondered why she was so upset. It would be many years before I found out that she had begged and pleaded with my father and the doctors for me to come back home, and had lost her argument to the men. My father told me, with great admiration for my mother's persistence, that each week, in Winnipeg, she would drag him over to the rabbi's house.

"Please rabbi, help me bring my daughter home," she would cry. "Please, my daughter needs to be home with her family."

My dad had tears in his eyes, many years later, when he explained that he and the rabbi would tell her to leave me there. The men would say they couldn't handle epilepsy and the other ways I had acted out, that it was better for everyone that I stay. Yet every week, week after week, month after month, year after year, my mother never stopped trying to get me out of the hospital. I never knew that when my mother was alive. I never got a chance to thank her for believing in me.

My mother came over to put her arms around me. "We need to go now dear, we'll be late for our plane." My mother pulled me to her again, kissed me on the cheek and then ushered my father down the hall where they descended on the clanking elevator to the strains of Mrs. Schwartz's lament, "I'm not left here, oh nooo, I'mmmm not left here."

I sat cross-legged on the daybed in Dr. Evanson's office and leaned against the wall in silence. He was engrossed in his tax returns. I thought of Dr. Doupe, Winnipeg, and all the events leading to this incredible situation.

Ruth Simkin

The first morning on the psych ward at Winnipeg General, I found myself being roused out of bed. "Come on, Ruthie J. Time to get up."

"Margie! What are you doing here?" Margie's older sister, Charlotte, was one of my best friends. I had known Margie for years.

"Well, I'm just doing my psych rotation now. One more year, and I'll finally finish nursing."

I sat up on the bed and Margie sat down beside me. I looked over at her and smiled; her curly blonde hair was escaping out of her student nursing cap. She had such a warm smile – I was really happy to see her.

"Listen, Ruthie, there is something I have to tell you. We have to write down everything important that the patients tell us. I'm telling you that now, because I don't want you to think that things will be confidential between us just because we know each other."

"Thanks for telling me, Margie. You just go ahead and do your job. I'm glad you're here. It's nice to see you, even if it is a little embarrassing for me to be on a psych ward."

"Well then, get up, get dressed, the doctors are coming to see you this morning."
"Doctors?"

"Well, yes, you are in a hospital, you know," Margie laughed.

I trudged down the hall to the shower room. As I was returning to my room, I saw Donna.

"Oh hi," she said, "how was your first night in cuckoo land?"

"Okay, I guess. The nurse said the doctors were coming this morning."

"Oh yeah, you have to get your admission history and all. Nothing to it. Come for breakfast now."

I had such mixed feelings about seeing Donna again. I desperately wanted the comfort she offered me. I also knew I possessed, but did not understand, strong sexual feelings towards her. Yet I had the uncomfortable feeling she would get me into trouble. I had decided to cooperate with everyone, sort things out, and get back to university. Donna's attitude was not consistent with my plans. I was confused.

We had barely sat down at the long table for breakfast, when a nurse came to get me. "The doctor is waiting for you in your room."

I walked into my room and saw a short, black-haired man dressed in white pants, white shirt and a white coat.

"Hello," he put out his hand, "I'm Dr. Singh."

"Hello," I shook his hand. I reminded myself that I had decided to cooperate as best I could. I had promised Glenda, the probation officer who had been so kind to me, and I wanted to keep myself out of trouble. And besides, I really did want to

get better, even though I had no idea what that actually meant.

Dr. Singh asked me lots of questions, which I answered as well as I was able. I felt the most uncomfortable with the sex questions, even though I tried to be honest.

"What is your sex life like?"

"Well, you know…" I shrugged.

"Do you have sexual intercourse regularly?"

"Yes, I guess I do."

"Do you have a regular boyfriend?"

"No, not now. I was married, but I'm getting divorced."

"Divorced? Do you want to talk about that?"

"No, not really. I really shouldn't have gotten married in the first place, and my husband, well,…."

I thought back to over a year ago.

Winnipeg, Manitoba, September 1962

I am standing with my father outside the Rosh Pina Synagogue doors, appropriately bedecked in full bridal costume. I am wearing a lacy white bridal gown with an enormous train that makes me laugh. My hair is curled and I have a little white cap on my head, its veil covering part of my face. I look at the last of my bridesmaids walking down the aisle, followed by the maid of honour, my sister Judi. They all wear peach-coloured, low-cut gowns. For someone like me, much more comfortable in blue jeans, it is a surreal, bizarre experience. The bridal party has finished making its way down the aisle and there is a slight pause, before 'Here Comes the Bride', courtesy of Richard Wagner and Lohengrin, heralds the entrance of bride and father. In that moment I begin dry heaving over a large ashtray near the doorway, my shoulders racked with misery and despair. I would vomit had there been food in my stomach instead of just alcohol.

"Ruthie, cut that out, quit fooling around," orders my father. "It's time for us to go."

"Oh dad," gasp, hack, heave, "I really don't want to do this."

"Don't be silly. Of course, you want to do this. Come on, stop this nonsense. It's time for us to go."

I take a deep breath, clear my throat, sigh deeply and take my father's arm. We start the long walk down the aisle and I feel the perspiration coming down my face. I see everyone smiling at me, whispering to each other.

Once I reach the chupah, *I realize there is nowhere to go but up the stairs to the altar of wedded bliss land. I look at my husband-to-be, grinning, reaching out* to take my hand. I don't even know if I like him, much less love him. I remember just two weeks before, telling my parents and my future in-laws that I definitely do not want to get married. They all reassure me that it is only pre-wedding jitters, and of course I want to get married. That night, I try to convince my best friend Susan to run away with me.

"C'mon Susan. Let's just get in the car and drive."

"Drive where, Ruthie?" Susan takes another swig of Jordan's crackling rose, our preferred drink of the year.

"Anywhere, I don't care. Texas. Let's go to Texas."

"Texas?! Why would we go to Texas?"

"I don't know. I don't care. You pick a place then. Let's just go. Please, Syuuuusan, please, let's go."

"Ryuth, no, I can't run away with you. I'm not that way. You know that."

"Please Syuuusan, I can't get married. Please, run away with me. I don't care if we're together that way or not. Just come."

"Don't be silly. Here, have another drink."

I do. I have many and stay drunk until, and during, the wedding.

Now, here I am, under the chupah, with the rabbi and Ricky, my grinning, idiotic husband-to-be, my sister Judi, the Maid of Honour, my best friend Susan, a brides-maid, along with Annette, Ester-Malka and Arlene, the groom's Best Man Arnie, my parents, Ricky's parents and the rest of the large bridal party.

What have I done? When Ricky asked to talk with me privately almost two years before, I had thought he was going to break up with me, not ask me to get married.

Pasadena, California, June 1961

"Ricky, I'm only seventeen. You don't want to marry me."

"Yes, Ruthie, I do, and I'll wait for you until you are ready. I love you and I do want to marry you."

I looked over at Ricky whom I thought very good-looking with his short light brown hair, well-built body and kind brown eyes. A year and a half ago I had been visiting my aunt and uncle in Los Angeles when my aunt decided it would be nice to arrange a New Year's Eve date for me. She asked Ricky, whom she knew through relatives, to take me out. He would only agree to take me on a date first and, if he liked me, then he would take me out for New Year's Eve. He was always somewhat prudent in areas that didn't really matter. We did like each other, especially since I won a pumpkin pie at bowling, which four of us devoured in the little Volkswagen belonging to George, his sister Annette's fiancé. We went out every night I was in Los Angeles, including New Year's Eve.

And then we wrote letters. Lots of letters. He came to visit his grandparents in Winnipeg, seeing me every day he was there. I went back to Los Angeles for Easter holidays. We tried to be together every chance we had. He was my first real boyfriend of whom my parents approved, so I reveled in the attention. Now I was back yet again in Los Angeles, staying at his house with his family. His sister was my age and the two of us had become fast friends.

I sat in the car and thought to myself, "Well, I've never been married before – maybe it would be worth a try." I turned to look at him. "Okay." I shrugged my shoulders.

"Okay? Okay yes, you'll marry me?" He seemed quite excited.

"Yeah, okay, I'll marry you."

"Great, let's go back in. My parents are waiting – they knew I was going to propose."

Once back in Ricky's house, I called my parents.

"Dad, hi. I'm engaged."

"How do you know you're engaged?" he asked.

"Well, Ricky asked me to marry him and gave me a ring."

"What do you mean, he gave you a ring?"

"I mean he gave me a ring, Dad. That's what people do when they get engaged. They get rings."

Within hours, my parents had driven down from Palm Springs where they were vacationing. Everyone seemed so happy and pleased with this turn of events, I didn't have the heart to change anything, so I went along with it. Finally, I had done something that merited the approval of my parents.

Winnipeg, Manitoba, September 1962

And now, here I was, under the chupah, this thing, this marriage, quickly becoming an inevitability.

I started to laugh. What else could I do? I giggled through the entire wedding ceremony. The entire turn of events struck me as ludicrous – the fact that everyone was standing here so earnestly when clearly life was full of surprises and turns one could not anticipate – I just laughed. I simply could not take this seriously.

"Shh," my cousins whispered. "Shhh, this is serious."

"I know," I whispered back and giggled some more. "It's very serious." I couldn't contain my laughter.

"Ruthie, be serious! Stop laughing!" this from my dad.

"Okay dad," snort, sniggle. I just couldn't stop the sounds from bubbling up out of me.

I looked down at the fading bruises on my arm, dark colours contrasting against the bridal white. Two weeks earlier I had been waterskiing at the lake. I was on the slalom ski, had just let go of the tow-rope and was coming in very quickly alongside the dock, where I was sure I would make a perfect landing. I did so love to show off. Just moments after I let go of the rope, a motor boat went by me far too quickly. Its wake picked me up and slammed me into the dock.

The next thing I remember is opening my eyes and looking into the deep, big grey eyes of a very handsome and curly-headed man. I looked down and realized that I was nude from the waist up, lying on a sofa. "Pity," I thought, "I don't even remember doing it with him." Just then, my mother's face came into view behind this Adonis. "Oh shit, my mom has caught us; and I am just two weeks away from being married!" I started to stammer some sort of excuse when the man said, "Just take it easy, don't try to get up. You are at the doctor's office. You've broken some ribs."

"Oh, Ruthie," my mother moaned, "how could you be so careless?"

"Mom, it wasn't my fault," I remembered the wake tossing me into the unyielding wood of the dock. "Really, it was going to be the perfect landing, if it hadn't been for that boat."

"She's getting married in two weeks, doctor," my mom explained, "and she just had a cast removed from her wrist last week! Before that, she had stitches in her leg. And now this. I just don't know what I'm going to do with her!"

I remembered my friends joking about the bride wearing a cast of silk, with bandages of beaded tulle and crutches bedecked in floral decals. We had a good laugh over that. And now, here I was in a very handsome doctor's office, needing to deal with several broken ribs. I really did not want to get married!

But I was standing under the chupah and it was actually happening. The rabbi was saying his stuff, I was trying not to giggle, and then it was done. Ricky stomped on the glass, and that was it. I was married. I put a smile on my face and tried to cover up the nausea that welled inside me. The only way I could abate that queasiness inside my soul was with alcohol, which I drank in prodigious amounts that night.

We got through it. I went off to set up house with my husband in a little apartment not far from my parents' home in Winnipeg, and lived one of the worst years *of my life until I finally sent him packing back to his mama. The only good things about my marriage were that I managed to finish third year university and we bought a little white toy poodle, Peppy, who lived with me and my family for fifteen years.*

Winnipeg, Manitoba, November 1963

Dr. Singh broke this reverie.

"What do you do so you won't get pregnant?"

"Huh? What?"

"What do you do about sex, so you won't get pregnant?"

"Well, I was on the birth control pill for a while, condoms, things like that."

"Do you have any homosexual tendencies?"

"What did you say?" I jerked my head up.

"Have you ever been attracted to people of the same sex?"

"Well, yes, I have, sort of, but I have never done anything."

As he carried on with the questioning, I worried about my honesty, because I knew at least four of the nurses who worked in the ward and was embarrassed to be talking about sex. I just prayed that the information would be between me and the doctor. I kept telling myself I needed to get better, although I didn't really even know what was wrong. I didn't mind partaking in sexual activities; I just didn't feel comfortable talking about it with a stranger, especially one who had on all his clothes.

When Dr. Singh finished examining me, he asked me to wait in the room, because all the doctors would be making rounds soon and they would want to meet me. I sat on my bed, swinging my feet up and down, up and down, up and down, feeling more anxious by the second.

Not long after he left, twelve people breezed into my room, led by a tall, white-haired competent-looking woman who reached out to shake my hand, smiled, and said, "Hi Ruth, I'm Dr. Doupe. How are you today?"

"Okay, I guess." I liked her at once.

Her warm, brown, intelligent eyes looked deeply into mine. I immediately felt that finally I had met someone who could help me sort out what was happening.

"I understand that you are a university student and that you have been having periods of black-outs, is that correct?"

"Uh, yes. Yes, that's correct."

"Well, Ruth," she smiled, "let's see if we can't sort things out a bit for you. Expect to be here at least two weeks so we can run some tests and get to know you a little better. Okay?"

"Okay. Sure."

"Good. See you later." Dr. Doupe swept out of the room followed by her entourage.

I stood in my doorway and watched them greet a few patients, peep into a few rooms, and then they were off.

I felt optimistic about my life for the first time in a long while. I knew that Dr. Doupe was the one who could help me. I felt she could see me, when most of the people I had met so far did not seem to be able to do that. I could hardly wait to meet her again.

Several hours later, I was alone in the TV room. Most of the old ladies were sleeping and Donna was taken off for some tests. All of a sudden, there was a news bulletin: the president of the United States had been shot.

"Oh my God!" I muttered. I watched just long enough to confirm Kennedy's shooting and then ran out of the room. The hall was almost deserted, except for Mrs. Garvey sitting in her usual place, tying her shoelaces to different parts of her clothing, and a nurse I had never seen before.

I ran up to the nurse: "The president's been shot!"

"That's nice, dear. What is your name again, Ruthie, is it?"

"No, you don't understand. President Kennedy's been assassinated!"

"Don't be ridiculous, dear. Here, come sit down with us for a while."

I sat down heavily, feeling stunned and devastated by her response and utterly deserted and alone. It had never occurred to me that my sense of reality would be questioned simply because I was a patient on a psychiatric ward. I was going to tell the nurse that I was a fourth year honours university student and could discern whether or not the president of the United States had really been shot. But instead, I was so shocked by her response that I had to wait for my heart to stop pounding, wondering how I could make contact and connect with someone, anyone.

Suddenly, the door burst open and Willie called to the nurse, "Alice, come quickly. President Kennedy's been shot! C'mon, it's on TV now. Ruthie, would you like to come watch with us?"

I was grateful for Willie.

I knew her before I came to the hospital because she was a good friend of Margie's. Alice looked at me, shrugged her shoulders, left poor Mrs. Garvey in her crouch and went quickly through the door.

"Thanks, Willie," I said. "I think I'll watch it here instead." I did not want to go with the nurses, especially when some were like Alice, whom I felt made fun of me and treated me like a mental patient. I felt I belonged more on Mrs. Garvey's side. I would just wait for Donna. I so badly wanted to be with her, as I remembered the comfort she gave as she stroked my head that day in the lock-up.

Soon Donna returned to the ward and the two of us watched TV for quite a while, in silence, holding hands and just feeling close. I seemed much more upset about the shooting of the president than anyone else on the ward, including Donna.

"Hey, want to play ping-pong?" Donna asked after a time.

"Sure. Where do we go?"

"Follow me, Ruthie J." She grabbed my hand and led me down the hall.

For a while we batted the ball back and forth without speaking, listening to the click-clack, click-clack of the ball on the table.

"Donna, why are you really here?"

"Ah kid, it's a long story. See, the welfare people took away my three kids…"

"Your three kids! How old are you anyway?"

"Thirty-one. Anyway, they took away the kids and my old man wanted to get back at the city so we planned some heists. We had a business where we were going into new houses where the people hadn't moved in yet and we were taking the appliances and stuff and selling them. And then we got caught and we got sent up for a while…"

"So you have been in jail before?"

Donna grinned. "Yes, many times."

I laughed. "And when we were in jail I said I would protect you!"

"Yeah, you were so cute."

We both laughed as Donna finished her story.

"So where is your husband now?"

"Oh, I won't see him for about another ten years," she winked. "Listen, Ruthie J., how about coming back to the physiotherapy department again tonight? You know, we could make a lot of money."

I didn't care about money. I let Donna do all the money arrangements, and even let her keep the money, as long as she bought my meals for me.

"Gee, Donna, I'm not sure. I want to get better. I don't think I should be screwing around right now."

Donna put her arm around me. "Aw, c'mon, Ruthie J., do it for me." And she leaned over to kiss me. That kiss — so sweet and tender, caused my entire body to fill with warmth. I thought I was falling in love.

That night found us stealthily sneaking into the physiotherapy department to meet the men once more. After we returned, I wasn't feeling so well and went right to bed. As I pulled back the covers on my bed, I noticed some lumpiness under the sheets. I pulled back the sheets and found many pictures cut out of magazines. All the pictures were of guns or rifles or cannons or tanks. It was a very violent collection.

I went out to the nursing station and asked a nurse to come into my room with me to see what I had found.

She took one look and said, "Oh, that's Mrs. Snell's stuff."

"Mrs. Snell!? The sweet little old lady? Are you sure?"

"Of course, I'm sure. She collects violent pictures. She also has a habit of setting apartment buildings on fire, which is why she is here. She shouldn't bother you any more. Goodnight."

I crawled under the sheets and pulled up the covers. I was exhausted from a day full of such varying emotions: seeing all the new doctors, learning about President Kennedy, being kissed by Donna for the first time and then screwing some stranger in the physiotherapy department. I wasn't so sure I liked this place.

Suddenly I became aware that I was not alone. In the darkness, I saw a shadow come towards the bed, then a hand reached over to pull back the covers and before I knew what was happening, a body was in bed with me.

"Mrs. Snell! What are you doing here?! Nurse! Nurse!" I yelled as loud as I could. "Nuuuurse!"

"Oh hush dear. Where are my pictures?"

"The nurse has them. Mrs. Snell, please get out of my bed."

The nurse came in and led Mrs. Snell away.

My heart was still pounding when, much later, I finally fell asleep.

The next morning, I was standing in my room when I became aware of a terrible racket. Suddenly I looked up, and there was Dr. Doupe, standing in the doorway, looking oddly at me. There were broken dishes at one end of my room.

"Why did you do that?" inquired Dr. Doupe.

"Do what?" I asked, feeling very puzzled.

"Break all those dishes," Dr Doupe indicated with a motion of her head.

"I didn't break those dishes."

"You did, Ruthie, I saw you."

Tears sprang to my eyes. I looked at the dishes, remnants from my breakfast which I had brought into my room to eat in preferred solitude, then at Dr. Doupe, then at the dishes again. I felt very perplexed and more than a little afraid.

"Have Ruth come to my office at two o'clock this afternoon," Dr. Doupe told the nurse who was with her. "And have someone help her clean up this mess."

Two o'clock found me in Dr. Doupe's office.

She smiled at me and said, "Tell me a bit about yourself."

I felt Dr. Doupe really cared about me, so I told her about the car accident and how puzzled I was about what had really happened. I told her about my family, and about my friends. I told her about my drinking sprees with Susan. I told her I thought I drank to cover up the fact that I couldn't understand a lot of my behaviour, and my forgetting whole periods of time. I told her about my other friends, about being on the basketball team, about poor Massey. I talked about my past marriage and my confused feelings about that. I related with some bitterness how my husband had not wanted me to continue university so I could stay home to keep house for him, and how university was so important to me. I talked about my hurt and confusion when I found out my husband had been lying about going to school and was really playing poker at his cousin's all day. I talked for over two hours. Dr. Doupe was so easy to talk with, and I knew that we both liked each other.

"And so throughout all this acting out, and all your escapades," Dr. Doupe remarked, "you've still been able to maintain relatively good marks at the university?"

"Yes, that's right. I'm due to graduate from an honours program this spring."

"Listen, Ruth, I normally don't see patients from the ward. I have a few private patients and spend the rest of my time being administrator of the ward. But I would like to see you for therapy if you would be willing. How do you feel about that?"

"Oh, I think that that would be great!" I smiled.

"Good. I also think that we need to do some special tests to find out more about these black-outs. I'll go ahead and order them for sometime next week, and I'll see you again Monday at two for another session. Okay?"

"Okay. That's great. Thank you very much, Dr. Doupe. Thank you for talking with me."

"Not at all, Ruthie. See you on Monday."

I returned to the ward feeling elated. At last, I had found someone who was going to help me feel better. I was sure of that. I pushed the buzzer to the locked ward and the door was opened for me. I didn't even mind being on the locked ward now because I felt so optimistic about my future. Dr. Doupe would help me figure things out. I laughed as I saw Brunhilda down the hall, preparing to enter her room: bump bump, bump bump, clap clap, slap slap.

Donna was waiting for me. "Well, how was it?"

"Oh Donna, it was great! Dr. Doupe is so nice. I really was able to talk with her."

"Don't let her snow you, kid. She's just like the rest of them here. Don't get sucked in. Hey c'mon, let's go sit on my bed and talk."

The weekend passed quickly. Mostly Donna and I sprawled on each others' beds, held hands and talked. My heart pounded deep within my chest every time she came close to me. I wanted another kiss so badly, but did not have a clue how to get it. I wished I knew more about real sex and real love. I was sure I was falling in love with her. Certainly, I already loved her more than I ever loved my ex-husband.

By Sunday night, I could hardly wait to get into bed, because then it would be Monday and I could see Dr. Doupe again. I changed into my blue and white striped pajamas and waited in line in the bathroom to brush my teeth. Back in my room, as I pulled back the blankets and saw the lumps, I thought oh no, not more pictures! But when I pulled back the sheets I saw soft white things, which turned out to be underwear. Mrs. Snell's underwear, I ventured. I went out to the nursing station holding white cotton underpants dripping from one hand and a soft white cotton undershirt dangling from the other.

"It looks like Mrs. Snell has a crush on you, Ruthie J.," laughed Margie.

"Well, at least it's not boring in this place," I chuckled, as Brunhilda exited in her usual fashion from the bathroom.

"So how're things, Ruthie; are they going okay?"

"Yeah, okay Margie. I'm seeing Dr. Doupe for therapy, so that should be a good thing."

"Great. She is very good. Everyone really likes her."

"Well, goodnight, Margie. Have a good night."

"Thanks. You too, Ruthie J."

Early the next morning, I was awakened and told to dress quickly. "Some special tests have been ordered for you," the nurse informed me.

I was taken over to the main hospital and up an elevator to a small room.

"Ruth Simkin?" asked a tiny young woman in a white uniform.

"Yes. Where am I?"

"This is the EEG lab. You are going to have an EEG, an electroencephalogram. That is where we measure your brain waves. It doesn't hurt at all. We just connect these wires to your head with some glue, and you lie down and the machine does the rest. Okay?"

"I guess so. I've never had one of these before. How do you get the glue out?" She smiled, and began attaching me to the wires.

The test wasn't so bad. The worst part was when the strobe light went off in my eyes, causing me to feel disoriented and distressed. The second worst part was washing the glue out of my hair.

That afternoon, Dr. Doupe casually said, "The nurses tell me you are spending quite a bit of time with Donna."

"Yeah, I guess I am. She's the only one on that side of the ward who isn't nuts."

"Ruthie, let me give you a bit of advice. Stay away from her. The woman is a sociopath. I know you want to get back to university as soon as possible. She is bad news for you."

"Don't try to tell me who my friends can be," I spat out angrily. I was feeling defensive and somewhat loyal to Donna. It seemed as though people were always trying to tell me who my friends could be.

"All right, Ruth, have it your way. Tell me about your family."

I sulked for the rest of the session, answering questions as briefly as possible without totally antagonizing Dr. Doupe. I felt trapped between Dr. Doupe and Donna, and wasn't sure which one of them was right about the other, although reluctantly I suspected that Dr. Doupe was the one who would prove to be correct in her assessment of Donna.

That night, Donna and I each had two partners in the physiotherapy department, as Don and Frank each brought a friend. I drank more than usual and, as soon as we got back, went straight to bed, holding onto the side of the bed as the room spun around until I finally lost consciousness.

Chapter Ten

One day at rounds, Dr. Stepford informed me I would be allowed to attend the movie at the Center the next evening – escorted of course. I had not been in the Center yet, though I had been at Chestnut Lodge for five months. I had only met the patients on my ward and those few, like Betty, who came up to play bridge, as well as a few from my very occasional trips to the dining room. I was terribly excited about going.

"C'mon, let's go Jorge, we'll be late," I jumped up and down for emphasis.

"Hold your horses. We'll go when we're ready." I was showered, dressed in clean clothes and looking forward to the outing. How could he not understand how much I wanted to go? At last I could meet some real people, have a real conversation with someone other than Lenore, who was becoming more and more important to my sanity, not to mention my alcohol habit, as the months slipped by.

It amazed me that I was still sane, according to my own evaluation. I listened to a lot of Miriam Makeba records, singing along in South African and Xhosa, not understanding a word of what I sang. But Pete Seeger's lyrics I did understand, along with those of his sister Peggy's, and they were my second favourite. I read prodigiously, being particularly fond of Kurt Vonnegut. I had read *Player Piano, The Sirens of Titan, Mother Night* and the new *Cat's Cradle*. And I played bridge. Max was an excellent teacher and within a few months I was one of the best players in the hospital. We played for hours during the day and in the evenings. And, of course, I drank – a lot. Yet in all those months, I still had not been in any of the other buildings except for Dr. Evanson's office. And now, finally, I was going to be able to go out! I was exhilarated!

Lenore told me she would meet me at the movie and save me a seat. Jorge took us all down the elevator – me, Janie, Max and Mrs. Kane, who could go unescorted, but preferred to come with us.

"Quentin," Janie moaned as the elevator clunked into action after the keys were turned.

"So, girlie," Max looked at me, "we're going to the movies, are we? Don't be fooled by them." I wasn't sure what Max meant. I wasn't sure if Max knew what Max meant.

Mrs. Kane, in her pink cardigan neatly buttoned up to her chin, stood in silence, immobile, like a statue.

The elevator reached the ground floor and Jorge pulled the steel grate open, collapsing the steel bars that made a fourth wall as we descended the elevator shaft. Where would we go without the bars, I wondered? I laughed at the lunacy of this lunatic asylum. Chestnut Lodge is a perfect euphemism, I thought, as I stepped out of the elevator, through the door, and into the open air at last.

We walked along the black-topped road surrounded by trees. It was amazing to me how beautiful the countryside was, the softly rolling pastoral hills, flowers peppering the landscape in bright colours, the fresh smell of spring in the air. I was struck with the incongruity of this nuthouse with its ugliness inside imposed upon this natural beauty.

We got to the Center just as the lights were dimming.

"Psst, Ruthie, over here." Lenore patted a stacking chair beside her.

"Thanks, Lenore. What's the movie?"

"Don't know. We'll see in a minute."

Just then the title came on the screen. "Oh no, I don't believe it! They must be joking, right?"

"No, I guess not. It's really that movie."

"Lenore, how could they do that? Is this a trick of some sort? They're not really showing that, are they?

"Yes, it appears as though they are. So hush now and let's watch."

I settled back into my chair as the movie, 'The Three Faces of Eve,' began to play.

I had already seen this movie when it came out a few years back. It was based on a true story and Joanne Woodward had won an Academy Award for playing Eve, a woman with multiple personalities. One of them, the evil one, tries to kill her daughter and Eve is then sent to an insane asylum. Under hypnosis, she brings out her different personalities and ultimately gets well, but the movie is scary at times – especially the parts with the abnormal personalities and the mental institution.

I looked around the room as my eyes adjusted to the darkness. There were ten rows of stacking chairs with an aisle down the middle, eight chairs on each side of it. Almost all the chairs were full. In front was a portable movie screen, listing to the right on its rickety tripod. The black and white movie flickered on the screen while a hissing sound came out of the one speaker.

I had trouble deciding where to focus my attention – the movie or the people. Across the aisle from us was a middle-aged woman who sat quite still, but every ten or fifteen minutes she'd begin grunting excitedly. Someone would yell, "Bella, shut up!" and she would sit still again until the next grunting episode.

Beside her was a long, lanky woman with stringy hair dangling down to her shoulders, who rocked up and back unceasingly.

Lenore leaned into my ear and told me that the long, lanky woman was Marsha. She had been a patient in a mental hospital for over twenty years and for most of that time, did not get off her bed. When she came here, she could not walk, because the tendons in her ankles had shortened. She had to have surgery to be able to walk again.

Bella had been at Chestnut Lodge for decades, where she had sat in silence. As the new anti-psychotic drugs came out, her doctors started her on some and she had just been on them a short time. Now she occasionally got excited and made sounds, usually grunting. She was starting to get better and could walk around on her own now.

George was a few rows behind her also rocking, sitting, staring straight ahead with a smile on his angelic face, black curls tumbling down his forehead, mumbling and moving: "Moov." Rock. "ie." Rock. "Moov." Rock. "ie." Rock.

Another woman began moving chairs around. Jorge yelled, "Daisy, sit down and be still!"

She yelled back, "I'm not Daisy, I'm Nancy!" but the threatening tone in Jorge's voice helped her to be still.

We turned our attention back to the movie. I was loathe to get too involved with the movie because I was frightened of all these strange people, patients and aides alike, and did not want to be off guard. I kept glancing over my shoulder.

I started to look around the room again as Daisy/Nancy knocked over a row of chairs. Lenore took my hand and gently patted it. "You get used to all this, you know. After a while, it won't even seem strange."

The screaming from the movie was echoed by the screaming in the Center. Several patients had to be taken back to their wards because they were too upset. There was a surreal quality to the whole evening. I couldn't believe that someone on staff had actually selected this movie to be shown here. It just reconfirmed my belief that this was truly an insane place – and I was not thinking of the patients.

By the time we came back to the ward, Janie was more upset than I'd ever seen her. She would make this low gurgling sound, turn it into a demented laugh and end in a scream. Her arms were flailing in front of her.

"Janie, here, drink this orange juice." Mrs. Decker pushed the glass towards her. With a scream, Janie flung out her arm and the glass smashed to the floor.

"Okay, Janie, settle down now," Mrs. Jackley urged.

Janie laughed and screamed more. It was amazing to hear that laugh – so deep and sinister, it did not seem to come from her slight body. She was wild now, leaping through the air and flailing her arms in a frenzied dance.

Her pink sweater hung off one shoulder, like a shawl wrapped around her. Her mauve slacks were wet between the legs where she had likely peed. Her blouse, neatly done up when she left the unit, was now partially undone and wrinkled and pulled out of her slacks. Her blonde hair was plastered to the side of her skull with perspiration. She couldn't seem to stop moving. Her arms and legs all moved but not in concert with each other; each limb seemed to be mobile of it's own accord, moving to it's own rhythm.

"Get a pack ready," Mrs. Decker ordered.

Mrs. Jackley followed Janie around the room, unsuccessfully trying to contain her.

"Call Main Three," she yelled over her shoulder, "we'll need help."

I watched as three large male aides ran up the stairs, picked Janie up and carried her to her room. I tried to shut out the screaming, but it echoed in my ears. As I walked to my room, I passed Janie's half open door and glanced in to see one of the aides whack her across the face with a wet sheet. The thwack echoed out of the room. He looked up, saw me and slammed shut the door. The screaming continued. I lay down on my bed and shut out the sound with memories.

Winnipeg, Manitoba, November 1963

I saw Dr. Doupe daily and almost every day had some sort of test. I was talking easily with her once more. Neither of us mentioned Donna again. I spoke very little to Donna about what happened with Dr. Doupe, and managed to keep the two of them quite separate in my actions and in my mind.

One Friday, Dr. Doupe said, "Ruthie, you have really been doing quite well.

How would you like to be transferred to the open side of the unit? You will have a little more freedom there to come and go as you please."

"That would be great. Brunhilda and Mrs. Snell and Mrs. Garvey are all really nice, but…" I smiled.

"Good. You'll be moved this afternoon. Have a good weekend."

I almost ran back to the unit. I went straight to my room and started gathering my belongings. Donna walked into my room.

"Hey, what're you up to?"

"Hey, Donna, guess what!? I'm going to the open side!"

"Oh, that's great kid, because I'm leaving here this evening."

"What? You're what? Where are you going? What are you going to do? When will I see you?" My heart started aching already at the anticipated loss of Donna, my best buddy. We hadn't had our second kiss yet, something I hungrily yearned for.

"Not to worry, Ruthie J. I'll leave you my number and you can call me as soon as you get out. I'm going to live with my friend, Curley. He lives with another guy, Locky. I know you'll like him. Come stay with us for a while when you get out."

"Well, my family…you know, they might not…"

"Never mind your family. Come. Then you and I can spend a lot of time together. Private time." She winked at me, put her arm around my shoulders and pulled me close to her. "Here's the phone number and address. Just call me as soon as you get out of here and I'll get you. It'll be great, Ruthie J., you and I, free, no cops, no nut cases, no nurses – just lots of time together." She squeezed my shoulder and my heart melted.

That evening on the open side, I sat on my bed in a room with three other beds, whose occupants were all young women like myself. They were all in the TV room, but I felt a little shy and out of place. I was afraid that they wouldn't accept me, that they would make fun of me. I had always been so awkward with girls my age, those who were "acceptable," – as though I could never measure up to them. I had to laugh at myself that here I was in a nuthouse feeling out of place with the very girls whom I, and more importantly, the rest of the world, perceived as being somewhat normal.

I wore my blue and white-striped pajama top over my shirt, a habit I had developed over the past week. It was soft and cuddly. I moved my little plastic glass with me to the 'open' side as well. Secretly, I talked to the glass and treated it as a substitute teddy bear. That way, I was beyond suspicion. The glass could sit on my night table and be a source of strength and comfort and no one would know. 'Glass' started to take on many anthropomorphic characteristics, but most of all, I loved

Glass and I knew Glass loved me.

That night, I could not fall asleep. About one-thirty, I wandered out to the nurses' desk, which was on the open side of the ward, with big windows looking over into the locked side.

"Hi, Ruthie, what's up?" My friend Willie was on night shift.

"Can't sleep. Can I sit here with you for a while?"

"Sure you can. Would you like a cup of tea? Here, help yourself."

"Thanks, Willie." I poured myself some tea. As we sat and chatted about nursing school and my courses at university, I eyed the nurses' desk. There was a big cardex sitting there. It had all the patients' names listed, so one could flip it open and read the most relevant things about each patient for quick reference.

"Willie," I asked hesitantly, "would I be able to read my chart?"

"Gosh, Ruthie, I'm sorry, but we're really not supposed to let any of the patients see their charts. It seems sort of silly, but I'd get into trouble if I gave you your chart. I'm really sorry."

"That's okay, Willie, I understand."

Half an hour later, one of the nurses from the locked side ran up to the window, banged on it and gestured urgently for Willie to come.

"Oops, gotta run, Ruthie. Be back in a flash." Willie let herself into the locked side, pocketing her keys as she ran down the hall.

The cardex file burned into my eyes. I knew I had to act fast. I looked around, and did not see a soul. I quickly flipped open the cardex where it said 'Ruth Simkin' and audibly gasped as I saw an asterisk in red, followed by red printing across the top saying: Watch closely. Has strong homosexual tendencies.

I closed the file as though the cards were on fire. I could not believe what I had seen. I remembered telling Dr. Singh that I had been attracted to women, but that I had never acted on it. He didn't know about Donna. Besides, nothing had really happened between us except for one kiss and lots of hand-holding. I was an active heterosexual. How could they do this to me? My face turned red when I realized that Margie and Willie and other nurses I knew must have seen this.

In the early 1960's, it was not okay to be homosexual. People got beat up or sent to jail if they were like that. I had yet to even hear the words "gay" or "lesbian." I did know that being homosexual was considered a shameful disease; yet another reason for locking me up in the hospital. I felt mortified and humiliated. I couldn't bear to ever face Willie again. I went to bed and pulled the covers up over my head, my tears dampening the sheets.

The next morning, I woke up angry and tired. I hoped that Margie and Willie would not be working on the weekend. Or ever again.

"Good morning, Ruth," I was greeted by Susan, the nurse in charge that morning. "How are you going to spend your first day of freedom? You know the patients on this side can come and go as they please?"

"Yeah, well, I'll probably go for a walk," I mumbled and walked away, leaving a puzzled Susan looking after me.

I showered and dressed, then ate my breakfast in silence, sitting apart from the rest of the patients. Since I was new on the ward, everyone just let me be, while they all carried on excited conversations about their plans for the day.

I was busy making my own plans. I knew exactly what I was going to do. I would show them. Late morning, I put on my winter coat and told Susan I was going for a walk. I walked right down the street to the liquor store and bought a six-pack of beer. I had it put in a bag and managed to get it back into the hospital and into the locker I had been assigned when I moved over to the "open side." I then opened one bottle and drank it down. I continued drinking, quickly finishing one bottle, walking around the ward to be seen, and then going back for another. After the sixth bottle, I could feel myself weaving.

"Ruth, are you all right?" Susan asked.

"Just fine," I snapped, and walked away to watch TV.

At the change of shift, Willie approached me.

"Ruthie, will you come with me please?"

My heart started pounding. I could not look at Willie. I was still feeling the mortification over what had been written beside my name. I wondered if Willie was disgusted or afraid to touch me. Willie walked into a small room with a sofa and two chairs, and closed the door.

"Ruthie, we found beer bottles in your locker. Would you like to tell me about it?"

I sat in silence.

"Ruth, is something troubling you? It's okay to talk about it. That's what you're here for."

I maintained my silence. How could I even begin to explain to Willie or anyone else my feelings about what was on the chart? My humiliation had locked that information up inside me.

"Well," sighed Willie, "we really have no choice. We have to put you back on the closed side for the weekend and then see what Dr. Doupe wants to do with you. I'm really sorry, Ruthie."

I put on my striped pajama top and carried my plastic glass. I didn't care about any of my other belongings. I went through the door, past the crouching Mrs. Garvey, around Mrs. Snell who was cutting out magazine pictures, past Brunhilda who breezed by, and back into my old room. Right where I belong, I thought. Aside from going to the bathroom, I did not leave my room nor speak to anyone for the rest of the weekend.

Monday morning, Dr. Doupe made rounds with her followers. When she got to my room, she said, "I hear you had a rough weekend. We'll talk about it this afternoon." And she was gone.

Entering Dr. Doupe's office, I was aware of a tension. I looked at Dr. Doupe who was frowning. "Ruth, I need to ask you something. I have just finished speaking with the nursing supervisor. Apparently, something happened here last Thursday evening that you have neglected to tell me."

I squirmed in my chair. I remembered last Thursday night with mixed feelings. Donna and I had been in the physiotherapy department with Don and Frank. Frank was lying on top of me, humping for all he was worth, when all of a sudden, the curtain was ripped open and there was the nursing supervisor.

"Just what is going on here?"

Frank lost his erection and slid off of me, jumping to the floor. I quickly dressed. I was glad that Donna had insisted that we wear street clothes and slide off our hospital bracelets. It worked.

"Just who do you think you are," the supervisor icily asked Frank, "that you can bring your girlfriend into the hospital and act like you're in a brothel? What is your name? What ward are you on?" She grabbed Frank's bracelet to read his particulars.

She heard the scuffling next door and opened the curtains just in time to see Don pulling up his pajama bottoms.

"Well, I never…" The supervisor huffed about. "Go to your room, at once. And you, young ladies, leave this hospital immediately. If I ever see you here again, I'll bring charges against you."

Donna and I walked out of the front door of the hospital under the staring eyes of the supervisor, and collapsed into gales of nervous laughter. We walked around the building and into another door, to go up to the psychiatric department, still holding on to each other doubled over with laughter – mostly, at least in my case, from sheer relief that I didn't get detained. I was very relieved, because now that our place had been found out, we wouldn't have to go to the physiotherapy department any more. I did not share that thought with Donna.

Dr. Doupe continued. "Apparently, the supervisor thought that you and Donna were from outside the hospital. She reported those two fellows to their doctors and to security. The next day one of the fellows told security that they had been asked by you and Donna to come, and he told them everything; how you were *patients on this ward, how you see quite a few men there, and how you took money from them. Ruth, is this true?"*

I gulped and slowly nodded my head. How could I possibly explain to Dr. Doupe that the only reason I ever went to the physiotherapy department was so that I could be with Donna. I didn't care about the men or the money. I had hoped that if I did what she wanted, maybe she would spend more time with me. I only wanted to be with Donna, to feel that comfort she provided, to feel that someone cared for me. Plus I had a sexual itch that needed scratching – it seemed irrelevant that I had no idea how to do that. Donna would know.

Dr. Doupe sighed and shook her head. "Well, I have had just about enough from you." She was angry. "First, you get caught prostituting yourself in the hospital, and then you go out to buy beer and get drunk on the ward. That's two things, Ruth. You will not get another chance after this. I am moving you back to the open ward. You will either cooperate with us and put some effort into getting better or you will be sent away. I will not waste my time on someone who does not take this seriously. Now get out of here. I am too angry to talk with you anymore today."

Rockville, Maryland; May 1964

One morning after I finished my breakfast tray, I left my rocker and stood by the window. There were large trees outside; we were on the fourth floor and if the window could open, I could nestle in the branches of this beautiful oak. It was springtime and the buds on the trees had already become leaves. I looked out past the trees and could see Upper and Lower Cottages and, beyond them, the Kiosk. Just behind Lower Cottage was apparently a music room. Although I had never seen it, today I could hear beautiful sounds coming from that direction, as Big John played *The Pier Gynt Suite*. I happily hummed along with John's playing as the mountain king marched about. I knew that the player had to be Big John because only he, from what I'd learned, could do justice to Grieg in such a magnificent fashion.

The road wound around the side of our building, turned west and then north all the way to Hilltop. Over to the left was a long, low white building which I was told had doctors' offices and group therapy rooms. The little tree sparrows flitted about the branches. I put my forehead against the window pane and tried to imagine what it would be like to be a bird.

"What are you doing there? Get away from that window!" Mrs. Jackson broke into my reverie.

The mouse-like woman in white quickstepped up to me and waggled her fingers in my face. "I've been watching you. You're sending signals out the window!"

"Signals! Mrs. Jackson, are you crazy? Who would I be sending signals to?"

She sputtered. "Why, to Lenore, or, or…I don't know. I just know you're doing it. Get away from the window."

"Mrs. Jackson, look, there isn't anyone out there."

"Of course there isn't anyone out there. They're hiding. Get away from that window. Don't make me pack you. Don't let me catch you sending signals again, young lady."

"If I can't be outside, I thought I could at least look outside." I slowly shook my head as I wandered back to the rocker and pondered how it was in life that some people got the keys and other people got the bars.

Chapter Eleven

Months passed. Lenore and I had became lovers, a fact she had confided to Hector so he could watch out for us. Hector found the idea of two women together titillating and often would stick his head around the corner to watch us make love. I knew he was there, but I didn't care.

At night, before we went to sleep, we sat on my bed looking through the bars and talking. We called the large, leafy oak outside our window our 'dream tree.' We confided all our secrets to the tree and each other.

I was almost always drunk, a state preferable to not being drunk in a mental hospital where it was almost unbearable to live sober. The staff suspected I was drinking and increased their vigilance, never letting me out of their sight. Lenore would go into our room when I was not there, filling up my water glass with vodka. I thought most of the staff was stupid. I craved the alcohol for the internal relief it gave me.

Twice a week, I was escorted to Dr. Evanson's office where we would usually sit in silence. Once I tried to say something meaningful. After getting up my courage for weeks, I walked into his office, sat down, took a big gulp and said, "Um, um, I think I'm a lesbian."

"No, you're not," he answered, without looking up from his papers, and we never spoke of it again. The rest of the fifty-minute hour took place in silence, except for the tapping of his paper piles on the desk.

I sat cross-legged on the daybed in Dr. Evanson's office and leaned against the wall in silence. He was engrossed in his tax returns. I thought of Dr. Doupe.

Winnipeg, Manitoba, December 1963

The rest of the week at the Winnipeg General Psych Ward went very slowly. Donna was gone, I had shamed myself in front of Dr. Doupe, I was embarrassed to talk with or even see Margie or Willie, I was having all kinds of medical tests and I was on a ward where I felt totally different from all the other girls. Strangely enough, I felt more comfortable with Mrs. Garvey, Mrs. Snell and Brunhilda than I did with the healthier patients on the open side. The locked ward demanded nothing from me and now that I had left it, I went into a deep depression, communicating in monosyllables only when necessary.

One day, my mom and dad dropped by in the afternoon for their usual visit. They had been coming faithfully every day to visit me. Usually, my mother would wait until my father was finished with work and would come with him. Often, he would leave work early to pick up my mother. This time, Dr. Doupe was with them. We all went into a small room to talk.

"Ruth, you know all the tests we have been giving you here," Dr. Doupe started. "Well, we have found the cause for some of your problems. You have epilepsy and you have been having psychomotor seizures. That would explain what happened the night of the car accident, the broken dishes, the other times."

I sat still in silence. My parents' faces betrayed expressions of concern, but I felt numb inside – like I was watching the scene from the ceiling, like I wasn't even there.

"We would like to start you on medication right away. We feel that the pills would keep you from having these seizures. However, as I explained to you before, and as I've explained to your parents, I feel you are having some emotional problems that need to be addressed and I would like to continue seeing you as a private patient."

"That would be fine," said my dad, adding, "I'm sure you wouldn't mind if we get a second opinion about this epilepsy, though."

"Dad, why do we need a second opinion? I think I'll be fine now."

"Your mother and I have discussed this with the doctor and we think that we should have some specialists check you. You can stay here to work with Dr. Doupe for now."

Not only did I feel totally invalidated, but also that the trust I had slowly been working to establish with Dr. Doupe was somehow violated. I hated my father for trivializing Dr. Doupe, the first person who had really tried to help me.

It had never occurred to me that I might have epilepsy. The only thing I knew about epilepsy was that it was a bad thing to have. In 1963, epilepsy was considered worse than having a mental illness; it was like mental illness multiplied. Epilepsy was a word that could barely be spoken by my parents and many others.

Personally, I was relieved that Dr. Doupe had come up with a reason for my behaviour as it had truly perplexed me. If epilepsy was the reason for my actions and feelings, so be it. As long as she could give me some pills to stop these things from happening again, I would be fine. But I was not fine with my father's dismissal of Dr. Doupe, the first person in a long time who had offered me hope for the future.

Throughout the rest of the session, when anyone asked me a question, I would just nod. I didn't speak a word.

There was one young girl named Susan on my ward whom I liked. Only fifteen, she had long blonde hair and was quiet and intelligent. We often sat together and chatted casually about being in the hospital, about the other patients, the nurses. We always sought each other out in the dining room and sat together. Even though she was four years younger, it felt good to have a friend. These days, I did not have many.

One day, I saw Susan being wheeled back on a stretcher, unconscious. I asked one of the patients what had happened to her.

"Oh, she's been getting insulin shock therapy. That's what they do to you when you don't cooperate. They give you all this shit medicine and then you have convulsions and then they think they made you better. She's probably going to end up at Selkirk anyway."

There is a Selkirk near every city, I imagine. It is where they send you when you are no longer 'amenable' to treatment. It's where you go for really long times, maybe even forever. It's where they put you away and throw away the key and forget about you.

I became fascinated and simultaneously appalled by therapy that would render a fifteen year old girl unconscious. How could this possibly help? For the next week, I pestered Margie, Willie, other nurses and Dr. Doupe as well, to tell me everything they knew about insulin shock or insulin coma therapy. I found out that it was used a lot in the past twenty years, mostly on patients who were diagnosed as schizophrenic. Many hospitals were beginning to replace it with drugs, but it was still in common usage in mental hospitals. A patient would be given insulin until a coma was induced, often preceded by convulsions. After being in a coma for about an hour, the patient would be given glucose and the coma would be ended. A usual treatment schedule would be fifty or sixty times. Patients almost always became very fat after insulin shock therapy. Apparently the medical profession was split in its assessment of the treatment. Many doctors, including Dr. Doupe, felt it only hastened a course of action that would happen anyway. If a patient went into remission, that patient would have gone into remission with or without medically induced comas.

I tried to talk to Susan about it once, but she was clearly uncomfortable with the subject; in fact it was the only occasion, in all the time I knew her, that she was rude to me.

"Mind your own beeswax," she snapped and stormed off, leaving me feeling guilty for bringing it up in the first place.

By the next week, I was feeling somewhat better. I had begun epilepsy medication and had been seeing Dr. Doupe. I had not told her or anyone else about what I read on my chart and my feelings about it; I also never quite trusted anyone there again. I had started helping around the ward with some of the sicker patients, just to keep myself occupied. I would pass out snacks to them, bring them juice, change their soiled clothes. It made me feel useful.

In my session on Wednesday, Dr. Doupe told me I could go home the next day. She said she would like to continue seeing me several times a week. My parents were making plans for me to go somewhere, but we would deal with that later.

Rockville, Maryland; June 1964

Janie and the invisible Quentin were having a very loud conversation. She was pacing up and down in the sunroom, both arms waving wildly over her head. Her loud voice soon became screaming and her movements became progressively jerky and violent. I sat in my rocking chair, not knowing what I could possibly do or say to help her. Soon, she was knocking down chairs and madly gesticulating in the air, her voice alternating from a high pitched squealing to a very low, "Quentin, oh Quentin, ooooooh." I could not believe that this tiny woman could make such a profoundly deep sound. Soon the alarm bell was ringing in concert with her howling and five male aides came running up the stairs, banging through the doorway on their way to grab and pack Janie. Mrs. Lohmer and Mrs. Jackson were spreading out the ice cold sheets on her bed. I shrunk back in the rocking chair, frightened for both Janie and myself, as I watched her fight off five large men. The screaming continued, punctuated by more than one of the aides yelling out in pain as Janie landed an unwanted kick or punch on one of her assailants. She just wanted to be alone with Quentin, but was having trouble controlling the encounter. It took forever for the aides to grab her and roughly carry her off, all four limbs flailing, to toss her down on the freezing sheets and hold her as they rolled her back and forth, to the right and to the left, as each limb was individually wrapped in freezing sheets and then her entire body rolled this way and that until she was thoroughly mummified.

Once she was enshrouded and restrained in the icy cold, her shrieking softened to a whimper. One of the aides, Wendell, loudly scraped a chair across the floor and sat beside the bed rubbing his shin. I watched all this from my rocking chair; by turning my head to the right, I could see directly into Janie's room, the first one after the nursing office. Privacy was not a popular concept on this ward.

The remaining four aides came out into the sunroom to "debrief," as they called it. One of them, Norman, had just started work at the Lodge the week prior.

"I just don't understand it," mused Norman, still panting. "How can a tiny woman like Janie fight so strongly? I mean, look, it took five of us to get her, and it wasn't easy. How is that even possible?"

"Well, mon," Hector piped in, "dis happen all the time."

"Yeah," Alvin agreed, "dese crazy folks is strong, man."

"Well, I just don't get it," Norman shook his head.

Mrs. Lohmer came out into the sunroom and sat down in front of Norman. "This is, unfortunately, a common occurrence," she explained. "When the patients get as upset as Janie, their adrenaline levels go up and they become amazingly strong. Don't be fooled by size, age or sex. Psychoses can allow for amazing feats. Always expect the patients to be stronger than they look; it's their illness that is giving them the strength."

"Wow, I never would have expected that," mused Norman, wiping his brown curly hair off his forehead. He rubbed a now-forming bruise on his forearm. I smiled, glad that Janie was able to give him such a painful introduction into the ways of the crazies.

Chapter Twelve

After many months of my sitting, waiting and silently remembering in his office, Dr. Evanson arbitrarily decided to give me privileges. I don't know what he based this decision upon, maybe pressure from Dr. Stepford, because we rarely spoke. I sat on the daybed in his office, usually cross-legged, for as long as he could stand it; sometimes he waited the full fifty minutes, but usually he terminated in thirty or forty minutes. More often than not he used the time to do paperwork. He was always straightening papers on his desk, filling out forms and shuffling folders. He never made any effort to talk with me and I never made any further effort, after the disastrous session where I deigned to mention the word 'lesbian.'

It was June and I had just been given grounds privileges. Finally, I could discover some of the other patients here who were not on my ward.

Lenore and I walked to the Center together. The sky was clear blue harbouring a bright yellow sun. There were no clouds at all in the sky. The grass was already summer green and the trees full. We passed a woman sitting in an oversized arm chair on the road, its stuffing popping out of the left arm and a coil poking through the upholstery on the right.

"Hello, Daisy," Lenore called out.

"I'm not Daisy, I'm Susan."

"Okay Susan. Why are you sitting here?"

The woman looked over at us. She had a sweet face, framed in curly light brown hair and the most impish smile I'd ever seen. "I'm sitting here," she paused dramatically, "because it's a beautiful day."

Somehow the image of Daisy in an overstuffed armchair in the middle of the road made us all laugh. "Of course," I added, and we walked around her.

As we walked, Lenore told me her story. From a wealthy Virginia family, Daisy ended up at Chestnut Lodge when, after a parade in downtown Washington, DC, she rode her huge white stallion up the White House steps. She was considered a security risk and could not go into DC anymore. The FBI kept special tabs on her. She was well-known in political circles.

"And," Lenore continued, "the strange thing is that she is not even political. She used to raise horses in Virginia and got it into her head to show off this beautiful stallion she was riding to the president. She doesn't care about politics. And now the FBI have labeled her as dangerous. Crazy, huh?"

We were still chuckling over Daisy as we approached the Center, the name for the activities building. "But here's the kicker," Lenore added, "her therapist worked originally in Maryland, but left to open a private practice in DC. After seeing him for eight years, she could not continue her therapy because the government would not allow her to cross the state line. Both the hospital and her therapist tried to reason with the FBI, begging them to allow her to continue her therapy, but I guess once you ride your horse up the White House steps, you are doomed for all eternity. Poor Daisy."

Outside the Center, we joined a group of other young people. Someone produced some marigold seeds and catnip, which they had heard could make you high. Someone else dissolved wood alcohol in orange crush. All of us were partaking. They were right about the marigold seeds. We started talking about sex.

I noticed a good-looking, dark haired boy who seemed to be about my age or maybe a few years older. Wearing pressed, dark blue Bermuda shorts and a crisp light blue shirt, he was lean and wiry, about five eight. I was taken with him immediately. From the conversation I gathered that his name was Pete. Lenore had told me about most of the people in the hospital so I knew a bit about him; that he lived at Hilltop and was from California where his family owned a record company.

Pete and I had both been eyeing each other.

"I'm horny," he said.

"So am I," I answered.

We grinned at each other and silently got up. Pete motioned with his head toward the road. Lenore was nodding off from the combination of marigold seeds and alcohol and smiled at me. I took Pete's hand and walked with him down the road. I was curious and looking for a new adventure. We came to the turn-off to the swimming hole and there, off a side road, was an old barn. I had no idea such a place existed, but Pete had obviously done this before. We went into the barn, into the straw and into each others arms. We weren't there very long, because we knew they would be keeping an eye out for me. But we were there long enough. I quickly put my clothes back on, reflecting just a bit about how numb my body was feeling. And I wondered if I really liked fucking Pete better than Lenore or just had to act that way.

For all the times I went to the barn with Pete, and there were many, I don't believe I ever had any significant feelings of love or even wanting to be with him. I had a physical ache, of which I was acutely aware, and being with Pete made the ache go away for a very short while. Walking down the barn road, I often felt like a zombie. Pete and I rarely talked or interacted other than our times at the barn. It helped pass the time and I felt as though I were defying the authorities, two pretty good reasons to continue. Truthfully, I wouldn't have cared either way if we had continued going to the barn regularly or stopped going. It was a thing to do in my stoned and alcoholic haze.

Winnipeg, Manitoba, August 1956

I remember the first time I was with a boy. I was twelve, Freddy was fourteen. I was alone in my home for the first time; my family were all at the lake. I was old enough to be alone now, although I wasn't really alone. I had relatives all around me – my dad's brothers lived in the houses on either side of ours and my aunt across the street. I was supposed to eat my meals at my aunt's and check in with the relatives daily or stay with them if I wanted. However, I told them I wanted to stay in my own house, alone, and I think they wished to respect my new independence. The houses were so close that if I had yelled, they would hear me.

Unbeknownst to my aunts and uncles, when I went home after dinner I had some friends over. They came down the alley and snuck in through the back door. We sat around the kitchen table, talking about school and our idiot teachers. About ten o'clock, they got up to leave. Everyone walked out the back door, but Freddy lingered. I did not want them all to go. I was frightened to stay in the big house all alone. I was already in junior high school, most of my friends were one or two years older and even though we were "teenagers," I was still frightened of being alone in the dark. I feared some unknown psychopath would kill me. It wouldn't have anything to do with me, Ruth. It would be quite arbitrary, but that psychopath was coming for me. It was only a matter of time until the psychopath would get me.

So when Freddy dawdled at the door, then put his arm around my shoulders and pulled me towards him to kiss me, I kissed him back. As long as he was there, the psychopath couldn't come. We stood in the doorway kissing for quite a while, until everyone else had long gone. Then Freddy whispered something about going upstairs.

"Uh, sure, I guess we could do that," I answered, and he took my hand and led the way. I kept the lights on so the psychopath wouldn't come. When Freddy started taking off his clothes and lay down on the bed, I followed suit. I knew what we were going to do and I really didn't care one way or the other. I just wanted to keep that psychopath away. My very first time was marred with thoughts of the psychopath and how he couldn't get me that night. Freddy stayed until it was light outside – by then I was safe. Just like being with Pete, my emotional feelings were almost non-existent. I had sex, I knew what I was doing, but the act itself was meaningless to me. I enjoyed the physical feelings, but, truthfully, I could have done that myself, without a guy, had I so wished. But that wouldn't have kept the psychopath away. I was almost forty before I could successfully banish the psychopath. But that is another story. Thankfully, he is now long gone.

Rockville, Maryland; July 1964

"Do I ever have a surprise for you," Ambrose said one day as he plopped himself into a chair on the sun porch.

"Oh yeah, what is it?" I didn't like Ambrose, even though he was Lenore's friend.

"Lela Marinides is coming back next week. You're going to love her. Everyone loves Lela," Ambrose smirked.

That was enough for me to hate this Lela Marinides. If Ambrose liked her, or loved her, God knows, I certainly wasn't going to have anything to do with her.

Ambrose still looked like an overgrown peach. He was round and fuzzy and he had that peculiar status of out-patient, which meant he had his own apartment and spent all possible hours out of it hanging around the mental hospital when he wasn't actually in therapy. I didn't think that was the initial concept inherent in 'out-patient' status, but Ambrose had honed that category to the loftiest heights. He would collect strings, winding them into huge balls, and old newspapers or pieces of cardboard. When his apartment was so full that one literally could not open a door, he was re-admitted to the hospital for a week while his social worker had his place de-collected. Then Ambrose was returned to an empty apartment, only to start all over again. He was always examining anything lying around, to see if it was worthy of being added to his wealth and his pocket. He was, what they called in the trade, an anal-retentive personality.

I realized I was now living in real life many of the things I had studied in one of my favourite courses, Abnormal Psychology. Ambrose was text-book classic and I would have loved to have brought him to class as Exhibit A. I had spent almost four years at university, but nine months at Chestnut Lodge eclipsed those in terms of getting an education, particularly in abnormal psych.

"Yep," Ambrose continued, his hands on his pudgy thighs, "she was here in this hospital several years ago. She was psychotic then. She's only neurotic now. Everyone loves Mrs. Marinides. You're going to love her, Ruthie. Just wait until you meet her."

I decided then and there that I wasn't having anything to do with this person and immediately abandoned the room, leaving Ambrose still shaking his head and telling anyone who would listen how much they would love Lela Marinides. He was bursting with his scoop. I hoped he would actually burst, exploding to expose pieces of string and old newspapers as his innards.

Those were good days for me. I had ground privileges, which meant I could come and go as I pleased. I did just that, having sex with Pete daily in the old deserted barn at the end of the property, after getting sufficiently drunk and stoned with the other young people at the Center. Lenore had recently become an out-patient and now had a boyfriend, so she didn't mind my going with Pete. In fact, she encouraged it.

A week earlier, we had snuck into my room to be together, asking Hector to be our look-out. He was more than happy to comply, especially since he knew we didn't care if he watched us.

"Ruthie, I think it is great that you are with Pete now," she whispered into my ear after we hurriedly made love. "You won't be so lonely now. And I will be here too almost every day." She kissed me gently. I missed her, especially at night when I was alone in my room with only the aides for company.

A week later, I strolled onto the ward, still immersed in the after-sex glow from the latest barn outing. I peeked into the sunroom to see who was there. Mrs. Decker called me over.

"Ruthie, I'd like you to meet our new patient. This is Mrs. Marinides," she pronounced it "mar-in-nee-dis" in her Southern drawl. Mrs. Decker was the charge nurse for the evening and clearly felt I needed to meet the new arrival.

I looked over to see the great wonder. There sat a frightened-looking, very skinny woman with thick, black hair streaked with gray. She was wearing an old, blue terrycloth robe with, it appeared, nothing on underneath. Her exquisitely sculpted face had very high cheekbones and she was beautiful in a haunting way. She smiled shyly at me. I turned on my heels and walked down the hallway to lie down in my room.

After Lenore moved out, our room was turned into one for male patients, and I became room-mates with Mrs. Kane. Mrs. Kane was fifty-seven years old. Her hair was now more grey than brown. She was a short, slight woman who always wore a skirt, blouse and cardigan sweater. She usually sat in the room on a chair, not speaking or moving, except for one leg, crossed over her knee, moving up and down, up and down. When someone told her it was mealtime, she arose as if being pulled by strings above her head and walked by herself to the dining room. After she filled her tray and quietly ate her meal alone in a corner, she returned to the chair in her room. If someone told her to go for a walk, she would go out for a short period of time. Other than that, she sat in silence. This made being in the room difficult for me. The tension of this half-alive body sitting in silence was too much to bear. Initially I tried to talk with her, but after a while I gave up in frustration and just felt uncomfortable in her presence. I did not spend too much time in my room those days.

When I got to my room, I pulled a cardboard box out from underneath the bed, opened the flap, dug underneath some clothes, pulled out a tee shirt, unwrapped it and grasped Glass, the plastic glass I had brought from Winnipeg. Glass had functioned in the capacity of teddy bear when I was in the Winnipeg General Psych ward. I took Glass with me to Locky's and when I left for Kansas, Glass was packed in my blue overnight bag. Lenore had filled Glass with vodka for months and months when we were still roommates. I focused my love on this little plastic glass and knew that it loved me, even though I was aware of how bizarre that was. I confided my secrets to Glass as I lay in bed at night. I felt good around Glass, who was completely non-judgmental, and I was a great deal less lonely in Glass' presence.

Three weeks earlier, I had been at a session with Dr. Evanson, begging for more privileges. Since I first got privileges – a result, I was sure, of pressure exerted by Dr. Stepford – I had become a bit more confident and started speaking again in my sessions.

When Dr. Evanson refused to increase my level of freedom, I muttered to myself, "The only friend I have is Glass."

"What? What did you say?"

"I said 'the only friend I have is Glass.'"

"Who is Glass? Why don't I know about this person?"

I sighed. "Glass is a little plastic glass I brought with me. Glass is my friend and stays by my bed. Sometimes I cuddle with Glass. It's no big thing."

"You sleep with a glass? That's entirely inappropriate! You can't do that anymore."

I sat up, putting my feet flat on the floor. "Oh Dr. Evanson, it's just a little plastic glass from my home town. It's not even breakable. It's all I have from Winnipeg."

"That is ludicrous, that one of my patients has identified with a plastic glass. You will do this no more. I will have that glass removed." He reached for the telephone.

"Oh no, please, Dr. Evanson, please. I won't sleep with Glass if you don't want me to, but please, don't take it away. Glass is my friend. Please, please, Dr. Evanson."

He glared at me as he spoke into the telephone. "Mrs. Lohmer? Dr. Evanson here. I believe there is a glass by Miss Simkin's bedside? A plastic glass. Oh, you know about it? Yes. I would like it removed. Send it to the kitchen. Mrs. Lohmer, I know it's not from here. Send it to the kitchen anyway. It will get lost there. I do not want it on the ward when she returns. Do you understand? Thank you."

He hung up the phone and smiled at me. I felt small and hurt. Silent tears fell down my cheeks.

"Well, that's that. Surely you understand it's not healthy to have an inanimate object for a friend. We're just trying to help you understand reality here." He grabbed a handful of papers and cheerfully began straightening them, tapping them on his desk one way, then another. He actually was smiling, something he rarely did.

"I want to go now." I looked over at him.

He shrugged his shoulders. "Alvin," he called. "Aaalvin!"

Alvin opened the door.

"Take her back now. Back to her glass-less room. Heh, heh, heh. Oh, that's a rich one."

I turned my back on this chuckling madman.

When I got back to the ward, I casually sat down on the sun porch for a while, feigning interest in a bridge game before I walked back to my room. Glass was gone. I looked behind the night table, under the bed, everywhere. No Glass. I felt such an emptiness inside. I sat on the bed with my arms wrapped around my body and rocked myself, alone, Glass-less, for the two hours before dinner.

In the dining room with Hector and the other escortees, I quickly ate a reasonable amount of dinner and walked up to Hector who was busy trying to feed

Janie.

"Hector, I'm just going over there for a minute. I need to get something from the kitchen. I'm not going anywhere, okay? Just to the kitchen."

"Sure Ruthie, go ahead. Here Janie, you have to eat this." Janie was off in Quentin-land as Hector lifted a spoon overflowing with mashed potatoes up to her mouth.

I went to the edge of the counter and called over to Mattie. "Mattie, I need some help."

The small black woman came over to me. "What is it, honey, y'all need something? Wasn't dinner good?"

I liked Mattie a lot. I felt much closer to her than to most of the patients or the staff.

"Mattie, I need a glass," I whispered.

"Well, sure thing darlin', here's a glass." And she took a plastic glass from off the shelf.

"No Mattie, I need a specific glass."

"What are y'all talking about? There are thousands of glasses in there." She jerked her head toward the inner kitchen.

"Mattie, please, I beg you, let me look for just a minute. I promise you I won't hurt anything. Please, Mattie." The desperation in my eyes helped with her decision.

"Okay, but don't y'all be long. Don't you be doing nuttin' you shouldn't be doin', y'hear?"

"Okay, Mattie, don't worry."

I slipped into the inner kitchen and felt my heart sink when I saw racks and racks of clear plastic glasses, all stacked up in piles. I knew that Glass was different; Glass had 'Made in Canada' around the little circle on the bottom, while all the others had 'Made in USA' on them. Glass was also just a tiny bit smaller than these glasses.

I walked over to the racks and ran my finger up and down the stacks of glasses trying to find a discrepancy in size. My heart was beating quickly; I knew if the kitchen or nursing supervisors came in, I would be kicked out immediately. If Glass ended up on some ward, I'd never get it back. I just kept looking and running my fingers up and down, up and down.

"Wow, here it is! Here's Glass! Oh Glass, I found you! Thank you, thank you, for being a little smaller." I picked Glass out of a pile. Sure enough, 'Made in Canada'. I looked at some others. They all had 'Made in USA' on their bottoms. "Oh Glass, it really is wonderful to be a little different, isn't it?" I put Glass in my pocket and pulled my long shirt over it.

"Thanks, Mattie, you're wonderful!" I slipped back into the dining room.

"You're welcome, Ruthie." We smiled conspiratorially at each other.

After I got back to the ward, I put Glass into the carton under my bed. Now as I was holding Glass and remembering, I knew I had to put Glass back. Glass was my friend. I liked knowing we were still together. And no crazy doctor was going to screw us around.

I lovingly replaced Glass and then re-emerged into the sunroom to play a record. There was a bridge game going on with that new patient Mrs. Marinides, Neville, Matt and Janie. I put Miriam Makeba on the record player, and sat down, feigning disinterest, singing quietly along to the "Click Song," one of Makeba's most popular songs, probably because hardly anyone could make the sound of the click in the Xhosa language, yet everyone I knew loved to try.

By the third song of the album, Janie started hallucinating again, "Oh Quentin, fuck me, Quentin, oh Quentin…" And then she would laugh that scary laugh of hers, coming out in a deep voice from down below somewhere and reaching a high crescendo. It was eerie.

"Snap out of it, Janie," said Matt, always the psychiatrist, even when himself a patient in a mental hospital.

"Oh, ho, ho, ho, Quentin, take me away, ooooooooo."

"C'mon Janie. It's your bid." This from Neville, the other psychiatrist-patient on the ward. We were a professional ward now. Soon we would be adding a third psychiatrist, John, to our patient roster. They were all male. Too bad Dr. Evanson couldn't make a fourth. Then they could have their own bridge game.

"She's a brittle diabetic," Matt explained to Lela, "and schizophrenic to boot. So whenever her blood sugar goes off, she gets worse." He turned to Janie. "Janie, drink your orange juice and play cards."

Janie fanned her cards out on the table, and almost as though she were being hoisted up by an invisible string, slowly rose from the table and followed Quentin into her room.

"Well, we need a fourth now. How about it, Ruthie, will you play?"

"Naw, I don't feel like it."

"Oh come on," Neville persisted, "Come play and get to know Lela."

"Yes, please join us," the new patient said in a whiskey baritone voice. She looked so sad sitting there, still in her blue terry towel robe. Her beauty shimmered about her, drawing and holding my eyes. There was something about the way she sat, knees up, arms around them, holding herself tightly, that tugged at my heart. I was intrigued.

I resented her even more after I heard her husky voice. This, after all, was *my* ward, and I was just starting to establish myself at the top of the pecking order; I didn't need or want any competition.

I played. We drew for partners and, of course, Lela and I drew each other, a feat we were to duplicate countless more times over the next while.

We won too, easily, even though Matt and Neville were both bridge masters. Max had taught me well. I played with my arm slung over the back of the chair, pretending not to care about the game, about this new person, all the while watching her every move. It didn't seem to bother her.

The game over, we all got up and went to our respective rooms. Outside of bidding, I don't believe I said one extraneous word to her.

The days went by. I continued screwing with Pete during the day and playing bridge at night. I always drew Lela. We always won.

Chapter Thirteen

I was getting to know Neville better. He was truly a remarkable person – a wonderful flautist and a masterful bridge player. He also played mandolin and ukulele at night when the "grown-ups" had their before-bed highballs. The "grown-ups," as I referred to them, were Matt, Lela and Neville – but really, I attributed the sobriquet to anyone older than me (whether warranted or not). Each adult got one and a half ounces of their favourite libation at night before bed, provided that they had previously bought the alcohol and given it to the nursing station. Lela and Neville were scotch drinkers, Johnny Walker Black; Matt drank Seagram's rye. Since I was under twenty-one, I was deemed not old enough to drink, a fact which amused me no end as I was drunk more often than not. I had to be content with a glass of coca-cola (usually secretly laced with vodka). Lenore was now an out-patient, but since I was no longer on "arm-to-arm special" I could easily sneak into my room and pour out some vodka from my stash in the closet.

While the "grown-ups" drank their nightly imbibement, most of the patients from our ward, Main Four, would sit in the sunroom singing bawdy limericks. I could always sing in an inspired way when we were doing limericks with Neville on the mandolin. But what I really loved about Neville was his sense of humour. He always made everyone laugh, often at ourselves, yet he had the potential to make everyone cry as well. He was forty-four years old, and pleasing to my eye – a little on the pudgy side, with brown hair that fell over his twinkling eyes, and a round face which more often than not sported a glorious smile. He reminded me of a cuddly teddy bear. He was, in my opinion, quite wonderful and I loved spending time with him. I felt more grown up when I was with Neville. He took me seriously, more than most other "adults." I never could understand how this psychiatrist with a wife and three kids at home ended up as a patient in the nuthouse. He seemed to be the most normal person I knew.

One sunny autumn day, Lenore and I were sitting in the dining room when Ambrose, the peach, waddled up with his loaded tray.

"We had a meeting on Main Three today. Yep, we did."

Silence.

"I said, we had a meeting today." The peach was frustrated by our indifference.

Lenore and I looked at each other as we raised our eyebrows, cocking our heads and looking at Ambrose. As she held her hand out in a grandiose gesture, I asked grandly, "And what happened at that meeting, Ambrose?"

Lenore signalled impatiently for Ambrose to speak.

"The boys are teaching George to swear and they're getting mad about it."

Lenore turned towards me extending her arm, indicating I speak.

"Tell us about it, Ambrose."

Ambrose settled into his chair, very methodically took each dish and utensil off his tray, moved the tray aside, straightened each dish into its correct position, placed his utensils around his plate, slowly spread out his napkin and tucked it into the neck of his vee-neck rust-coloured sweater and began. "Well, the boys, Big John and his gang, have been teaching George to swear. So he swears and people get upset and then George goes crazy. Today they told us that the whole ward will be held responsible if he keeps swearing. Of course," he smiled as he fingered a piece of lint to add to his collection, "I am an outpatient so I'm not really part of the ward. And…" he straightened his chair, "I don't swear." He then proceeded to cut up his pork chop into equilateral triangles.

I followed suit, but only cut my pork chop into digestible hunks as opposed to algebraic shapes. I smiled, disguising swallowing something that tasted like fried shoe. Poor George, unknowingly swearing, upsetting all the nurses and Big John and his cronies laughing uproariously. I wondered exactly what words they were teaching him.

Just then, George stood up. He was six feet tall and I was always surprised to see a beard shadow on the face of someone whom I thought of as a little boy. An innocent, he always reminded me of an angel. Rocking agitatedly he yelled, "F!" Rock.

We all looked up.

He rocked again and yelled, "U!" Rock.

There was now silence in the dining room as all eyes focused on George – everyone, both patients and staff, holding our breath.

Lenore and I looked at each other. I whispered to her, "I don't think I've ever heard anyone say "fuck" out loud in the dining room." I was still having trouble saying that epithet myself, as I had only just uttered it out loud for the very first time a few months earlier, shocking myself more than the nurses. I turned back to George, waiting anxiously for his next utterance.

And then with a particularly vigorous rock, he yelled, "Q!"

Boisterous laughter echoed throughout the room. Poor George was roughly led back to the ward by Lane and Stan, two of Main Three's larger and less gentle aides.

The next evening, Lenore was visiting and we were sitting on my bed talking, looking at our dream tree through the bars in the window.

"Lenore, I'm worried. I haven't had my period for two months."

"Oh Ruthie, do you think you're pregnant?"

"Yeah, I do, and I don't know what to do. I can't tell them, because then they will take away my privileges. Do you know anyone in Rockville who can give me an abortion?"

"Gee, I don't," Lenore frowned. "But I bet Lela does. She lived here for years last time, so she must know someone. Why don't you ask her?"

"Oh, come on, Lenore, I can't do that! I don't even like her!"

"Well," Lenore shrugged her shoulders, "I don't know what else to tell you. If you don't ask her, you have nowhere to go and they'll find out and you'll lose your privileges. Go on, Ruthie, ask her. Do you want me to come with you?"

"No," I sighed, "I'll do it myself."

That night, when the group got up from the sun porch and prepared to retire, I knocked on Lela's door.

"Come in. Oh, Ruthie, hi."

"Uh, Lela, can I talk to you for a minute?"

"Sure. Come in. Sit down." She patted a spot beside her where she was lying in her bed. "What's up?"

"Well, Lela," I took in a deep breath, "I just wanted to know if you could tell me where I could get an abortion in Rockville."

"You're pregnant?"

"Yes."

"You sure?"

"Yes, I'm sure."

"Well, you must tell Dr. Stepford first thing in the morning."

"*What?*"

"You heard me. You have to tell Dr. Stepford in the morning."

"Forget it, Lela. Thanks for nothing." I stood up and faced the door.

"Furthermore," she continued, talking to my already turned back, "if you don't tell him by nine o'clock tomorrow morning, I will."

I turned around and stood over her, my hands on my hips, my heart pounding.

"Look, I came to you for advice. I don't like what you're telling me. I don't want to tell anyone because then I'll lose my privileges. Please, if you can't tell me where to go, at least forget what I said. Lela, I can't go back to living with no privileges. Please."

"Do you think I am going to stand by and let some hack chop you up for money? What kind of a friend do you think I am?" Until then, it had never occurred to me that Lela might be my friend.

"Please, Ruth," she took my hand, "Ruthaiki," the Greek diminutive of my name almost whispered, "please don't hurt yourself. Please tell Dr. Stepford tomorrow."

I felt as though I were hypnotized. I did not want to let go of that hand. "Okay, Lela, I'll think about it tonight. Thank you." My knees buckled and I sat heavily down on the bed, with her naked body under the sheets wrapped around me. We sat there like that, holding hands, together, in the stillness of the night for another ten minutes. I gently slipped my hand out from hers, stood up, walked out and quietly shut the door behind me.

"Dr. Stepford, I'm pregnant." This at individual rounds the next morning.

"How do you know you're pregnant?"

"Well, I haven't had my period for two months."

"And have you been sexually active?"

"Yes, I have."

"You must tell me who it was. Was it a staff member?"

"Dr. Stepford, I can't tell you that. I'm only telling you because I was going into Rockville for an illegal abortion and decided that I would be better off to confide in you." I thought that might be worth points.

Dr. Stepford turned to Mrs. Lohmer. "Order a pregnancy test and confine her to the ward until further notice."

Then he turned to me. "I suggest you think very hard about telling me who it was. You will regret not doing that." With that, he got up and stormed out of the room, leaving me sitting there with a disgusted Mrs. Lohmer.

"Hmmph, how could you?" she mumbled, not looking at me as she wrote furiously on her clip board.

I stood up and walked out.

When the pregnancy test came back positive, Dr. Stepford summoned me to the day room for another meeting. He sat in one of the armchairs, I sat in the other and Mrs. Lohmer stood in front of us with the ubiquitous clip board.

"Miss Simkin, you are pregnant. Now, you need to call your parents and tell them and you need to tell me who you did this with."

"Don't be silly. Why would I tell my parents?"

"Because you are going to have an abortion."

"No, I'm not. I want this baby. I'm not having an abortion." I figured since I couldn't hide the pregnancy from them and wouldn't retain my privileges once they found out, I might as well keep the baby. The only reason I wanted an abortion in the first place was to keep the whole thing a secret and maintain my long waited-for privileges. "I'm not having an abortion," I repeated with resolve, my chin jutted out, my lips pursed.

"Yes, you are. You may think you want the baby, but you can't raise it here."

"So I'll leave here."

"No, you won't. You will call your parents and you will tell me who did this to you. If you don't, the entire ward will be confined until you do, and you will be committed. If you feel you can tolerate the other patients being confined to the ward because of you, then you can keep the silence."

I knew I would lose. I could not imagine even one day with Matt or Max on my case, not to mention Margaret Bullard.

But still I said, "I'll think about it."

That night, a whole group of us were sitting on the sunporch, waiting for the nightly alcohol dispensations. Bruce, one of the young men who had recently joined us as a patient, had been reading the book *I Never Promised You a Rose Garden*. "Hey, check this out," Bruce looked up from his book, "this is from 'Rose Garden.' Listen."

He read out loud, "'Of all the D-ward women, how many would be free someday?' D-ward women really refers to this ward, Main Four, you know." In fact, all of us did know, as everyone who could focus long enough had read that book since arriving at the famous location.

Bruce continued, "'In her three years there many faces had come and gone, and many had stayed. Of those who had gone, maybe three-quarters had left for other hospitals. Some had improved enough to live a kind of half-life as out-patients. How many were out, alive and free? You could count them on your fingers! She shivered.' That's pretty gloomy," Bruce concluded.

"Wow," chimed Rick, another new young patient, "I had no idea the odds were so stacked against us."

Matt drew on his pipe. "Don't let that bother you, guys. Everyone reads that book when they come here and everyone focuses on that. You will get out, especially two clever young lads such as yourselves."

Bruce and Rick looked at Matt, then each other, and got up to leave the room to continue this conversation in the TV room.

Matt, Neville and Lela were still sitting in the sunroom, anxiously eyeing the alcohol cupboard. I took a deep breath and began to say what had been on mind all day.

"So, I have some news today. I wanna know what you guys think."

Mrs. Decker came around with the cart of alcohol, and dispensed it just as though it were cardiac medicine. Lela was sitting beside me in her blue terrycloth robe, her scotch in her hand. She raised her eyebrows at me as Mrs. Decker lumbered out the room, wheeling the alcohol cart to be locked in the nurses' office.

"I told Stepford today that I was pregnant."

Neville laughed. "Really? Are you?"

"Yeah, I really am. But the thing is, Stepford wants me to tell my parents. And he wants me to tell him who did it or else he said they would commit me and they would lock everyone up on Main Four and not let them out until I did."

"Oh, oh," Neville took a deep puff of his cream-coloured Meerschaum pipe.

Matt slowly put his glass down on the little table beside him and tapped his corn-cob pipe in an ashtray. He filled the bowl of his pipe with tobacco and tamped it with his index finger. Then with the pipe between his teeth, he flicked a lighter and lit the fresh tobacco. While the room filled with aromatic smoke, he took a deep puff and looked at me.

"They can do that, you know. Commit you."

"Oh, c'mon. How can they do that?"

"I've seen it before. They get three of their cronies to come up here, other psychiatrists, maybe from St. E.'s."

The mention of St. Elizabeth's, the state mental hospital, was unsettling. We had all heard nightmarish horror stories from those who had actually experienced its atrocities. Patients received electro-convulsive therapy, also called electroshock, for just looking sideways. They would be made to convulse through electric shocks to their heads, with the crazy notion that somehow this would get rid of their so-called disease. I had also met, just last month in the dining room, a patient who lived in Upper Cottage, who had been sterilized at St. E., just for having the diagnosis of schizophrenia laid upon her. I did not want anything to do with St. E.'s – it was a scary place.

"Yeah, but aren't they real doctors? Don't they have to make up their own minds whether or not I'm crazy?"

Everyone in the room laughed. Neville said kindly, "Ruthie, you need to remember that we are we and they are them." He smiled. "It's them against us. They have the keys, they have the power and they are always going to win."

"The three psychiatrists know before they even get here that they are going to commit someone. It's just a formality to have them come. You would absolutely be committed and then you would need a court order to get out," Matt continued.

Lela, who had been sitting quietly sipping her scotch, set her glass down. "Ruthaiki, I think they have you on this one. You can't take a chance on being committed. Besides, think what would happen to you if everyone on the ward were confined here. Max would not understand. Nor would Margaret. Your life would be unbearable. You have to tell them."

"So who was it?" Neville grinned.

"Why? Wish it was you?" I grinned back.

Neville and I had started flirting lately. He was forty-four years old and I didn't care that he was married with kids. I loved being around him. But I hated the way this conversation was going.

I stood up abruptly.

"So, what are you going to do?" Matt asked.

"Do I really have a choice?" I spat as I stomped down the hall to my room.

"Mom, hi mom, this is Ruthie."

"Oh, hi dear. How are you?"

"Mom, I'm pregnant."

The pause, filled with a heavy, uncomfortable silence, seemed to last forever. After what seemed like an eternity, my mother finally responded, "Oh, Ruthie, how could you do this to us?"

The conversation went downhill from there.

"Look Dr. Stepford, I already told my parents. That should be enough." We were once more sitting in the armchairs in the day room, not really facing each other, both of us staring straight ahead towards the door. Mrs. Lohmer, of course, stood just ahead of us, clipboard against her chest, right arm slightly raised with pen in hand, ready to write down the words of the wise ward administrator.

"You will tell me who did this to you, Miss Simkin, or I will confine you and everyone on this ward until you do."

"Oh, Dr. Stepford, please. Don't make me do this."

"Was it an aide?"

I understood his concern now. "No, I promise, it wasn't an aide. It was another patient. There, that should be enough. No one did anything wrong, really," I ventured.

"Which patient was it?" he demanded. "What ward does that patient come from? From here?"

"No, Dr. Stepford, not from here, not from your ward. You're okay." I smiled at him. "You see, you're off the hook."

"We're waiting, young lady," Mrs. Lohmer looked up at me. "Do I have to write an order confining everyone to the floor?" She turned to Dr. Stepford. "We'll need more staff if we do that. Everyone will be real upset."

They both looked at me angrily. I knew they had me. If I didn't tell them about Pete, then everyone on my ward would make my life a living hell by yelling at me, hitting me as I passed them and I did not want to imagine what else. If I did tell them about Pete, poor Pete would get into trouble and I didn't want to be a squealer. Pete lost when I sized him up in my mind against a furious Max, Margaret and the rest.

"It was Pete, Pete from Hilltop," I sighed.

Dr. Stepford snapped shut the chart, smiled a tight little smile, got up and turned back to Mrs. Lohmer. "Don't let her out anywhere. Maybe Evanson can come up here for a while."

"You, young lady," Mrs. Lohmer pontificated, "are going to rue the day you ever met Pete from Hilltop." She turned on her heels and swished by me.

"Lela, I don't *want* an abortion," I whined. I really didn't. For the very few times that I allowed myself to feel anything, I felt as though a baby would be nice. It would get me out of here. It would love me. But most of the time I just went numb inside, something that came very easily to me these days. I didn't want an abortion now that everyone knew about the pregnancy. The only reason I ever wanted it before was to keep it all a big secret. Now that everyone knew, I preferred a son to a surgery.

"I want a baby, Lela," I whimpered. "I don't want an abortion where they hack you up."

"Ruthaiki," she took my hand, "you don't have a choice."

Since that first night I approached her, we had ended every night by my sitting on her bed beside her, hand in hand, talking about the day's events. Each evening it got progressively more difficult for me to pull myself away from her. I didn't know what it was, but I felt so comfortable beside her, so safe, and especially, so loved. Every time she took my hand, my heart speeded up. I made sure it was she who took my hand, not the other way around, although I always made sure my hand was excessively available to be taken.

"Look," she continued, "what would you do with a baby?"

"Oh Lela, I would have a son. His name would be Jacob. Wouldn't that be cool? And I could help him grow up and not screw him around the way I got screwed around. I want to have a baby, Lela." At the time, I perceived my upbringing as wanting. Several decades later I would not generate the same opinion.

"*Chriso-mu*, my golden one, you are too young to be a mother. How about when we both get out of this joint we go to Greece together? Would you like that? To go to Greece with me?"

My heart was overflowing. I was imagining being with Lela without having a shadow outside the door. Being with Lela where we could laugh, lie down together in bed, maybe even…. I stopped the image from playing out in my head. What I had done with Lenore I did for booze and out of boredom. Same thing with Pete. But being with Lela was different. I was filled to bursting with an emotion that was new to me, that of feeling loved and cherished and valued by this person. I would rather sit and hold hands with Lela then go all the way with anyone else. Every time I was around her now my heart would speed up. My body yearned to be close to her and my hand hungered for hers. Her deep voice was music inside of me. Going to Greece with her? Could she possibly be serious? I wondered.

"Oh, I don't know Lela. You don't want to go to Greece with me. Your family lives there. I would get in the way."

"Ruthaiki, I would love to show you Greece. We would go to our little cottage in Piraeus and the large family home in Phaleron. I could introduce you to my friends there."

I picked up the thread. "And we could get a boat. And go to all those Greek islands."

"Absolutely," Lela smiled. "Just you and me and a handsome male crew of five."

I laughed. "And lots of ouzo."

"And lots of ouzo," she agreed.

Two days later, I was told to get up and shower quickly. I was not allowed to eat anything. With an aide on either side of me, each taking one of my arms, an aide in front and another one behind me, I was half-walked, half-dragged into the open elevator, out the side door of the large brick building, into a waiting car and driven to Suburban Hospital for the euphemistically named D & C. A close first cousin in Winnipeg had had a D & C. When I asked what the surgery was, I was told it stood for dilation and curettage, a common procedure for women where the womb is "scraped out." Now I wondered if this cousin did indeed have a 'real' D & C or did she simply do away with what might have been a second cousin?

I knew my father had come down yesterday to sign the papers. I was still considered a minor by law and not allowed to make a decision for myself. It was against the law for me to have any kind of surgery without the signature of one parent. I refused to see my father. I knew he would be okay with me, but I was simply too ashamed and embarrassed to see him.

"You killed my baby," I muttered to no one in particular, just barely awake from the anaesthetic. "You killed my Jacob. I want my Jacob." I started to cry, the tears drying on my cheeks as I fell asleep again. I allowed myself to feel the loss, even though I barely understood the implications of what had just happened. I felt violated by everyone. The son I would never have was taken away from me. My youth, both in years and emotions, did not allow me to view this episode of my life in a realistic manner. I had wanted that baby. And now it was gone.

Groggy non-pregnant me was returned later that day, still surrounded by aides. I was walked-dragged down to my room, put into bed and told I was totally confined to the ward until further notice.

Winnipeg, Manitoba; December 1963

The day I was released from Winnipeg General Hospital Psych ward, I was not at all ecstatic. I felt like a condemned person. And I was only nineteen. I'm not sure if I felt condemned because my dad insisted on taking me to Kansas for a "second opinion" or because I had epilepsy in the first place or because something inside of me drew me to Donna and I knew in my heart of hearts that Dr. Doupe was right about her. But I knew that I would still see her.

My mother came to pick me up at the hospital and take me home. I went straight up to my room and called the number Donna had given me.

"May I please speak to Donna?" I asked the male voice who answered.

"Yeah? Who's callin'?"

"Well, I'm a friend of hers, Ruthie, I met her…well, she gave me this number…she said I should call…"

"Yeah? Well, just a second. Hey," he yelled away from the phone, "Donna, some broad, Ruthie, wants to talk to you."

Soon Donna was on the phone. "Hi kid, where are you?"

"I'm at home. I just got here."

"Good. You want to go to a party tonight?"

"Gee, Donna, I just got here. I don't know…."

"Look kid, let's just go have some of the good times. Lots of booze and laughs, you know what I mean. Life is good here. I'm living with Curley, the guy I told you about. He and his friend Locky have a little business at home here. Look, I'll be out tonight. Why don't I meet you and bring you over here for a few drinks?"

"Well, okay, maybe for a while, Donna." We made the necessary arrangements while my heart started pounding at the very thought of seeing her again – maybe she would hold me and comfort me like before.

That night at dinner, I told my parents I was going out for a while.

"Who are you going out with, dear?" my mom asked.

"Just friends," I responded. We sat in a difficult silence.

I opened the cab door and gave the driver the address written on a small sheet of white notepaper. My heart was pounding with excitement at the thought of seeing Donna again, although I wished I could share this with my family instead of keeping it such a secret. I knew my parents would not approve.

"Here we are," said the cab driver after a twenty minute drive on icy roads lined with piles of snow. I paid him, got out of the cab and walked across the street to the house that showed 547 on it. I walked up the steps to the little yellow bungalow and rang the bell. The door opened on what seemed to be hundreds of partying people.

"Helll-o," one man put his arm around me. "What have we here?"

"Is Donna here? I'm supposed to meet her."

"Sure. She's tied up for a minute. Come on in. Have a drink."

He led me into the kitchen. I saw him walk over to a couple other men and tell them something. I overheard the word 'chicken'. Then he came back to me to get me a drink. I remembered that Donna had also referred to 'chicken' when we were *in the hospital; it meant someone underage – young, like me.*

One of the other men came over and held out a fifty dollar bill.

"Here," he said, "take it. Go on. It's a joke, I'll show you. Just take the money and I'll show you the joke."

My hand reached out to take the money just as a flash went off in my face. The men laughed as Donna stormed into the kitchen, threw the money down and grabbed the camera.

"Leave the kid alone. She's with me. No funny business. Come on, kid. I'm finished. Let's get out of here."

We started walking down the street to look for a cab.

"Donna, come to my house. We can spend some time together there without going to a party."

"You mean your parent's house?"

"Yeah, but it'll be okay. Nobody will bother us. We can just go to my room."

We got into a cab and I gave them the address where we were going, "5 Seven Oaks Place, please. In West Kildonan." The driver grunted and headed out into the snowy streets.

"Donna, what was all that business with the money back there?"

"Oh, they were going to try to blackmail you. You know, if they have a photo of you taking money, they say it was for work, you know, like I do. They won't bother you now."

We sat in silence. Donna took my hand in hers. The warmth of her gloved hand and bundled body penetrated all my layers of clothing in the wintry air. The tires of the taxi crunched on the snow as we drove.

"Ruthie," she whispered, "you don't want to get involved with me."

"Yes, I do. Why do you say that, Donna?"

"Because I'm a lesbian." As soon as I heard that word, my heart started pounding with excitement. It didn't really bother me that Donna was a lesbian and was also married and working as a hooker. It didn't even seem that contradictory; it just was – and I just wanted to be with her.

"Yes, Donna, I do want to get involved with you." I squeezed her hand.

We got to my parents house. Everyone was already in bed and the lights were out. We tiptoed up the stairs.

"Ruthie, is that you?" from my parents' bedroom.

"Yes, mom."

"Are you alright?"

"Yes, mom. I brought a friend home."

"Who is it?"

"It's Donna."

Silence. My parents had met Donna in the hospital and were not impressed.

They were especially not impressed that her husband was in jail for stealing appliances from new houses that my dad's construction company was building. We had a huge fight over Donna's involvement and her being my friend and then decided the best way to deal with it was to ignore it.

We got into my room and I asked Donna if she wanted pajamas or something. She said she would sleep in her underwear. We crawled into bed and I nuzzled against her.

"Donna, I love you," I whispered against her neck.

She rolled over, gave me a light kiss on the lips and a big hug, then rolled back over on her side, her back against me, and promptly fell asleep.

I lay there with my arm around her body, thinking there must be more to being a lesbian than this. I loved the feel of her body next to mine, loved her smell, loved to have her touch me. It felt so different from being with a man. I lay awake for a long time, wondering what it would be like to explore being a lesbian with Donna.

The next morning, we woke up and stayed in the bedroom to talk for a long time. By the time we went down for breakfast, everyone had already gone out. We lazed around most of the morning, till Donna said we had better go to Curley's house.

We took the bus downtown and walked eight blocks in the Winnipeg cold, eventually ending up at a little white house on a residential street. There was a white picket fence around the house, but it was dirty and the paint was peeling off. Every few feet one of the pickets was missing or crooked. The whole house looked as if it might tip over at any moment.

We walked around the side to the rickety back door, which squeaked as Donna pushed it open. A small vestibule was strewn with empty liquor bottles, old cigarette butts, bags and garbage. We walked through an equally slovenly kitchen to the living room. On one wall was a door leading to the two bedrooms and the bathroom. Against the other wall was an old, torn rust-coloured sofa and several large beige armchairs with springs sticking through the seats. I couldn't imagine anyone willingly wanting to sit on those chairs. There was a small, enclosed front porch off the living room. Sitting in the living room were two men, quietly talking.

"Hi," said Donna. "This is Ruthie. Ruthie, this is Curley and this is Locky."

Curley sat slouched in an armchair. He had lush black hair which was carefully combed. I thought he looked to be in his 30's. He was very handsome. "Hi", he waved.

Sitting at one end of the sofa, with one leg slung over the edge, was Locky, a rather slight man, about the same age as the other, in brown slacks and a white undershirt. His straight brown hair fell over his eyes. Although he was sitting still, *he looked like he had energy overflowing from his body.*

"Hi, Ruthie," he said. "How're ya doing?"

"Okay." I ventured.

"Great. Come on in. Have a seat. Wanna drink?"

I immediately liked Locky. His eyes sparkled when he talked and almost everything he said made me laugh or at least smile. When he spoke, his whole body became animated, his dangly arms waving in the air and his legs swinging over the sofa. The four of us sat around for a while chatting about the weather and the previous night's party.

Donna stood up. "C'mon," she motioned to me, "let's fix us some food." I followed her into the kitchen.

Locky came to stand in the doorway. "Are you going to help us work tonight?" he asked me.

"I guess so. What's happening?"

I already knew that they had a bootlegging operation and an after-hours joint.

Locky talked about what needed to be done, how to always take money first, as he explained the workings of an after-hours joint to me. After a quick tuna casserole, both Curley and Locky said they needed to get some sleep, because they were usually up until morning. Donna followed Curley into his bedroom and I went into the living room and sat down.

I didn't want Donna to be with Curley. I wanted to be with Donna. What was I doing here anyway?

After about ten minutes of my sitting there pretending to read the two-day old Winnipeg Free Press, Locky appeared in the doorway of his bedroom, dressed only in his shorts.

"Hey," he jerked his head, "come on over here. You probably need some rest too. No, I'm serious. I won't jump you. Not unless you want me to," he winked.

He came up to me and took my hand. Gently, he pulled me up and smiled. "Come on, it'll be fine. We'll have a little rest before the party starts."

I followed him into the bedroom. I could hear Donna and Curley making love in the next room. I was irritated that she could do that with him and not with me, although I still wasn't sure what it was that two women did together.

"Which side of the bed do you like?" he asked. He had such a sweet smile. He leaned over to kiss me. I kissed him back. He was very gentle and soft, not at all rough. We sat down on the bed together and kissed again. He started unbuttoning my blouse.

"Okay?" he asked. I nodded my head and he smiled. "Ah," he whispered, "I haven't had chicken for a long time. Just a joke, just a joke." He skillfully removed my blouse, and then removed my slacks. We lay down together in a tight embrace. He reached around my back and undid my bra. My arms immediately went up to

hide my breasts.

"What are you hiding? Let me see," he said.

"No, Locky, leave me. I don't want you to see."

"No, I have to see."

He wanted to know my biggest secret, the one I lived in fear of being found out. I had only one developed breast, on my right side. My left breast never grew. I had become very skillful at hiding it, covering it up so no one really knew. It was a source of mortification for me, the one thing that meant to me that I was not a real woman. I felt I would fall through the earth if anyone discovered this secret. I braced myself for when he would kick me out of his bed and out of his house for being so malformed.

"Oh, so that's it," he said. "Ruthie, this one is so beautiful, you only need one anyway. Besides, my mouth can only be at one place at one time." And he started kissing my nipple and fondling my right breast. It felt so good; I felt so endeared to him. We slowly and gently and sweetly made love for the next few hours.

Chapter Fourteen

The abortion had been in early August. Dr. Evanson actually came up to the ward for a few weeks to see me, as both he and Dr. Stepford said they didn't want me off the ward at all. Dr. Evanson rarely stayed for the full fifty minutes. Usually he just went into the long room off the sunporch with me, pulled the folding door closed, stared at me, sometimes without even sitting down, and after a few minutes, shook his head in disgust and left.

I knew that this was not the way psychotherapy should be, but it seemed there was little I could do to alter the situation. Whenever I would complain or otherwise comment about Dr. Evanson's actions, I was told I was having very normal negative transference. I knew deep within myself that this was not true. It was true that I did not like Dr. Evanson, but that was mainly due to the fact that he was incredibly incompetent as a physician and even more so as a human being. I did not feel I was "crazy" or mentally unbalanced in the least, but I certainly felt that he was. His lack of emotion and empathy was striking. He rarely spoke more than a sentence or two at a time and seemed completely disinterested in anything that I said. I felt trapped in a cage with no egress. And the only one who had access to a key did not have the ability or the desire to find it.

The days passed slowly. Lela and I spent most of our time sitting in the sun porch talking. The late summer light reflected along the walls and I loved to watch the shadows of the leaves wave within that light. At least I could look at some movement. I was confined to the ward except for my bi-weekly hours with Dr. Evanson. He had only lasted a few weeks coming up to the ward before his laziness overcame his meanness and he once again had me escorted to our sessions.

Lela refused to go out, although she had privileges. She would come out to the sunroom in her blue terrycloth bathrobe, wearing nothing underneath, and sit in a corner of the sofa. A small wooden end table stood between her and my rocking chair. Every morning found us sitting with each other and our coffee. We began to talk more frequently and I found her more interesting every day. She was one of the few people I could actually talk with and be believed and understood.

"I'm the baby of my family," she said, taking a sip of coffee. She laughed her husky laugh. "That's funny, because I'm seventeen years older than you are. I should be the oldest. I'm old enough to be your mother."

"Well, I'm the oldest of my family and guess what? I had the temerity to be born a girl. In the Jewish religion, that's not good. The oldest should be a boy. In fact, everyone should be a boy. Girls don't count for anything, except cooking and making babies. After me, my parents had another girl. Uh-oh. Then finally, six years later, my brother Jack was born. At last, a boy. And I think they thought our family was complete. But when I was eleven years old, my grandfather died. My father said to my mother, 'I want a son called Samuel Simkin.' And a year later, my brother Sammy was born. Good thing he turned out to be a boy. Can't imagine what his life would have been like if he would have been a girl." We laughed. We talked about everything.

Aside from the distractions my conversations with Lela provided, I was feeling terrible. I was totally confined to the ward except for my so-called therapy sessions, and Lenore had left. After achieving out-patient status, she was now busy moving into her own apartment in Rockville. Lela was still a relatively new patient and although I really liked being with her, I still wasn't completely sure of her, although our evening goodnight chats were beginning to change that.

After ward rounds one Monday morning, Lenore stayed behind to visit with me. Even though she had recently become an out-patient she was still required to attend rounds. The hospital did not let go of its patients lightly. Lenore was cheerfully telling me about her new apartment and her new freedom.

"I like my new boyfriend, Stanley. He is good to me, takes me for dinners and to the movies." I had met Stanley several times when Lenore had brought him around. He seemed nice enough; freckled face under a thick crop of red hair and a friendly grin. He never said too much during the few times we met;

usually he just sat quietly beside Lenore while the two of us chatted.

Lenore reached out to touch my cheek. "But I miss you, Ruthie," she smiled at me, "especially in the evenings. I miss our talks under our dream tree, and well, you know, everything else." Her face turned pink when she said this.

"Oh Lenore, I just have to do something, or I really *will* go insane. I can't stay here any more. It's driving me crazy. If I have to listen to Janie or Mrs. Schwartz for one more day, I will freak out."

"Oh, you poor thing. I know what you mean. Listen, I've been thinking about this idea. It's Labor Day week-end next week. Tell me what you think of this plan." And we put our heads together and talked.

Rockville, Maryland; September 1964

It was the Friday of Labor Day weekend – a beautiful, bright autumn day, with orange, red and yellow leaves colouring the trees and grass. I was on my way to my therapy appointment with Alvin escorting me. Alvin always made Dr. Evanson feel safer because of his size and strength, so the good doctor requested that Alvin be my escort as much as possible. I actually found Alvin to be a gentle, calm man, very good looking in a football linebacker sort of way – but not overly bright. As usual, we walked along the tarred road, under the trees, greeting people on the grounds as they passed.

"Hey, Alvin, come here for a minute, *mon*." Hector was calling Alvin from the Center.

"No, man, I can't. I'm escortin' de wild woman here."

"Hey, *mon*, come here for just one minute. She be okay."

"Just keep walking down the road. I be right behind you and I'll catch up in a minute. No funny business, y'hear?"

"Okay Alvin. Don't worry."

I began to walk quickly down the road and look nervously around the corner. Then, just like clockwork, there it was – Stanley's red convertible – just as Lenore and I had planned.

"Quick," Lenore hissed, "hop in the back and lie down."

In a flash, I was on the floor in the rear of the car as we drove out the back gate of the hospital. Before I knew it, Lenore told me it was safe to sit up and we headed down the turnpike for Virginia.

"Oh Lenore, that worked out so well! I'm so excited! This is my first time away from the hospital since January. Well, not counting the abortion. Or that dinner with my folks."

I sat back and grinned. Autumn in Maryland and Virginia is beautiful. It was warm, a clear, blue sky was above us. Trees were lining the turnpike on which we sped away from the hospital. The wind blew my hair across my face. Lenore looked back at me and squeezed my hand.

I had not been sure of Stanley before, but I sure liked him now. He sat with both hands on the wheel, a contented look on his face. Every once in a while, he turned to smile at Lenore. She had started dating him almost as soon as she became an out-patient. He didn't seem to mind that she was an ex-mental patient and he was always very good to her. And now, he was good to her friends too, I thought with a grin.

As much as I loved sitting in that convertible with the wind whipping through my hair, under a sunny sky, headed towards freedom, I would be lying if I didn't say that my heart was pounding as the fear of what I had just done rose to my throat and was palpable in my chest. As badly as I felt deceiving Alvin and running away, the wind and the freedom won. I wanted to be where I was, away from that insane asylum that was driving me into insanity.

A few hours on the turnpike, forty-five minutes on winding, country roads, and we turned into a driveway. Straight ahead at the end of the road was a large, faded green, wooden one-story house. To the right was a pasture full of horses, and to the left, a large corral and a barn.

"Wow, look at this place!" My eyes hungrily took in the animals, the peacefulness, the colours.

"Yep, this is the family farm," Stanley informed me. "My brother Charles is waiting for us."

I knew a bit about Charles. Lenore had already prepared me. She said all I had to do was 'be nice to him.' We both knew she was speaking euphemistically. Then we could have the long weekend at the farm. I knew Charles was a Colonel in the US army, but that was about it.

I hopped out of the car and ran around the yard with my arms spread open wide. "Yeehaw! I'm free! I'm free!" I ran and ran.

Lenore and Stanley went into the house. After a few minutes, Lenore called, "Ruthie, come on in. Charles wants to meet you."

I walked in and saw a fat man who looked to be in his early sixties, dressed in khaki trousers and a white, cotton undershirt. He was sitting in an overstuffed armchair, looking a little overstuffed himself. His hair was light and thin. He had his hand around a glass, a bottle of bourbon on the table beside him.

"Charles, this is Ruthie." Stanley introduced us.

"It's ah pleasure, ma'am." Charles had a heavy southern drawl.

"Oh, Charles, I'm so happy to be here. Thank you so much for letting us come!"

"It's mah pleasure, ma'am. Enjoy. Have a drink!" He motioned with his overly pendulous jowls toward the bottle.

"Uh, Charles, maybe Lenore and Ruthie can rustle us up some dinner." Charles grunted in assent and took a swallow from his glass. Lenore and I walked into the country kitchen.

"Wow, Lenore, this is too much!" I smiled at her as we sliced vegetables on the wooden counter top, alone in the kitchen.

"How did you get Hector to divert Alvin?" What did you have to do to him?"

Lenore shrugged. "Blow job." She shrugged again.

"Oh Lenore, I really owe you. I really love you. You are so wonderful. Thank you, thank you, thank you!"

I had been so excited about being away, that I hadn't paid attention when cutting up the carrots, and accidently sliced a small tip off my left index finger.

"Ow! Fuck! Oh Lenore, I just cut my finger! Aw shit!"

"Let's see. Hmmm, it's really bleeding. Here, wrap it up."

"You know, Lenore, maybe I should call Lela. She's probably worried about me."

"Hey, you can't do that. They'll try to trace the call."

"Oh, I'll be quick. I need to tell her I'm okay and that I cut my finger." I realized with a pang that Lela was now the one I wanted to turn to when I was hurt. Although my finger was not badly injured, it was still bleeding profusely.

"I don't like it. You better be fast."

I dialed the number, and in a disguised voice, asked to speak with Mrs. Marinides.

"Hi Lela, it's me."

"Where are you?"

"Doesn't matter. Just wanted to let you know that I'm okay. Cut my finger, but it's okay. I'll be back on Monday after the weekend."

"Oh, Ruthaiki, they have a thirteen-state APB out for you. Be careful. They're looking all over for you."

"They won't find me. Gotta go. *S'agapo*, Lela." Only she knew that I had just told her, in Greek, that I loved her.

"No, wait…"

I hung up.

I lay in the grass looking up at the stars. Between them and the moon, it was light enough to see the outlines of the horses grazing around me. I breathed in deeply, savouring the smells of the grass and hay and fresh air. I reviewed the day: the escape brought a big grin to my face. I had hoped that Hector and Alvin weren't in any trouble, but I was sure they could somehow manage to blame it all on me. I missed Lela, but other than that, I was thrilled to be here. Even doing it with Charles wasn't too bad. It helped if a guy was old and he drank; it went a lot faster. Charles said he didn't care if I wanted to sleep outside, but to come back to bed in the morning for a pre-breakfast poke, as he so gallantly put it. I figured one or two hours a day with Charles was a tiny price to pay for all this. I rolled over on the grass and smiled at a horse who nickered softly. Then I got up and ran all around the perimeter of the pasture. I ran and ran until I could hardly breathe. Still panting heavily, I plopped down in a bale of hay and promptly fell asleep.

I spent three blissful days in Virginia. All I had to do was help with the meals, have a few drinks with and fuck Charles once or twice a day, and the rest of the time I could run in the pasture or lie under the stars. I knew I was going to go back. Lenore had explained what an APB was, an all-points bulletin. She reckoned they told the police I was dangerous and maybe for the ride back, I should stay hidden. She said that sooner or later they would catch me. I couldn't stay here and her place would probably be one of the first places they would watch. I was grateful to be out here. I felt I had received a new breath of life. I would go back and convince them to let me change therapists. Then I could tell my new therapist that I was not crazy and they would let me go home. I felt certain that would happen.

I mulled over the thirteen-state APB with a sense of pride and confusion. Why on earth would they think I was that dangerous? I had never hurt anyone except myself. Well, maybe I had bruised a few shins in self-defense, but I certainly wasn't a dangerous person. I was now in the same category as murderers, for heaven's sake. On some level, I was appalled that my reputation was so different from my actual being. I knew if I were to be caught, I would not be treated kindly. And this confused me even more, since I thought of myself as a gentle person, who truly abhorred violence. I knew Dr. Evanson was afraid of me, but I had never done anything to him to foster that belief. It was all coming from his own insanity, but he was the man with the power and the keys and because of that, a huge police hunt for me was unleashed across the entire Eastern United States.

To keep me occupied on the way back while I was lying on the floor of the car, Stanley and Lenore gave me a case of beer. They let me off a few blocks from the hospital and I took a few bottles of beer with me for good luck.

"Thanks so much, both of you. I feel like a new person. Thanks. See you soon. Bye now." I headed for Chestnut Lodge.

I decided to walk up the four flights of stairs to Main Four to surprise everyone. I opened the door quietly and walked in. Strange, with the one-way locks on the doors, how easy it was to go in, yet impossible to get out. The door clicked locked behind me loudly. I peeked around the corner to see Lela, sitting in her spot, arms around her blue terrycloth covered knees.

"Hi, Lela. I'm back."

"Oh, Ruthaiki!" she leaped up and enveloped me in her arms. "I was so worried about you. Are you okay?" She started looking me over. "Oh, your finger, my God, look at your finger, it's infected."

"Lela, it's nothing, just a little cut."

"Oh, I'm so glad you're back." She stopped. "But oh, you're in big trouble. Brace yourself for a few rough days." We stood facing each other, close, her hands holding mine gently. We were smiling, happy to be back in proximity with each other.

"Hey Lela, you know, I'm fine. I was on a farm in Virginia, and I slept outside and played with the horses and breathed fresh air and ran in the fields and smelled flowers, and I just know I am going to get out of here soon. I am going to talk to them again about a new therapist, and…"

I was ripped out of Lela's arms. The alarm went off. Footsteps echoed on the stairs. Within minutes I was rolled over and over in wet sheets, the ice cold of the packing displacing the warmth of the Virginia farm and Lela's touch. Tighter and tighter they wound me in the cold sheets, Jorge and John and Harry and Allen and some aides I had never even seen before – none of them gentle, all of them acting out the wrath of the hospital on my body. When they were done packing me in my ice cocoon, they stood around the bed glowering at me. It had happened in just three minutes. My insides went from a gentle warmth to an ice cold hatred. Soon Dr. Stepford strode into the room.

"Where were you?" he demanded. His face was red and he was puffing from having run down the hall. I had never seen him this angry. My cold pack got even colder under his enraged scrutiny.

"On a farm."

"Where? What kind of a farm?"

"In Virginia." I had been quite proud of my escapade, but the chill of the sheets and voices were quickly taking over.

"Whose farm?"

"Hey, look, I came back, didn't I? What's the big deal? I said I'd be back, and I came back. If you didn't treat me like this maybe I wouldn't have run away."

"Miss Simkin, we do not allow people to run away here."

"Look, Dr. Stepford, how about a new therapist? Please, I beg you. Just give me a new therapist and I won't run away again and I will be okay. I promise. I am not working well with Dr. Evanson. All his patients are getting worse. His other patient Petey ran away. David has not spoken in years. Maybe it's him. Please give me a chance with someone else."

"Miss Simkin, you are out of line here."

"No, really, I am in pack," I muttered, making myself laugh.

"You are confined to the ward. You are back on arm-to-arm special. One more stunt like this and we'll have you committed and throw you into St. E.'s."

"Hey, you can't do that."

"Don't push me, Miss Simkin, don't push me." With that, he stormed out. Only Alvin was left as my guard.

"Now, whatchu go and run away like dat for? Get us all in trouble. Why you go and do a t'ing like dat?"

"Hey, Alvin, tell them I tricked you or beat you up or something."

Alvin laughed, his huge frame shaking with the chuckles. "Naw, me and Hector be okay. We blame it all on you anyways."

Lela came to the door. "Alvin, can I sit with her for a while please?"

"Sure thing, Mrs. Marinides, she ain't going nowhere. I need a smoke anyway. Hector will be just outside the door." Alvin lumbered out while Lela slipped in to sit beside my enwrapped body.

The next morning Alvin escorted me to Dr. Evanson's office for my therapy appointment. I had not seen Dr. Evanson since the week before. Tuesdays and Fridays were my appointment days and last Friday I was on my way to Virginia before he even realized I was gone.

"Alvin, wait outside the door," he instructed sternly.

"Sit down!" he yelled at me before I was even inside the door. I chose the daybed by the wall – as far away from him as I could get. I sat, legs crossed, a cup of tea in my hand.

"What the hell do you think you are doing?" he exploded. "You are trying to get pregnant again, aren't you? You are doing that to ruin my reputation. You are trying to ruin my reputation!" he screamed. His face was red and his ears seemed bigger, sticking out from his closely cropped hair. His breathing was heavy and his body rigid. He banged his fists on the desk as he spoke.

"Dr. Evanson, I don't really care about your reputation. I didn't even think about you when I went away."

"You're lying!" he was yelling now. He stood up and came towards me waving his hands. "You're trying to ruin me! Why are you acting like this?"

He seemed such a contradiction, dressed in a fashionable blue suit, white shirt and pale striped blue tie, yet yelling at me, his face purple with anger and indignation, spittle coming out the side of his mouth, his limbs jerking in an involuntary manner.

"Dr. Evanson, sir, calm down, you are frightening me, sir." I spoke in as calm a voice as I could muster, yet my heart was pounding loudly and quickly in my ears. I was afraid of this man. I knew he had the potential to seriously hurt me, both physically and psychically.

He banged his fist on his desk. "You piece of slime. You are not fit to be with people ever again. I will see to it that you never breathe fresh air again. I will keep you locked up until you die!" As he was yelling I watched a small drool of white spittle come to the edge of his lip.

"I'll show you. I'll get you for this." He started to approach me. I thought he was going to hit me. I got frightened and threw the cup against the other wall to distract him. I purposely threw it in the opposite direction from his approach so he would not be threatened by this action, merely startled into sanity. The white china shattered and fell. I sat still and did not move.

"Alvin! Alvin!!!!" he screamed. "Help! Help, I'm being attacked."

"Now Dr. Evanson, I'm not attacking you, you were just scaring me."

Alvin opened the door and quickly put his arms around me, softly. I felt safer.

"Grab her Alvin, grab her. Remember, she's dangerous."

"Now calm down, doc, I got her. She won't hurt you."

"Get her out of here. Lock her up on the ward. Get her out of my sight!" he screamed, his voice at least an octave higher than normal.

"C'mon, Ruthie, let's go." Alvin held both my arms behind my back, but gently. I was not struggling. We both stared at Dr. Evanson as he huffed back around his desk and started straightening his papers. His face was still a blotchy red and he was breathing heavily. Beads of sweat stood out on his brow. He would not look at us.

"Oooeee, you sure did get him angry. C'mon, let's walk back together." Alvin put his arm around me and we walked back in silence that way.

The following week, my parents came for a visit. They had been called by the hospital, told of my "escape" and were asked to come down for a meeting.

"How are you ever going to get better if you don't cooperate with them?" my dad asked.

I rolled my eyes and counted to ten before answering. I was really angry. I couldn't understand why my parents would believe these strangers and not believe me. I felt invisible to my parents, especially my dad. My mom seemed more and more like a robot each time she visited me, going through motions with no feelings – on automatic. I didn't understand until many years later that she had been working so hard to try to get me back home, yet my father overruled her. He was positive he was doing what was best for me because the doctors had said I needed to be there. He refused to look at me as an individual, a person with a life to live. If educated men said something, who was he to disagree? My mother and I simply could not understand this, yet we were both helpless in our own worlds to do anything other than comply with the men who had the power.

"Dad, there is nothing wrong with me. They are crazy here."

"Ruthie," my mother added, "you can't run away just because things get a little difficult."

"A little difficult!!! Mom, give me a break. This place is nutso. I can't stay here. Don't you understand?"

"Now, Ruthie, we have met with the doctors. Dr. Tatelman said…"

"Dad, Dr. Tatelman never sees me. He is the P.R. doctor for the hospital. He hasn't seen me in months. How can he tell you how I am doing? They just want me here because of the money. People are left here by rich families. Don't you get it?"

"Now, Ruthie, I'm sure Dr. Tatelman has your best interests at heart."

"Mom, *I* have my best interests at heart. And they are to get me out of here. Why don't you understand?"

"Now listen here." My father was sounding stern. "You are to cooperate with these doctors. We want you home too. But we cannot take you home until they say you are ready to come home. Do you understand?"

"Your father is right, dear. We do want to bring you home. But only when you are ready."

"But I *am* ready. I was ready nine months ago!" And with that, I stomped down the hall into my room and slammed the door. I never wanted to see my parents again. If they could leave me here, it had to mean they didn't love me.

I lay on my bed, thinking about those I thought did love me: Lela, who couldn't help me now, and Locky and Curley and Donna.

Winnipeg, Manitoba, December 1963

That first night at Curley and Locky's I was a little frightened, but excited. At about twelve-thirty, people started to arrive. Some came just to buy a bottle and then leave, but most stayed and danced and drank. Donna and I were encouraged to dance with them.

"Keep 'em happy," Locky winked at me. "They drink more and we get more money."

At six-thirty in the morning the last person left. The house was in even more disarray then before, glasses and dirty ashtrays and used cigarette packages strewn about, but we were all so tired we fell into bed. Locky put his arms around me and nuzzled into me. I was becoming very fond of him.

Curley was exceptionally good-looking, but Locky was, well, interesting. He looked like an adventurer, sandy hair falling over bright alert eyes. They were both very romantic – my pirates of the snow. They stole from the not-so-good perhaps, and gave to themselves and others. I could see Locky with a black patch over one eye – it suited him. Captain Locky of the Pirates of the Snow.

At seven a.m. there was a terrible noise. I heard the back door being smashed down and all of a sudden three men appeared in the bedroom. My heart started pounding and I grabbed Locky tightly. I had no idea what was happening.

"Vice-squad. Okay, everybody out of bed. Now!"

"Locky?" I whispered. I did not think I could tolerate having the police laugh at my body. Plus I was terrified of these strangers bursting into our room. Locky was my hero. I was confident he would take care of me.

"Get out of this room so the lady can get dressed!" Locky snarled at them. "Go on, get out now. We're not getting out of this bed until you give the lady some privacy."

The men retreated to the living room. We got dressed and met them and Curley and Donna in the living room.

The police asked a lot of questions – our occupations, who came to the house, what did they want, what did we do last night, how many people were over at the house, and on and on. It was apparent that Locky, Curley, and Donna were old hands at this. They asked me a few questions, but after lying about my age saying I was twenty-one and satisfying them that I was a university student, they left me alone. After about an hour, they left. We went back to bed.

"Don't worry, they do this all the time. Dumb cops." Locky was soon fast asleep.

Later that afternoon, after Donna and I had cleaned up the house, she said she had some business downtown and asked if I would like to come.

We went to the Salisbury House Restaurant and ordered coffee. Just as our cups were being refilled, a man came up to Donna and gruffly said, "Let's go."

We walked next door to a motel where he opened the door to a room. He didn't seem to mind my being there in the least. Donna and he poured drinks for all of us and after we had all knocked back several glasses, he and Donna began fucking on the bed. They were on one side, naked, sexual, and I was on the other side of the bed, fully clothed, with my back turned to them, listening to the sounds and wondering why I couldn't be the one to be with Donna.

Back at the house, Donna was in her bed resting and the men were in the living room. I was sitting on the side of the bed, holding her hand and talking softly with her.

"Hey, you butches, what are you doing in there?" yelled Curley. I pulled my hand away. I was scared that they would guess my true feelings. I enjoyed Locky, maybe I even felt I loved him in my teenage way, but my heart really speeded up when I was near Donna. I knew that shouldn't be the case and was terrified that Curley would guess how I was feeling and kick me out or hurt me or even kill me. Yet my hand slowly crept back into hers.

"Ruthie, it's okay. He's just teasing us." Donna kissed me as she got up to get ready for the nightly customers.

I stood there feeling very confused.

The next morning, at seven o'clock, the repaired door was once again knocked down. Into the room burst the morals' squad. The whole event was very similar to the previous day. After a week of early morning visits, I was calmly reaching for my clothes and padding out into the living room with a bored look like the rest of them.

Locky and Curley had just bought a huge shipment of alcohol and that day we had no money and no food. Donna said she and I would go out and make some quick cash. I had been going out with her, occasionally being with my own johns and turning the money over to her who in turn gave it to Curley.

"Don't take the kid with you, Donna," said Locky. "I don't want my woman with other men."

This was the first time I had ever heard Locky refer to me as his woman. It was true that from the very beginning, things were extremely good between us. We got along well, we laughed a lot, we had great sex. But I thought I was just hanging out, and was even periodically going to classes during the day at university. I could-

n't allow myself to fall in love with Locky, because I felt sure that he would eventually get bored with me and ask me to leave. But I did fall in love with him and he did call me his woman. Locky always made me laugh. He used to love to shock me – using very obscene language in the tales he told me about being a safecracker. He would wink at me, lean over, and make very lewd suggestions. I loved it. He was always gentle and loving, especially when we were alone. I loved to run my hands over his body and feel and see him becoming aroused and feel good that he was with me. I thought life was good with Locky.

Donna had gone out early that day. I told Locky I was going to go to my parents house for the night. My parents were out of town, and I was going to be with my sister and brothers. I missed Judi, Jack and Sam and my dog Peppy. Although I had been living a wild life, spending as much time away from my parents' home as possible, I still missed my family very much. All these feelings swirled in a confusing mass in my head; I couldn't understand myself. How could I ever expect anyone else to understand me?

"I want to come with you," he said. "I want to see where you live."

I was very nervous, especially because I never heard him say a sentence without an obscenity in it, and my brother Sam, the youngest, was only seven. But from the minute Locky walked into the house, I knew he'd be fine. He and Sam started playing, and Jack and Judi seemed to like him. He said he was taking a holiday, that Curley could handle business that night, and that he was staying the night with me. We all had dinner together and watched TV. It was like a real family, except my parents were gone. I made up the fold-up sofa-bed in the guest room for Locky, went into my room to change and then snuck into his room. He wanted to make love immediately.

"No, Locky, we can't. The kids…"

"Don't be silly. They don't care. They're probably asleep anyway."

I could feel him hard against me. He started kissing me, turning my "No, Locky" into "Yes, Locky."

In the morning, we were still in bed, and Sam opened the door and jumped into bed with us. I was somewhat shocked, but Locky was delighted and he and Sam played for an hour.

"Don't be such a prude. It's good for the kid." He smiled that beautiful smile of his. I melted.

We went back to his house later that day. I was falling more and more in love with him. We both seemed to be enjoying each other so much. That day, he told me about his wife and his two kids, and how he missed his kids so much. His wife left him after the first time he went up. He spent two years that time in prison. He never saw his kids after that. He really wanted to have more kids.

The weeks passed. I told my parents I was staying with friends and made sure to call them every day to say I was fine so that they would leave me alone. At night, we served drinks. In the early morning, the police raided us and knocked the door down. In the afternoon, Curley and Locky fixed the door and Donna and I cleaned up. Locky and I spent more and more of the time in between talking and making love. I never wanted to go back to school. I just wanted to be with him. But he used to send me to classes occasionally, "We got to have one smart one in the family. Now go. And hurry back."

Chapter Fifteen

Rockville, Maryland; October 1964

Lela never dressed. She would go days without putting anything on other than her old navy blue terrycloth bathrobe. She usually sat on the sofa with her feet tucked up in front of her, knees bent upwards with her arms around her legs. She was from an extremely wealthy Greek family and spoke Greek fluently. Very quickly, she began teaching me and soon I could haltingly speak one or two appropriate words, then sentences in Greek.

It was very hard to have any privacy, especially when Lela and I started getting quite intimate in our conversations with each other.

"Well, Ruthaiki," she mused one day, "you are just going to have to learn to speak Greek so that we can communicate in private."

I've always had a proclivity for other languages – in fact, Yiddish was my first spoken language. I grew up in a home with two grandmothers, one grandfather, boarders and friends, none of whom spoke English – so Yiddish was the language of the house. My parents spoke English with me and Yiddish with their parents. When they didn't want me to understand something they usually spoke Ukrainian or Russian. I then decided I had to learn Ukrainian as well. I never did master Ukrainian, although I did learn Russian in later years. By then, speaking in secret codes was no longer necessary to me and I learned solely for the love of the language.

It was Monday morning, and ward rounds were just finishing. Dr. Stepford was standing in front of the elevator consulting with Mrs. Lohmer, who stood erect, clipboard at the ready. Many of the patients were preparing to go out on the grounds for various activities, tying shoes, putting on sweaters, dating and initialing the sign-out book. Through the open window wafted a warm breeze and the lovely strains of *Morning* from Pier Gynt, courtesy of Big John who hogged the piano room cottage as much as possible to play his beloved Grieg. I always enjoyed his music and this morning was no different.

Lenore was still obligated to come to ward rounds as an out-patient and she usually stayed behind afterwards to have coffee with Lela and me.

Lela had just excused herself to use the washroom and we shared a few secret sentences in Greek. I got a brilliant idea. I asked Lenore to go out on an errand for me. When she returned later that day she handed me a package which I excitedly took back to my room. The next morning, when Lela came out for coffee I had already been hard at work for several hours with the book Lenore found me. I had taught myself to read and write the Greek alphabet as a surprise for Lela.

"Ruthaiki, I'm amazed!" she beamed. "You need a regular teacher now."

"Hey, Lela, what a good idea. I think I'll find me a real Greek teacher and take lessons."

I thought I might as well take advantage of the fact that I lived very near Washington, DC and so immediately telephoned the US State Department and asked for the Greek office to see if I could hire a tutor. I explained to the gentleman on the telephone that I wanted to learn Greek and he agreed to come talk with me about it. I gave him the address, set up a time two days hence, and anxiously awaited the appointment.

Wednesday evening came and Dr. Stepford had kindly given me permission to meet the new Greek teacher at the door of the main building and sit privately with him in the main sitting room, while my guard lurked in the hallway.

I waited for him at the front door.

"Hello, are you the Greek teacher?"

He looked anxiously about him. "Yes, my name is Panaiotis Sapountzsis. But you can call me 'Taki'." He inclined his head, raised his eyebrows and waited for my introduction.

"My name is Ruth. Ruth Simkin. I am the one who called you on the telephone. I am very anxious to learn to speak Greek and I hope you will be able to teach me. Would you like to come in please?" I walked into the front sitting room.

"Please, have a seat." I indicated the sofa.

He sat on the very edge of the sofa and looked about the room nervously. He and I were the only people there, although my 'guard' was quietly slinking about the hallway.

The room was just the way I remembered it from the first day I arrived ten months ago; doilies neatly in place over the backs and arms of overstuffed chairs, furniture spaced in conversational groupings; as though it was all prepared for a Victorian tea party.

"What kind of place is this?" he asked.

"Well, it's a hospital. Quite a famous hospital, actually. It's for…" here I dropped my voice down to a mumble, "mental patients."

"What? What did you say?"

"I said that the hospital was for people who, maybe have a few problems, but they all get better, and it's a very good hospital and I'm just here for a very short time."

He started to stand up. "Perhaps I should leave."

"No, please, please, don't leave. It's okay, really. Please, I beg you, please, stay. It's perfectly safe, really it is."

"Why do you want to learn Greek?"

I looked at this man, perhaps in his early thirties, sitting perilously close to the edge of the sofa. His slick black hair was oiled and neatly combed over to the side. He had on a pinstriped dark blue suit and a matching light blue tie over a starched white shirt. He took out a crisp white handkerchief and dabbed his perspiring forehead.

"Well, I have always loved things that are Greek and I have a Greek friend and I just thought it would be a good idea."

I leaned forward, assuming it was a positive stance.

"Well," he dabbed at his face, "I think it is not such a good idea. Perhaps I go now." He started to stand up.

"Oh no, please, just give me a chance. Please." I gently touched him on the arm. I felt him recoil from the touch.

"Look, just give me one short lesson. Right here. If you still think after the lesson it's not a good idea, I won't bother you again. Okay? Please? Just one lesson. I *really* want to learn."

He sat down again, looked at me and smiled. "Okay. We begin."

Lela had coached me a bit and I was very focused. I guess I did okay, because he agreed to come back for another 'trial lesson,' as he tactfully put it.

"So Ruthaiki, how was the lesson?" Lela was waiting for me in the sunroom.

"Oh, Lela, *thavma*, excellent!"

She laughed. "So what's he like, this teacher? What's his name?"

"His name is Panaiotis Sapountzsis."

Lela burst out laughing in that deep, rumbling infectious laugh of hers. "Oh Ruthaiki! Oh ho ho." That was how Lela laughed, a deep oh ho ho, coming from very low down.

"What's so funny? He said to call him Taki."

"Oh, nothing, oh ho ho, it's just that if you translate his name into English from the Greek, his name is 'Peter Soapsuds'."

From then on, no matter how much I protested, Lela called Taki 'Peter Soapsuds.' But as my Greek improved and he kept returning to teach me, she said it with more and more respect.

Within a few months, Lela and I could converse in the sunroom in full view and hearing of anyone and they could not understand us. We talked for hours and days at a time, usually in English if we were alone, but in Greek if anyone else was there. I took to the language quickly. Taki was an excellent teacher, and I could practice with Lela as much as I wanted. Taki was acting above and beyond the call of duty by giving me my lessons on the ward, in the long room off the sunporch. Dr. Stepford had let me meet him that first time downstairs, but when Dr. Evanson heard about that, he insisted on restricting me to the unit. So I had lessons off the sun porch to the accompaniment of Quentin and Mrs. Schwartz, while Lela and I worked hard initially to keep Taki from bolting in terror. It helped that she could calm him in his first language, and she was obviously an intelligent, well-brought-up Greek. She creatively explained away many of the loonies on the ward, trying to assuage his fears.

Lela called me the diminutive 'Ruthaiki' all the time now, or *chriso-mu*, my golden one. We developed a ritual at night which we called our Jesus Prayer. Someone must have been reading Salinger those days. I remember that when *The Catcher in the Rye* came out, there were lots of references in ordinary conversation to Jesus Prayers from that book, and Lela and I just adopted the name and adapted the prayer. Our prayer was an elaborate ritual, consisting of blessings and good wishes in English, Greek and Hebrew. It had a very specific form and order to it, and we composed it in the three languages so that no one could know or pronounce it except us. We said it to each other every night for as long as we knew each other. *Kali nichta, kali spera, laila tov, leyl m'nucha*, it began in Greek and Hebrew, and went on and on from there. Those words were very precious ones to me – we said them with love and they contained all the emotion that we couldn't express physically or otherwise.

Lela and I still played bridge together and developed quite a reputation in the hospital for being virtually unbeatable. We would speak Greek together, but would rarely cheat. Sometimes if we were bored or felt the competition was unworthy, we would cough out signals to each other in Greek. Couples would come to our unit, Main Four, to challenge us to bridge games. We thought the whole thing was a lot of fun and those games certainly acted as a diversion for these very boring times.

Lela's voice was exceptional; soft, and very deep and musical even though it cracked in the lower registers. It was the sexiest voice I had ever heard. I was falling in love beyond anything I had ever experienced before.

We seemed to be able to communicate more and more by just looking at each other. Aside from the eight or so hours we were in our bedrooms at night, my two hours a week of so-called therapy and her two hours with her therapist, we were inseparable. We ate together upstairs, me out of necessity because since the abortion and the Labor Day excursion, Dr. Evanson vowed to keep me locked up for life. Lela stayed on Main Four out of choice, since she never wanted to get out of her blue terrycloth robe and leave the ward.

Lela had lots of friends, both patients and staff, and everyone brought her treats which she always shared with me. If I had to be locked up, then things could be worse, I thought. I was head over heels in love with Lela and could not get her out of my head nor heart for even one second.

I now had my own room because the administrative staff thought I was too disruptive a roommate for Mrs. Kane. I began having grand mal seizures and psychomotor temporal lobe seizures with regularity and was packed almost every time I raised my voice, courtesy of Dr. Evanson's orders. Sometimes when I was fighting off an aura, which came pre-seizure, they would not believe me. Usually, if I had a seizure, I was also packed to "settle me down."

Exactly why these seizures started to increase at this time I do not know, and I believe the doctors did not know either. I suspect that my being locked up in a place where I was treated with psychological and physical disrespect might have had something to do with it. Perhaps, as I was truly epileptic, my disease was now declaring itself. In those days epilepsy was considered as much or more of a mental disease than a neurological one. The administrative staff from Chestnut lodge, Dr. Stepford and Dr. Tatelman in particular, insisted that I see neurological specialists in an attempt to treat this. Dr. Evanson, however, was opposed to any further medical investigation. He expressed the belief that the seizures were my way of acting out and we should ignore them. Thankfully, no one at Chestnut Lodge listened to him regarding this particular aspect of my disease.

I did see neurological specialists at NIH, National Institutes of Health, and had many more EEGs, x-rays, blood work, physical and psychological exams. I didn't mind most of these investigations because they took me off Main Four for a short time – always a pleasure even if it meant getting my brain wired up to a huge machine that blinked bright lights in my eyes. I was placed on medications – first dilantin which caused my gums to bleed profusely (and didn't really stop the seizures), then other combinations of medications – tegretol, phenobarb, mysoline and others, some of which made me feel as though I were a zombie, robbing me of energy and affecting my capacity to think. The worse the side-effects I experienced from these drugs, the happier Dr. Evanson seemed to be. If I were feeling particularly ill one day in a session with him, he would be positively gleeful – rubbing his hands together, tapping his papers on the desk in a rhythmic way, almost trying to smile. When he was like that, I knew he was a madman. I just didn't know what I could do to extricate myself from his clutches.

With each seizure, whether it was a full-fledged grand mal convulsion or a temporal lobe seizure of confusion or anger or even a petit mal seizure where my face went blank for seconds, I was packed – on the order of Dr. Evanson. I spent a great deal of time wrapped in cold wet sheets contemplating my pet seal, a stuffed animal my parents brought me. Lela and I had christened it Aristophanes. My twenty-year old self thought that having a stuffed seal named Aristophanes after an ancient Greek playwright was terribly sophisticated.

One day, Lela and I had a terrible fight. Lela's temper was as bombastic as mine and it's a miracle we fought so rarely. I don't even remember what the specifics of the fight were, only that a short time after we both stomped off in opposite directions, Lela sent me a note which said, "*Charitsa* (little joy) dear – I'd rather switch than fight," – the motto lifted from the package of cigarettes sitting on the table. And that was the end of that.

We wrote each other many notes. Lela wrote to me in Greek. I usually drew cartoons to say whatever it was I was saying. Some of the notes and cartoons were very complex, others simple, many just plain silly – all very funny. Our communications showed clearly the mutual love we shared.

I often drew a little cartoon character I called CLO (the C and L standing for Chestnut Lodge). Usually, each cartoon was four panels consisting of little CLO talking about the hospital, patients, doctors, etc. She was basically a round head with a curl at the top, two little feet coming out the bottom and her head had expressive eyes and mouth. I used these cartoons to work out some of my frustration at the hospital. I remember one cartoon with CLO saying in the first panel, "I have a brilliant plan." It continues in the second panel, "When the patients want to get rid of hostilities and tensions... (third panel) There is really only one thing to do..." The fourth panel shows CLO's eyes criss-crossed and her mouth wiggly and weird and she yells, "Pack the staff!"

Another one had CLO saying, "There really is nothing wrong with me."

Second panel, "I'm convinced of it."

Third panel, CLO looking very sad, "It's all in my mind."

Last panel (even sadder), "The temporal lobe."

I made about one hundred of these little cartoons. They did allow me to feel as though I was doing *something*! Had Dr. Evanson ever seen them, I feel certain he would have banned me from using pencil and paper.

Lela and I had a friend, Jefferey, whom Lela had known when they were both patients in the hospital six years earlier. Jefferey was now a private patient and had his own apartment in Rockville. A private patient was one step ahead of an out-patient and did not have to attend ward rounds or have anything to do with the hospital really, other than continue in therapy. Jefferey still saw his therapist whose offices were at Chestnut Lodge, but other than that, he had nothing more to do with the hospital. Like most of the out-patients and private-patients, he did like to hang around with old friends from the hospital. A gay man in his early twenties, Jefferey was very lively and entertaining, regaling us with great stories and jokes which we loved to hear.

When Jefferey found out Lela was back, he started sending her flowers and, as our friendship developed, I was included on the flower runs. It was a given that everyone staying at Chestnut Lodge came from money – it simply cost too much to stay there for those who were not on the wealthy side.

One sunny day Lela and I were sitting on the sun porch in our usual places: me on the rocking chair, her on her corner of the sofa, the small wooden table between us. The table was small enough for us to hold hands if we were so inclined, and large enough to place our coffee mugs and our books there. It was home. We were waiting for our lunch trays to come up.

Mrs. Lohmer came out to the sun porch to dispense pills to Janie who was wandering about muttering to Quentin. Lela and I were generally oblivious to her and the others who wandered through our space.

Suddenly, the elevator started grinding its upward passage and an aide emerged with two large bouquets of red roses, one for Lela and one for me. Mrs. Jackson took them from the aide and the elevator. "Look how lovely these are, aren't they lovely? Here, I will put them in vases for you." She took them off into the small kitchen and brought back two vases filled with roses.

"Aren't you two lucky. Look how beautiful these are."

Lela and I looked at them and shook our head. All day, everyone who came into the room kept commenting on the beauty of the flowers. We decided not to follow suit – we ignored them completely.

Three days later, Mrs. Jackson came into the sunroom where we were sitting, wilted flowers between us.

"Well, it looks as though these roses didn't last very long." She moved towards the vases.

"Don't you dare take our flowers," Lela warned her.

"But Mrs. Marinides, they are dying. They don't look good any more."

"They look lovely," Lela answered. "They are our...our morbidities. Look Ruthaiki, this morbidity is Angus, and this one, Philomena..." She then proceeded to name each flower, and I repeated the name after her.

"Our morbidities," she smiled upon them. "Our morbidities," I echoed.

We kept those dead flowers between us for three weeks. We would not allow anyone to throw them out. Each day, we would come out to the sunroom and make a big fuss over our morbidities, our dead flowers.

"Oh, look at Phillip this morning. He's drooping even more than yesterday."

"Yes, and Saralee is turning all brown. How wonderful!"

We would ooh and aah and gush over them while Mrs. Jackson would harrumph and shake her head. She was afraid of both of us and so was not really able to challenge us, since we were not hurting anyone or ourselves. Lela and I felt that we were terribly blasé.

After the fourth week, when Lela and I were each in a therapy session, someone took the vases of dead flowers and we had a relatively empty table between us again – until Jeffrey sent us more flowers, and we would go through the entire process with the morbidities all over again. We spoke about our morbidities a lot. We saw anything fresh or blooming only as a future morbidity.

Lela had been a professional actress in New York. Her latest boyfriend there was Desmond, who used to come to visit her once in a while. He'd slink off the elevator, black hair greased down to one side and combed back so that it was short on his neck and longer in the front. He usually wore a plaid cotton short-sleeved shirt, a pack of cigarettes stuck under the left sleeve, and stained khaki pants. How Lela could even look at him, much less go out with him, was absolutely beyond me. They would leave the ward on occasion and I would rock in my chair, not talking to anyone until Lela came back to her spot on the sofa to tell me about her outing.

Lela had her own apartment in New York, as did Desmond, but he was always hanging around her place. After several good years, her illness returned. Lela's first instinct was to call Dr. Will, her therapist, but Desmond talked her out of it and told her she could rely upon him. She told me she had become completely dependent upon him, even to cross the street. She knew that was a sickness, but only now did she begin to realize that he was the sleaze ball I knew him to be who had taken advantage of her by convincing her she couldn't get along without him at all, for anything.

One night, very late, I got out of bed as though called by some powerful yet unknown instinct and slowly walked down the hall. Lela was in the TV room alone, wearing her terrycloth robe, sitting in the dark with her legs pulled tightly up against her chest. I went in and sat down on the floor beside her chair. She brought her legs down and I wrapped my arms around them and leaned into them. I kissed her legs.

"Ruthaiki, you're like my child."

"I want to be your lover."

"No, you don't. You don't even know what you are talking about."

"Yes, I do, Lela, I love you."

"I love you too, *chriso-mu*, but like a daughter, a son, a mother. I don't know any other way. I'm strictly with men."

"Lela, I love you. I want to be with you."

Suddenly, she jumped up. "What do you want?" she yelled, ripping open her terrycloth robe, exposing her naked body. "This?"

I sat on the floor in stunned silence, flabbergasted, not knowing what to say or do. Lela did up her robe, sat down and took my hand. We sat in quietude.

There are always a few times in life one wishes one could replay and alter from the irrevocability of history. This time was one of them. Why I did not embrace that vulnerable, emaciated body and smother her with yeses is something that will forever elude me.

Two weeks later, Lela was in bed in her room. She had a roommate who was snoring away soundly. I was sitting on Lela's bed beside her and we were chatting and laughing. I turned to look at her face; we melted together and kissed, softly. Then not so softly. Soon our passions were unleashed as we were kissing furiously, rolling around in the single bed.

"Oh, Ruthaiki-mu."

"Lela, I love you so much, *s'agapo*."

I felt like my heart would burst from emotion and happiness.

In lurched Mrs. Decker.

"Okay missy, get back to your room right now or I will call the aides and we will have you cold packed faster than you can say your name." She turned to Lela. "Sorry to bother you, Mrs. Marinides." Everyone deferred to Lela! Lela and I said a few quick words to each other in Greek and I left.

The next day I was on my way back from 'the silent hour,' as I now christened my sessions with Dr. Evanson. Since the throwing of the cup episode, he virtually refused to acknowledge my existence and vigorously pursued his paper work. As Hector, my guard for the day, and I were walking back to the locked ward in the big brick building, we came across Lela on a very rare outing, and Jefferey. It was late fall and there were many beautifully coloured leaves on the ground. We all started tromping around on the golden leaves and singing in the sun. Jefferey was just leaving and was in his car. Lela and I hopped on the front hood of his car. Hector sat in the front seat while Jefferey drove slowly around the crescent, winding past the low-sitting Center, the large brick building that housed Main Four, back around Upper Cottage, Lower Cottage – as though we were in a one-float parade for all the world to see. Lela and I held hands tightly. She wore soft, thin, black leather gloves which held my hand so lovingly. The sun shone, the sky was blue and our laughter filled the air. I forgot about the silent hours and that I was returning to be locked up again. I just looked at her thick, dark hair, heard her deep laugh and felt the joy of love inside. It was a magic moment I will never forget. It's strange how one magic moment like that can overshadow the pain of the packs and the beatings, the times with a doctor one knows to be insane, all the other negatives of a grotesque life. It's strange, this glimpse into the face of optimism, of hope.

Rockville, Maryland; November 1964

The weeks and months continued to pass. Early November, I told Dr. Stepford that I wanted to sign myself out, that I saw no benefit to my continued incarceration. He said he would get back to me. The following day, he told me that if I were to sign myself out, he would call a hearing to have me committed. Three psychiatrists from another hospital would come to interview me. If they all agreed, I would be committed and if my family would not pay for me to be there, I would then be sent to St. Elizabeth's. Did I still want to sign myself out? I said I would think about it again.

That evening, a group of us sat around on the sunporch discussing this.

"Look, Ruthie," offered Matt, "these guys are going to listen to the other doctors before they listen to you. Once you're committed, two years have to go by before you can have another hearing. It's barely been two months since your

Labor Day escape. We've already had this discussion once before. You know they will commit you."

"Jesus, I didn't even do anything bad. I just ran away for the weekend. I had to get away."

"Matt's right, Ruthie," added Neville. "They'll listen to Dr. Evanson before they'll believe you."

"But Neville, everyone knows Dr. Evanson is cuckoo."

"Yeah, we know, but they don't. Doctors protect one another, don't we, Matt?"

Matt puffed deeply on his pipe and nodded slowly. "Most of the time we do. I think you'll be committed."

"But I'm not even crazy! I don't have delusions. I don't hear or see things. There's nothing wrong with me."

"You are a trouble-maker. Nobody likes trouble-makers."

"Margaret Bullard, how can you say that! I have never caused you any trouble."

"Not me," answered Margaret, "but the doctors. Look at all these letters I've written and nobody answered me." She proceeded to put her basket on the table and, after pulling out her typewriter, showed me pages of letters.

"Margaret, not now, please. I need to decide my future."

Matt and Neville puffed at their pipes and sipped at their drinks.

"Ruthie, look at the facts." Neville shifted in his chair. "For some reason, Dr. Evanson really has it in for you. You are an epileptic. You have grand mal seizures. You are considered violent. You..."

"Violent! Oh, for Christ sake, Neville, I am not violent! What is it with these guys and epilepsy? Are we in the god-damn stone ages or something? Epilepsy is a neurological disease, so why does everyone, especially the bloody doctors here, keep thinking it's a mental disease?"

Matt smiled. "Saying it is a mental disease is better for this hospital, right? More patients, more," indicating quotation marks with his fingers, "psychiatric problems to deal with. Of course we know you as the sweet young girl you are, but they consider you violent."

"Jesus, Matt," I yelled, "I am not violent!"

"But you are packed a lot." This from Max. "Yessiree, you sure are packed a lot. Don't let them get you, girlee. Then they take away everything. They are always trying to kill me, yessiree, trying to kill me, they are." Max began his paranoid rantings which I was beginning to think were not so paranoid after all, and stormed down the hall.

"Well, we all think you'll be committed. So be careful."

"Okay, thanks, Matt, Neville. Good night."

Lela walked with me to my room and we stood outside in the hall softly talking.

"I think it's taking a big chance. Maybe you can get out, but what if you're committed? Then you have two years here, or worse, at St. E.'s, before you can get out again."

"But Lela, what about here? I'm not getting out here. I've been here almost a year, and nothing has happened."

"Well, *chriso-mu*, let's keep trying to get you a new doctor. Maybe that's the answer. I don't think you can afford to take the chance of commitment."

"Dr. Stepford, I have decided not to sign myself out and to stay voluntarily."

"Good for you, Miss Simkin. We like to see cooperation."

"Dr. Stepford, please, I beg you, please can I have a new therapist?"

Dr. Stepford sucked on his pipe. What was it with these psychiatrists that they all sucked on pipes? Likely some kind of oral fixation, I grinned. He paused.

"Please, Dr. Stepford. I am anxious to get better. I will try almost anything. But I really don't think I can do it with Dr. Evanson. I know he does not work like the other doctors here. I've talked with other patients. Please, sir."

"I'll think about it. I'll discuss it at our staff meeting in the next few weeks. Perhaps. But in the meantime, don't count on it and keep working in your therapy with Dr. Evanson."

"Yes, sir, thank you, sir."

That evening in the dining room, Ambrose came rushing up to our table, breathing heavily. He was not carrying a tray – this must be really important news.

"Guess what! Guess what!!!! Big John just killed himself!"

"What!?"

"Yeah. On the ward. He slit his throat. What a mess! What a mess! Blood all over the place."

I thought of John, lowering his huge body onto the piano bench to play Grieg for hours on end. He was a brilliant pianist, and could caress the piano so softly, yet when away from it, he could be so violent. I wondered what pushes someone to slit his throat.

Lela and I went upstairs and played Peer Gynt for John and sat in silence.

Chapter Sixteen

One month had now gone by since I spoke with Dr. Stepford about changing therapists and he still could not give me a positive response. I had been exceptionally "good," which meant I was quiet and polite. Perhaps the medication I had been taking kicked in, but I didn't have any seizures and had not been packed for a month. I spent almost all my time talking with Lela or sitting with her and reading.

Jefferey was having a special Christmas party at his house and had invited Lenore, Lela and a few other friends. They also wanted me to go. Much to my surprise, Dr. Stepford gave me permission to go to Jeff's apartment for the day, provided I stayed with the group and had an escort. Hector had volunteered to come with us.

At the appointed time, Jefferey picked up Lela, Hector, myself and Lyons, another friend of his who was at the hospital, and drove us down the Rockville Pike to his apartment in Bethesda. He lived in a beautiful complex called Grosvenor Place, three large apartment buildings, each over twenty floors high, all with balconies that overlooked parks and a large swimming pool.

"Ooooh, Jefferey, I love this place. It's so cool."

Jefferey was a wonderful cook, and soon there were more people at his home, all eating and drinking and listening to Barbra Streisand wistfully sing "Happy Days are Here Again." That song did something to me – the words said one thing and the feelings expressed were the antithesis. I felt it was about me and I loved listening to it. I would usually find tears welling up in my eyes when it was playing.

We weren't supposed to drink, but we did anyway. At first, we were hiding it by drinking spiked eggnog, but when we saw Hector drinking and we knew he wasn't supposed to be, we just all became very open about it. Over the hours, we all got quite drunk. The other guests left, but we were going to stay until the last possible minute before our eleven p.m. curfew. Hector slipped off the couch and started giggling. Lela began teasing him, telling him what a big penis he had and he lay there smiling and drunk, content with his sexual fantasies. Everyone was laughing. Lela and I were getting closer and closer. The lights were lowered and muted voices could be heard from around the apartment. Soon Lela and I fell into an embrace, kissing and holding each other for a very long time. Hector just lay on the floor, with his eyes partially closed, smiling. His long penis was visible under his brown pants, lying along his left leg, anxiously waiting for some sort of action which did not seem to be forthcoming. Lela and I didn't care. We were grateful for every second we could get together. The lush feel of her hair, the softness of her lips, her arms gathered around me, her wonderful Jean Naté smell, her favourite and the only fragrance she ever wore, the touch of her body against mine – all these relegated the soft lights, music and the other people to just background murmurings in the distance. I floated on love, vaguely aware of, but not caring about anything except Lela and myself.

The loud ringing of the phone jarred us all.

"Hector, it's for you," Jefferey called.

Hector groaned and took the phone.

"What? How do you know? Well, she was here. Just a minute… Jefferey, is Lenore still here?"

"No, she left about an hour and a half ago. Why? What's up?"

Hector turned back to the phone. "Okay, we'll check it out. We're on our way." He hung up the phone and turned to us. "That was the hospital. Some neighbor of Lenore's called to say that there is screaming coming from her apartment. The hospital is short-staffed now, so asked if we could check it out on our way home."

Jefferey drove us straight to Lenore's. Her apartment was five blocks from the hospital. Lela and I ran to her door and banged on it.

"Lenore, open up. It's us, Lela and Ruthie, open up." She banged on the door with her fist.

"Go away!" came from inside the apartment.

"Lenore, we're worried about you. Let us in. Please." I pounded on the door.

"Go away. Go be with Lela. Get out of here and leave me alone."

"Lenore, it's Hector. Let me in at once."

"Get the fuck away from here, you drunken asshole. Leave me alone, all of you."

"Okay, Lenore, this is Ruth. We're getting serious now. Let us in or we will bash down the door."

There was silence. I took a run and threw myself into the door. It did not budge. The alcohol disguised my bruised and painful shoulder.

Suddenly, the door opened a crack and Lela and I rushed in. There stood Lenore, blood dripping down both arms. "Oh my God, Lenore, look at you. Hector, call an ambulance, right away. Ruthie, get me some towels. Lenore, come here."

Lenore walked into Lela's arms and began sobbing. She held her while I wrapped her arms. Soon the ambulance came and took Lenore off to the hospital to be stitched up. We cleaned up her apartment, stalling for each extra minute before we had to go back.

The next morning, a glum Lenore came out of a room down the hall for coffee. Both arms were bandaged in white.

"Gee Lenore, what happened? Why did you do that?" I confronted her in the small kitchen.

Lenore stared hard at me. "Don't you know? How could you not know?"

"Know what? What are you talking about?"

"I was in love with Lela. Until I saw her with you. I loved you too. I guess I couldn't stand seeing the two of you together and I was alone."

I was stunned. "Gee, Lenore, I'm really sorry. I didn't know you felt that way about Lela."

"Ruthie, *everyone* is in love with Lela. You're the only one she's ever gotten really close to. I guess that's what started it."

"Lenore, I'm really sorry." I reached over to touch her gently on her shoulder. "Still friends?" I smiled at her.

She smiled back "Still friends." We hugged and kissed each other and went out to drink our coffee.

In the meantime, Lela and I continued to be close physically whenever we could grab a private moment. We couldn't go to each other's rooms, because ever since that night I was caught in her bed, they posted someone on hall duty just outside the doors. We'd spend long hours devising ways to be alone. We decided that as soon as we were both out of the hospital, we would charter a yacht together and sail around the Greek Islands. We both knew we would go to Greece together. Lela already told me about all her family and friends there and I felt as though I knew them well. We planned the trip in detail, reveling in the sumptuous ways we would enjoy each other under the Greek skies. I was never more grateful that we both came from families that could financially support our fantasies and make them true. Money would not be an issue for either of us. We just needed to be free.

"Was your family always rich?" I asked one day as we were planning our Greek trip.

"As far back as I can remember," Lela answered. "I'm not even sure how it started, but my brother owns most of the entertainment industry on the west coast. He likes doing the work, but I just sit back and enjoy the benefits," she smiled. "And it helped that I got married when I was twenty to a very rich man. He was in Greek shipping. I stayed married for about five years and when we divorced, I had a nice hefty bank account left for me. How about your family? Did you always have money?"

"Nope," I answered. "In fact, when I was born my parents didn't even have their own home; we lived with my dad's parents, aunts, uncles, my mom's mom and a bunch of boarders, all in this big house. Then my sister Judi was born three years after me, and my mom and dad and grandmother and me and my sister all moved into our own house.

"You know, my dad came back from the war kind of freaked out. I think he was shell-shocked or whatever they called it. He didn't see me for the first three years of my life."

"Really?"

"Yeah. The family story is that when he was finally coming home, all the families of the soldiers were at the train station awaiting the arrival of his platoon. The train had just come in, the soldiers were all standing in formation while speeches were being made, when my dad heard this voice, 'Daddy, daddy' and he saw this little girl in a yellow dress pushed towards him. I guess I was rehearsed for weeks for this moment. Anyway, he broke rank and ran to pick me up. Once he did that, all the other soldiers did that too, and all hell broke loose. I guess he had seen me once twenty-four hours after I was born and then he was shipped overseas until I was three.

"So he came back from the war, no home, no job, no money, hadn't finished high school, and he had a wife and three year old me. He and my uncle borrowed two hundred dollars and a bulldozer and ended up building one of the biggest construction companies in the city. My dad worked like a madman – he was hardly ever home in the summer – always out on the jobs. And soon their company was one of the biggest in the province. And then in the country. And then they sold it to a huge European company and went public. And that's when we became rich. So my brother Sam who is twelve years younger than me always remembers growing up in a big home and having money for things. It was different for me. You know, we got our first big home just before I turned twelve. And then I was in junior high school. I was ashamed to bring friends over to our house because I thought it was too big and fancy. I told my friends my dad was a cop who would arrest them if they came over. Really."

We both laughed.

"It took me a long time to get used to the fact that we had money and to not feel embarrassed about it. My dad turned out to be very generous. I guess he was always grateful for the way things turned out. He puts people through school all the time and he has a reputation for hiring convicts, just to give them a chance to rehabilitate. I guess my dad had a rough time growing up. They all lived on a farm."

"How did they get a farm?"

"My dad's parents came over from Russia when they were in their early twenties. They were homesteaders – you know, if they farmed the land, they could live there, so that's what they did. It was a place not too far from Winnipeg, called Pine Ridge. My grandmother had six kids on that farm. Every few years my grandfather would hitch up the horse and buggy and go into Winnipeg to register the new kids born. They lived there until the farm burned down when my dad was a teenager. Then, the whole family moved into Winnipeg and my grandfather sold wood and coal for fuel. That's why my dad's nickname is Blackie – well, two reasons. One is that he has very black hair, but the other reason is that he was always black from working in the coal yard."

My Greek lessons continued on a regular basis. Soon I was completely fluent and Taki and I began reading Kazantzakis together in the original. He was very proud of my accomplishments and I was trying to feel proud about it too. It certainly had helped a lot in my relationship with Lela, allowing us to speak privately anywhere, even when surrounded by people. Not too many people, other than Lela's family, who rarely came, could speak Greek – in fact, no one else we knew of, so we had found the ideal way to continuously tell each other how wonderful we both were, and how much we meant to each other, all in perfect privacy in the midst of a crowd.

Rockville, Maryland; February 1965

My first year anniversary at Chestnut Lodge passed, then another month – and only then was I summoned to an individual meeting in the TV room with Dr. Stepford. He looked over at me thoughtfully.

"Miss Simkin, we have considered your request for a new therapist and are willing to let you try therapy with someone else. Your new therapist will be Dr. Frances Brennecke and you will be starting with her this week. Do you agree to be in therapy with her?"

"Oh yes, of course, thank you, thank you, sir." My head was reeling with excitement. Dr. Brennecke was my third choice for a new therapist, but still, she was a choice. She was an older woman, short, with one leg smaller than the other. She walked with a cane. She was tiny, yet she was administrator of Main Three, the all-male, most violent ward in the hospital. I knew that she had worked at St. Elizabeth's and had a reputation for being tough, but the few times I saw her, she looked at me as though she had seen me and there was something about her that I liked. I thought the fact that Peter, a patient of Dr. Evanson's, had hung himself over Christmas probably had helped this change to occur. Dr. Evanson now had no patients who were doing well. All his patients were getting worse.

I ran out of the small room, leaping in the air, shrieking with excitement. "A new therapist. I'll be free at last. Yahoo. A new therapist." I ran to the sun-porch to tell Lela.

Within the mental health community, Chestnut Lodge was known to have progressive policies regarding rehabilitation and therefore had many diverse therapies, including drama therapy. The drama director of Georgetown University had long been involved in various activities over the years at the hospital. When he heard that Lela was back, he proposed starting a drama group with the idea of mounting a play with the patients. Lela had an excellent reputation in the theatre community, and he had approached both the hospital and her long before anyone else. Everyone knew that Lela was a serious actress and had appeared on Broadway in many roles, to wonderful reviews.

Lela would not even consider a play or being involved in a drama club until the new year, and now, early in February, Donn returned to form his drama group. Besides Lela, the group included Jefferey, who sort of qualified as a patient, even though he was a private one; Jefferey's friend Lyons, from Hilltop and his girlfriend Barbara, from Main Two. There were about twenty others who came and went depending upon their mental status. Janie was involved with the group, but rarely could stay "in contact" as they called it, for very long. We didn't feel Quentin qualified for a role. The group approached me to ask if I would join them. Dr. Brennecke suggested to Dr. Stepford that it would be an excellent idea.

Months passed and the drama club was getting ready to mount a play, "The Importance of Being Earnest" by Oscar Wilde. Lela, the only patient who had any professional acting experience, was to play Lady Bracknell and Jefferey was Ernest/Jack. Lyons played Algernon and his girlfriend Barbara played Gwendolen. They wanted me to play the ingénue part of Cecily. I would have done anything to be near Lela, so readily agreed, all the while insisting that I could not act. The play was indeed fun to work on, and Donn, the director, was wonderful. I saw my participation in this play as a turning point in my stay at the hospital, because now it seemed as though I was doing everything right. I was given unescorted privileges on the grounds, which meant that I could go to rehearsals in the Center, where we met for read-throughs – going either alone or, as was more often the case, with Lela. We were either in rehearsal or were practicing our lines almost all the time. We barely had time for bridge. We would rehearse all day in the Center, then go to the cafeteria for dinner, and come up to the ward to rehearse our lines some more. And I still saw Dr. B. four hours a week. I looked forward to those sessions and missed the days when I did not see her.

The play was to be performed at the beginning of April. Donn was so impressed with the calibre of the acting and the production in general, that he had arranged for us to perform it twice at the hospital and then once at Georgetown University in their main theatre, for the general public. We were all very excited about that.

A lot of my scenes were with Miss Prism, played by Claire, from Main Two. Claire was a quiet woman, maybe fifteen years older than I. She was tall and very thin, her grey-brown hair pulled austerely back into a bun. She looked just as I would have expected Miss Prism to look like, even though she was not in costume. She really came into her own in this play. She said more as Miss Prism that she ever said as Claire, and since Cecily liked Miss Prism, I liked Claire.

The Rev. Chasuble was played by Ward, an elderly man from Main Three whom I didn't know well before the play. I always felt that Ward reminded me of a fuzzy teddy bear with his close cropped white hair, round, pudgy face, soft, plump body and an almost permanent grin. Sid, who played Merriman, the butler, lived in Upper Cottage and looked like a shoe salesman I used to know. There was something disruptive about his large body indicating business that needed to be dealt with – "Open toed or closed sandals today, ma'am?"

Both Ward and Sid were manic-depressives and both were in their normal phase. We were all hoping that they wouldn't go manic until after the run of the play. It was something that could just not be predicted. Before the days of lithium and other drugs used to treat this illness, manic-depressives would be perfectly normal one day, then manic the next, or else depressed and non-functional for months on end. It always lent an element of surprise to go for a visit to Upper Cottage where most of the manic-depressives lived, because neither we, nor the doctors, nurses or staff ever knew what we would find. Anyone might be peacefully sitting around chatting or playing bridge, or throwing things and screaming, or lying on a bed in a catatonic stupor.

Going completely manic was usually preceded by a kind of speeding up, a hyperwarp of time for that person. The newly manic person had excessive energy, never slept, felt she or he could do anything, spoke faster, moved faster and performed grandiose acts. This situation would escalate until that person was completely out of control and, for some patients, this stage could be fairly violent. For others it would just be living in an altered reality and wanting to save the world by their actions. Manic-depressives were fascinating people and I enjoyed being with most of the ones I knew.

By mid-March, I felt as if I was becoming the real me again. I could come and go pretty much at will, I was very engrossed in the play and being part of an accepted group, and I was very involved in my therapy. It wasn't always pleasant, but I always wanted to see Dr. B. Things were wonderful with Lela and we drew even closer as the days and weeks sped by.

New York City; March 1965

For my twenty-first birthday, my parents came to the hospital and took me to New York for a few days. It was the first time I had been out in over fourteen months. Dr. Brennecke had encouraged us to go and her opinion prevailed over Dr. Stepford's and Mrs. Lohmer's hesitation. My parents were excited and I was even more elated. Five days in New York – I could hardly believe my good fortune.

We flew into La Guardia and took a cab to the Plaza. There was a telegram waiting upon my arrival when we checked in. It was from Lela and it said in transliterated Greek, "Tuesday Wednesday Thursday Friday Saturday," and then the Jesus prayer was transliterated out in its entirety in all our languages. I was so much in love with her. I kept that telegram with me the entire trip. And for the rest of my life.

We had a full five days, going to one or two plays a day and shopping most of the rest of the time. The day before my birthday was St. Patrick's Day, so after the theatre we went to an Irish pub in the village for some green beer. I was dressed in a black silk dress, hemmed quite short, in the style of the times. Lord knows, I wanted to be fashionable. My hair was piled high up on my head, in the then-trendy beehive style. I thought I looked quite sophisticated and at least looked older than my twenty-one years. My parents and I were at a small table in the very noisy bar. At the next table was a large party with over a dozen people, the focal point of which was the cutest looking guy I had seen in a long time. At first glance, I was attracted to his curly brown hair. As I looked at him more, I noticed the collar around his neck. My ears perked up when I heard the people at his table address him as "Father" and I realized he was an Irish priest. This man of God was now looking back at me most lasciviously. As the music became livelier, the priest pushed back his chair and walked toward me.

He smiled at me, smiled at my parents and then started tapping out the rhythm of the lively music on my hair. He was laughing and I was laughing and my parents were laughing, and then his hands moved below my head and he was drumming on my shoulders, then my breasts, then my sides. I was pulling each hand off of me almost as soon as it landed, feeling suddenly like I had been attacked by an army of unwelcome octopi. My father jumped up, put out his hand and said, "Hey now…"

Just then a bouncer went over to the priest's table and spoke to one of the men who immediately got up and grabbed the priest. "Come on, Father, these people don't want you bothering them. Come back to the table."

By now, most of the people in the restaurant were staring at us. I was beginning to feel distinctly uncomfortable and somewhat defiled. The priest smiled sadly at me, went back to the table, grabbed a huge mug of green beer, lifted it to me in a toast and drank it all down.

My mother asked me if I wanted to leave.

"No, I'm fine, mom. He's just a little drunk. I like it here."

Shortly after, a few couples from the priest's table got up to leave. One woman glanced at our table and turned to the priest, "Father, be good," she pleaded as she touched him on the shoulder.

He winked and turned back to his beer. After that we all left. I felt both flattered and contaminated at the same time, not an unfamiliar feeling for me. I never discussed those feelings with my parents, although later Dr. Brennecke and I got several good sessions out of the good father's behaviour towards me and my feelings about it.

We continued to have a great time in New York and returned Sunday night to Chestnut Lodge, my bags crammed with new clothes and books. I had taken Aristophanes, the stuffed seal with me; it was a way to bring Lela closer to me – as I hugged Aristophanes, I pretended it was Lela. My parents flew back home early the next morning, feeling much better about my being there, and I fell once more into my routine of play rehearsals, therapy and loving Lela.

Rockville, Maryland; April 1965

The next few months sped by. This new year of 1965 promised to be a good one for me. Almost immediately, Dr. Brennecke had recommended I be let off the ward and given ground privileges. Her office was in the same building as my ward, and she suggested I be allowed to come and go on my own, a suggestion to which Dr. Stepford reluctantly agreed.

I saw Dr. Brennecke four times a week, for fifty minutes each time. We had both requested that I see her more often than the usual twice a week and the hospital agreed. We talked, mostly about my family and my growing up. She listened, but actively, not like Dr. Evanson. She remembered what I told her, and made reference to things. I was starting to look forward to my therapy sessions and to depend upon them and her.

"I hate him, I just hate him!" I was yelling one day.

She just nodded at me.

"Well? He's an asshole, isn't he?"

She smiled at me.

"Look, Dr. B., I can't go on living with him like this. I can't stand to see his face."

"Ruth, just what is it about Matt exactly that you find so upsetting?"

"He's so, so….fatherly!!! And sure of himself. And he's such a shithead. I hate him, hate him!!!! He's always telling me what to do," I continued, "as though he knows what's best for me. He doesn't know. I hate when he talks to me like that."

"Does he remind you of anyone?"

"No!!! I hate him!"

My early therapy sessions were somewhat rudimentary.

One session, very early in our relationship, I was particularly frustrated with the way things were going on the ward. Having to step over a masturbating Janie lying in the middle of the hall before my morning coffee was starting to get to me. Max had been particularly paranoid recently, which always came with increased shouting at everyone and everything. Mrs. Schwartz was noisier and more annoying than usual with her, "I'm not left here, oh nooooo," emanating non-stop from her room. Everyone, including the staff, seemed to be a bit on edge. My therapy sessions offered a respite from this insanity.

"Oooooh, I would just like to throw something, to break something!" I stood up and paced around the room.

"Why don't you heave a Kleenex?" she asked quietly.

"What? What are you talking about?"

"Heave a Kleenex. Go on. Give it a try. You can't hurt anybody, including yourself, and it may help. Go on." She nodded towards the Kleenex box.

I stormed over to the box, grabbed a Kleenex, wadded it up and heaved it with all my might, only to see it fluttering slowly to the ground. I grabbed another, which also floated on wafts of air until it landed softly beside the first. I tore out another Kleenex, kneaded it into a ball and threw it as hard as I could, watching it float benignly to the floor. There was something about the enormity of my efforts of throwing and the gently fluttering piece of tissue that so intrigued me that I began to laugh. Now, instead of anger, a sense of fun prevailed as I took yet another Kleenex, and another, and threw them all into the air. We were both laughing out loud by the time the box was empty. I felt a temporary release of emotion. I have never forgotten to heave a Kleenex when overcome with total frustration.

My therapy sessions with Dr. Brennecke very quickly started becoming real – and work – and more often than not, painful. But she was always there for me – calm, intelligent, observant and frustratingly neutral in her perceived alliances or lack of them. I knew I could always count on her to be objective, yet to support me when it really counted.

"I feel really used – and dirty," I started off one session. "I don't really know why."

"Well, let's talk about that," from Dr B.

"I just want to be ordinary. But I am non-ordinary. A non-ordinary outcast." I sighed.

Dr. B sat still and waited.

"When I was a little girl, I felt like…. I was…. well look, if I could draw it, this is what the picture would be: a tiny little girl, confused, perplexed, standing in the middle of an enormous tornado swirling about her. I guess that means lonely too.

"I was so lonely as a kid. I remember once my sister Judi had a particularly bad asthma attack. We were in our big house then, but just, so I must have been barely twelve and she was nine. She was in the bedroom and my parents were running in and out and calling the doctor and Judi was wheezing and practically dying. I was so scared for my sister and for my parents and I also wanted to do something to help. I stood in the hallway outside the closed door where my mom and dad were running in and out of the room, wanting to be involved somehow.

"'What are you doing out here?' my mom yelled at me. 'Can't you see we're busy? Why are you bothering us?'"

"Tears came to my eyes – I didn't want to bother them, I just wanted to help – and to find out how my sister was.

"'Get out of here, Ruthie,' my father yelled at me. 'Don't be a pest, can't you see you are in the way here? Go!'

"I slunk back to my room, closed the door, lay down on the bed and thought I would die from the hurt of it all. I was so misunderstood, and so frightened for everyone. I wanted my parents to care about me too. But I knew they didn't."

I dried my eyes with some tissue, took some deep breaths, and continued.

"The confusion is less now than when I was young, but I see that some-times I manufacture big diverting gusts to compete with the tornado. Now, when that little girl's hurt comes, it comes with such a vengeance...like it was trying to make up for the times I didn't feel it.... because of my defense mechanisms."

I smiled, thinking about how we patients, living in the mental hospital, couldn't help but pick up psychiatric jargon and tended to use it in everyday conversation.

"You know, I just remembered something."

Dr. B. raised her eyebrows in a question.

"When I was five, I was in kindergarten, and was going to be a tree in a school concert. I was very excited about this. My mother put on my best dress and I felt so pretty and loved and a valuable part of our kindergarten forest. I was going to walk the two blocks to school to prepare for my role and get into my tree costume and my mom, maybe my dad too, would meet me at the school in time to watch the play.

"I left the house. It was a lovely spring day, warm and bright, and I was a beautiful, excited, happy little girl. I felt so pretty. I skipped along, thinking of wonderful things. All of a sudden I slipped and fell into a mud puddle. I mean, I *really* fell into a mud puddle. Briefly, I was stunned, as if the air had been knocked out of me. With a painful clarity, I knew I was no longer pretty or happy or worthwhile. I ran home, crying, tears covering my mud-flecked face.

"When I got home, my mom was so supportive. 'There, there' she said to me, 'we'll put a new dress on you and you'll be good as new.' But I knew that it would be my second best dress, not my best one, and I knew that I would only be pretend okay, not really okay. I knew I was filthy and degraded and an embarrassment and everyone just pretended I was a nice little girl."

I sat back in my chair, fighting tears that had welled up unexpectedly.

Dr. Brennecke looked over at me. "And you've been digging and falling into your own mud puddles ever since, haven't you?"

Over the past few months the character of our Main Four ward had changed. We now had more younger people and others less obviously psychotic. In the evenings a group of us would sit in the sunroom, singing limericks and extemporizing, accompanied by Neville, still playing the mandolin or ukulele. On occasion, he would switch to the flute or recorder. I liked Neville more than ever. He was even-tempered, bright, an extremely talented musician and very good at making up limericks, particularly off-colour ones. I thought he was quite outstanding, one of the few men in my life I truly adored. He was a psychiatrist-patient, as were Matt and John. No one could figure out why he was a patient; he seemed to be the most normal person I knew.

Three months after Neville had come to the hospital, we found ourselves alone in the kitchen. We were preparing coffee and, all of a sudden, we both stopped and looked at each other, hands still on our respective cups. We moved closer together. My heart sped up and a warm feeling perfused my body. Our lips came closer and closer together. We kissed. It was a sweet, long, tender kiss. Our hands still remained over the counter but our lips melded into each other. It was such a sweet moment. Then we disconnected ourselves, both smiled and made our coffees. Neville was old enough to be my father, but every time I saw him I got that warm feeling inside of me. He was such a gentle person. We both looked forward to hanging out together and always laughed a lot when we did.

Rick and Bruce, both in their early twenties, were still there. Rick was an English student at Amherst and Bruce was from Winnipeg. They seemed pretty normal too.

And then there was Rachel. Rachel, with her bright red hair flecked with white, was in her fifties. She was a grandmotherly type and was always fluttering around. Usually she spoke in non-sequiturs:

"I got a letter from my daughter today."

"Oh," I asked, "the red-headed daughter?"

"No," Rachel answered, "she's only twelve."

Lela, Neville and I would howl with laughter almost anytime Rachel opened her mouth. She didn't sing with us at night because our songs were a little too raucous for her, especially the one about the fucking machine, but she loved to play bridge. We had so many bridge players now we often had two tables going at the same time.

Lela, Betty, Rachel and I were playing bridge. We chatted amiably. Betty was somewhat frustrated because Lela and I were winning by a lot. They were playing a hand and, as Rachel went to take a card from the dummy, Betty whispered, "Think, Rach."

"But we're in no-trump!" exclaimed Rachel.

"We need to win at least one hand," whined Betty.

"You can't beat us, Betty," I smiled.

"You don't think this game can be good for us?"

"If it is, then it has to be, but it's not, so it isn't." I was very philosophical.

"Tell me, Mrs. Philosopher, if you are so smart, what is faith?" Betty asked.

"Faith? What are you talking about?"

"Well, my doctor and I were talking about faith. What do you think it is?"

"Hmmm. What do I think faith is?" I scratched my head, and threw one arm over the back of the chair. "Well, when I get high, I *know* I am going to come down okay. That's faith. When I'm in an airplane, I don't know if I'm going to come down okay."

Just then there was a ruckus in the elevator. The doors opened and an angry Margaret Bullard was led out by two aides. Jorge had his hands on Margaret's arm and she was trying to shake him off.

"I demand to be let off this ward!"

"Now, Margaret," Mrs. Lohmer came up to her, "you know we need to keep you here for a while, at least until we talk with Dr. Stepford."

"Well!" huffed Margaret, as she stormed to her room. Jorge collapsed on the sofa in a fit of laughter.

"Jorge, what happened?"

"Well, you know the public offices in Rockville, the civic offices?" We nodded. "Margaret went into them at lunchtime. She picked an empty desk and set up her typewriter. When the guy came back from lunch, she wouldn't give him his desk back. She said they were offices for the public and she was the public and she was using that desk. They finally called the police. Still Margaret wouldn't budge. She was sitting there typing away. One of the police recognized her and called us. We had to drag her away from the desk." He was doubled over with laughter.

"Oooh, hoo, hoo," he laughed. "Those guys must really wonder. Last week Ward took that new aide, Barry, into Rockville. When they got in front of the civic offices, Ward saw a police officer and put a citizen's arrest on Barry for stealing his money. Barry tried to tell the police that Ward was a mental patient and he was just holding his money, but the police believed Ward and took them both down to the station while they tried arresting Barry. Oooh, hoo, hoo," he laughed.

We turned back to our bridge game and tried unsuccessfully not to giggle as Margaret came onto the sun porch and set up her typewriter.

Chapter Seventeen

Rockville, Maryland; April 1965

Excitement mounted as our play's opening night drew near. Sid and Ward were still doing well. Only some patients on the production crew had flipped out and they were replaced. We were now rehearsing with the sets and costumes. Donn had sent away to a costume house in New York for our costumes and we had all gone to the Center for fittings. Two more days to go. The whole hospital was abuzz about this production. There hadn't been one this big for years.

Every night I fell into bed exhausted from rehearsals and from the stress of not wanting to do anything that would cause me to lose my privileges. I was very excited about the play and did not want to jeopardize my participation. One night, the week the play was to be performed, just as I was falling asleep, my door quickly opened and shut and someone approached me in the dark.

"Ruthie." It was Bruce.

"Bruce! What are you doing? Get out of here!"

"Ruthie, I just want you to be my Jewish mama." And he lay his head on my breasts and grasped me with his hands.

"Bruce, are you crazy? Get out of here before I lose my privileges!"

"No! Just be my Jewish mama for a while. You know if you call them and they find me in your room, they'll pack you. You're a troublemaker. C'mon." By now he had dug in and I felt I would never get his head off of me.

"Okay, Bruce, two minutes. Then leave."

We lay still for what seemed like a very long time.

"Bruce, go, please." I was getting frightened.

"Okay, but I'll be back." He left. I did not sleep the rest of the night. In the morning, I quietly told Mrs. Lohmer what had happened. She said she would post an aide in the hall at night.

The night of the first performance was upon us.

"Come here, *chriso-mu*, let me help with your mascara." Lela looked stunning. She had put make-up on, albeit theatrical make-up, for the first time since she'd been at the hospital, and she was such an expert at it.

"Ooh, look how long your eyelashes are! Do you know you have beautiful eyelashes?"

She leaned over and kissed my eyes, then my cheeks, then my mouth.

Sid burst into the makeshift dressing room. "Break a leg, Lela. Break a leg, Ruthie." He had just learned that expression and was eager to show everyone how theatrically inclined he was. We wondered if he was starting to go manic.

My heart was pounding. Although I knew my lines well, I was petrified that I would forget them. Donn assured all of us that there were many prompters in the wings and we should just do our best. We did. The performance was a huge success. A lot of the staff and their families came, as well as people from the Rockville community. We had many curtain calls. These were enhanced by cheering coming from the patients allowed to see the play. Many were not really aware of appropriate theatre behaviour, but we didn't care – we loved hearing Bella gurgle, and Marsha yell, "Yay, team. Yay!" and George stand and rock, loudly vociferating, "Play." Rock. "Over." Rock. "Play." Rock. "Over." Rock. The insane cacophony was music to our thespian ears. We knew they were pulling for us and we were grateful for that.

The second night, we were even better, although by now, Sid was definitely beginning to go manic. Ward had perked up a bit as well, though still in character for the Reverend Chasuble. We had one day off, then we went to Georgetown Theatre, in downtown Washington, DC, to get ready for the big performance there.

We arrived at Georgetown University in the morning, and spent the day going over blocking for the new stage. We had a light dinner there and performed that night. It was a very stressful day for everyone. Sid was now completely manic and Donn had to decide whether or not to pull him from the show. We helped him decide not to pull him, promising that we would all cover for him. Ward was acting a bit strange, but still seemed okay.

And there we were, playing to a sold out crowd at Georgetown University Theatre in Washington, DC. Donn had encouraged his drama class to come out and there was not an empty seat in the house.

The first act went very well, with one exception. Sid and Ward got into a vigorous discussion backstage and knocked over a set. When the noise of the wall crashing down hit the stage, Lela raised her eyebrows in a very Lady Bracknellesque way and carried on. It could have been part of the play.

Donn was visibly nervous between the first and second act after he had talked with Ward and Sid. Ward was now giggling and couldn't stop. Sid was just moving fast.

Claire and I were alone on stage as the curtain rose on the opening scene of the second act. When Rev. Chasuble, aka Ward, made his entrance, he skipped up to Miss Prism and giggled, "And how are we this morning?" Giggle. "Miss Prism," Giggle, "you are," giggle, "I trust," giggle, "well?" Giggle. Giggle.

There was something endearing about the Rev. Canon Chasuble/Ward, his thick white beard covering an angelic face, looking as though he had just become a character of saintly proportions. His giggle was quite infectious and soon the entire audience was giggling. I tried very hard, and succeeded, as did Claire, not to giggle at all and to carry on. But by the time Ward made his exit, the whole audience was giggling and gave him a rousing hand of applause. He tried to come back for a bow, but Donn pulled him back.

There I was, alone on stage for just a moment before Sid, as Merriman the butler, came out carrying a calling card on a silver tray. Sid was a large man, almost six feet tall, looking quite portly in his morning suit. His thinning hair was combed over to one side and he appeared quite distinguished.

I glanced over to the wings and saw Lela watching anxiously.

Sid looked around, held out the tray towards me and said at record speed: "Mr.ErnestWorthinghasjustdrivenoverfromthestation.Hehasbroughthis-luggagewithhim." Then he curtsied.

This brought the house down. I had to wait quite a while to deliver my next line. Luckily, Merriman had few lines this scene, but all were delivered at break-neck speed – to the delight of the audience.

The play continued on its strange course. Ward aka Rev. Chasuble giggled on and off stage, and Sid walked and talked as though he were in a time warp. The rest of us just carried on normally. There were no more 'incidents' until the very end, when all of us were on stage. Jefferey, effeminate naturally, was extremely good in his role – seemingly born to act in Oscar Wilde plays. He made only one error, but one none of us were likely to forget.

At the end of the play, Jefferey, as Jack, has his final line: "I always told you, Gwendolen, my name was Ernest." Jefferey takes Barbara's hand. Ever so dapper, he looks deeply into her fluttering eyes and blurts out: "I always told you, my name was Gwendolen!"

Everyone howled with laughter. Funnier than Jeff's mistake was the look on his face when he said it. His eyes almost popped out of his head. Everyone on stage, except Lela, broke up! It took us several minutes to compose ourselves to finish the last thirty seconds of the play. That didn't much matter because the audience was hysterical and up on its feet bestowing accolades. Well after the play was finished the audience was still applauding, still laughing. This continued even more when Sid insisted on curtsying instead of bowing and Ward could not stop giggling.

By the next morning Ward and Sid were both completely manic and restricted to their units. I don't believe they could have even remembered any of their lines, but by then the run of the play was over. We were just grateful to have made it through the scheduled performances. The play was actually reviewed in a DC paper and we got very good reviews overall. Donn came to the hospital the next day for our wrap-up party and told us all how proud he was of our group. He suggested we take a few weeks off and then work on a new play. We felt so good, so proud. Dr. B. had seen two of the performances, one at each venue, and she was beaming with praise. I felt wonderful, a part of something substantial. The fact that I was in a mental hospital did not seem so disturbing now.

Rockville, Maryland; June 1965

Desmond had come to stay in Rockville for a while. He had rented a small apartment. Lela would go out with him occasionally. I would wait up for her and we would talk about the evening, sitting together on the sunporch. Once, Lela had asked Dr. Stepford if I could go out with her and Desmond. To our amazement, he agreed.

We pulled up in front of the Howard Jackson's in Desmond's car. I remember the fried clams sitting on the plate. I smiled at the people eating their meals and smiled at Lela. I did not smile at Desmond. I did not like Desmond. He made inane chitchat as we sat there.

"Peter walked through Central Park last week and saw some nice horses," he remarked.

"Who's Peter?" I asked.

"Just some guy from my building," Lela responded.

"Clams are good." Desmond put a clam-filled fork up to his mouth.

"Uh-hmm," Lela and I both nodded, while keeping our eyes on each other. We couldn't seem to take our eyes off each other. Ever.

We went back to Desmond's apartment and had a few drinks. My head spinning from the alcohol, I went into a small bedroom to lie down. I was also being considerate, leaving Lela and Desmond alone. Within minutes, Lela was on the bed with me, holding me and smothering me with kisses. It didn't take long for Desmond to come in and drag her off the bed. He took us back early.

Two weeks later, my father came down for a short visit. He took me and Lela and Desmond out for dinner to a lovely country inn. We all had a few drinks; maybe a few too many. My dad was trying to be so compliant that evening and not have any fights. It was difficult for us to get along and on those occasions when we did, we both tried to maintain the positive warm feelings as long as possible. It was normal for my family to have one or two highballs before or with dinner, and the three or four we all had were a sign of our nervousness. I don't believe my father thought that anything untoward was happening. We were all getting along well, chatting, laughing – truly, it was a very pleasant evening.

My dad drove us back to the hospital, with Desmond in the front seat talking business with him. Lela and I were sitting very close to each other in the back seat. We could not keep our hands or lips off each other, even though I knew my father was trying hard not to look in the rear-view mirror. I knew he saw us and I knew Desmond did too. I wanted to be respectful to my father, I really did, but I had so little chance to physically connect with Lela without being torn away from her and thrown in a pack, that I just couldn't waste this opportunity; it was as though my body and hands and lips were not mine, they were attributes of Lela's body and they were just going home where they belonged.

Neither my dad nor Desmond ever spoke of the kissing that went on in the back seat, either to me or to Lela. That night was the last time I ever saw Desmond. He went back to New York City the next day.

Rockville, Maryland; July 1965

"Guess what, Ruthaiki!"

"What?" Something told me I did not want to know.

"I'm getting out of here soon."

"When?"

"Well, Dr. Will says soon, this summer, maybe two months."

"Lela, that's great." Tears came to my eyes.

"Ruthaiki," she put her hand on my arm, "I will go back to New York and get settled and wait for you. When you get out, you can join me. Then we will go to Greece together, okay? *Endaxi, chriso-mu?*"

"*Endaxi*, okay. But Lela, what about Desmond?"

"Now Ruthie, you know that I broke up with him. He had me thinking I couldn't do anything without him. I won't let him back into my house. My brother Bill is arranging to change the locks on my apartment and the doorman won't let him up. It will be okay, you'll see. Come, let's go for a walk."

By now, the two of us walking on the grounds holding hands was a familiar sight. We walked to our favorite tree, a huge oak tree not far off the road. We always sat against it, facing the woods. Low hanging leaves made a private little house for us. We would sit there holding hands or with our arms around each other and talk.

On our way back to the ward, we passed by Daisy sitting in an armchair just off the road. Beside the chair was a small table with a vase full of crocheted items.

"Hi Daisy, how are you today?"

"I'm not Daisy, I'm Mary."

"Okay, Mary, how are you today?"

"Just fine, thank you. And how are you?"

"Fine. What are you making?"

Her hands moved quickly and expertly. "I'm knitting a penis," she said.

"Oh yeah? Can we see?"

"Sure." And she handed over an anatomically correct crocheted yellow and red penis for our inspection.

"I also have here a kidney and a liver. Look." She pulled out a crocheted kidney and a crocheted liver. "I'm doing all the parts."

"Great, Mary. Keep at it. Good work." We continued on our way. Encounters like this were no longer unusual for any of us.

I walked into the low white building, and into Dr B.'s office. She had recently switched offices, into a new building which did not house patients and consisted only of offices. It was a quieter building and I liked these offices better than the older ones.

"Why do we always have to talk about the past?" I yelled. "Why is it always the past and the future. What about the now?"

"Well, what about the now?" Dr B. asked.

"In a weird way, the now could be good," I calmed down a bit. "Being with Lela is all I want anyway, after getting out of here, of course."

"Of course," Dr. B. echoed sardonically.

"Listen, Dr. B., living you in the now is the real." I really did imagine myself quite the philosopher.

"That may be true," she countered, "but no more real than the past and the effect that it has had on your 'now.'"

"But being with Lela is so....so...." I groped for the right word, "so gentle. It's so gentle, and when I'm with her, I feel so beautiful – and so loved. What's wrong with that?"

Dr. B. sat in her usual expectant silence.

"I mean, if I could redraw that picture, you know, the one of the little girl in the tornado, now it would be a beautiful woman with a very small tornado in the background, growing smaller."

"That would be very good. If that were all. Tell me some more about growing up."

The next day, I bounced into my session, all excited.

"Wow, Dr. B., you should have seen her!" I was describing Janie's latest meeting with Quentin and the resulting pack. "This time it took six aides to get her into the pack. Amazing, she's just amazing," I shook my head in wonder.

"But you know," I continued, "I don't get it. I'm not like that. I don't have hallucinations and I'm not out of contact with reality or particularly paranoid – at least, no more than normal," I smiled. "So why am I even here?"

"Ruth, not every patient here has to be psychotic. Many patients here are simply neurotic, have just had problems in their lives that need sorting out."

"Yeah, but problems that need Freudian psychotherapy? Is that what we're doing here, anyway?"

"The process we use here is psychoanalytically-oriented psychotherapy, but it's really not very relevant what we call it. What is relevant is getting you better and out of here. Therapy like this can benefit anyone wanting to learn more about themselves. Tell me about growing up in Winnipeg. You have barely mentioned that."

"Well, maybe that's because I can barely remember things," I suggested. "But I do remember a few things."

As I sat back in the comfortable armchair, I thought about the difference between sessions with Dr. Evanson and Dr. Brennecke. In the former's sessions, we rarely lasted the allotted time – he would always send me away early. He sat in a chair behind a very large desk, papers stacked up in seemingly important piles in front of him. I sat across and to the side on a hard daybed covered in an ugly patterned red and yellow blanket, and leaned against the wall. I was rarely comfortable, physically or psychically. Dr. Brennecke's office was warm and welcoming. We each sat in an armchair, made from a soft fabric in a mellow brown pattern, not directly facing each other, but more side to side. The chairs were plush and large and I was very comfortable in mine. I could slink down into it, or sit forward, or cuddle up in it with my legs underneath me. There was a wonderful landscape painting on the wall across from me – warm, golden meadows with brown and white cows languidly grazing under a blue sky. I could almost hear them contentedly chewing their cud. I had given them all names and would, on occasion, refer to them by name. Dr. B. understood. Dr. Evanson likely would have had me packed for doing such a "crazy" thing.

"Growing up in Winnipeg…." Dr. B. reminded me.

"Oh, yeah, growing up. What a bummer. My dad and I were always fighting, you know, because I hated the Jewish kids and didn't want to hang out with them."

Dr. B. raised her eyebrows in a question.

"Well, they always made me feel so fat and stupid. And the girls were always talking about boys, and who kissed who or who held their hand. It was so stupid! I hated them. I felt so…. so ugly around them. And stupid too. Besides, I was really into sports and nice Jewish girls didn't do sports."

"They didn't?"

"Oh, no, never. Not in Winnipeg. Nice Jewish girls went out with nice Jewish boys. Sports was never something they would do. Might get their pretty skirts dirty," I sneered. "I loved basketball. I was even captain of our team, several years. I played basketball all through junior high and high school, and then was on the University team for four years. We played all across Canada. My parents never –I mean never – saw me play basketball. Not once. Of all the times I asked them to come, they never came once. Oh, my mom came to see me in school plays and to hear me debate on the debating team. But they never, ever saw me play basketball. Or do any other sports. I even won the provincial medal in track and field. I remember coming home very excited. For me, it was a big thing. To win provincial, first you have to win your grade, then your school, then your district, then your city and so on. And I did. I won them all. I was a discus thrower and a runner. I trained really hard, running every morning for hours before school. And when I went to the provincial track meet, I was really sad that my parents were not there with all the other parents. Most of them seemed so proud of their kids, and my folks acted as though I were doing a bad thing. So when I won the provincial track meet, I was so excited. I ran home. I remember running down our street, exhilarated, waving my trophy in the air, yelling, 'I won! I won!' My mom and dad were just leaving the house to go out somewhere. 'That's nice dear,' my mom said. 'We're going out, please take care of the kids until we get back. We'll be back in about four hours.' And that was it. They left. And my win was never mentioned at home again, even though I was written up in the paper."

"You must have felt hurt by all of that," Dr. B. observed.

I looked up at her through the tears now forming in my eyes. "Naw, it was okay. I get it. Jewish girls just don't do sports. But I wish just once, they would have seen me do something in sports, any sport – you know, watch me do something I was good at. Just once. But they never did. Yeah, I guess I was a little hurt. But mostly I hated those stupid Jewish girls. And I hated that I was so different from them."

We sat in a comfortable silence for a while as I remembered.

Winnipeg, Manitoba; October 1957

"*Mom, I have to eat early tonight, okay?*"

"*Oh, Ruthie, why? It's* Shabbas *and you know your father likes the family to have dinner together on Friday nights.*"

"*Yeah, but mom, there's a Young People's dance tonight and I really want to go.*"

"*Oh Ruthie, for heaven's sakes, that's at the church! How can you go to the church on* Shabbas, *our family dinner night? What will your father say?*"

"*I don't care what my father says. He doesn't understand. I don't like being with my family and I like being with my friends. These kids are my friends.*"

"*Oh Ruthie, don't be silly. They are not even Jewish!*"

"*Mom, I hate the Jewish kids. I hate them! All the girls want to do is sit around talking about the boys. They are so stupid. I don't want to do that. Anyway, I don't care what dad says. I'm going to the church tonight, whether he lets me or not. I don't care about stupid dinner.*" *I stamped out of the kitchen and up the stairs to my room, slamming the door behind me.*

I tried to sneak out of the house before my father came home from work but as I came down the stairs, I saw my parents whispering urgently together.

"*Where do you think you're going?*" *boomed my dad.*

"*To the church. To the dance.*"

"*Ruthie, you have to stop going out with gentile kids. What's wrong with the Jewish kids? Why can't you go to dances at the synagogue?*"

I replayed my conversation with my mother just ten minutes earlier. "*Dad, I hate the Jewish kids. They are dumb and boring and I hate them. The other kids, the ones at the church, they are my friends – the kids from the team, the kids I hang out with at school. I like being with them. They ask me to dance. They are more fun.*"

"You will join us at the table for Shabbas. *I will not have a daughter of mine leaving the* Shabbas *table to go to a church!"*

"Dad, no!" I ran back upstairs and slammed the door to my room.

Soon, I was eating as quickly as I could, ignoring everyone at the table so I could finish and go to the dance. The second I finished eating, I asked to be excused. I went up to my room, opened the second story window, slipped out onto the roof, climbed down a conveniently close tree and ran all the way to the church.

I knew that the next day we would have another one of our massive arguments. My relatives had all stopped dropping in on Saturdays because my dad and I would usually be screaming at each other. The house was always tense. If we weren't arguing at any one time, we would be very soon.

Rockville, Maryland; July 1965

"I'm glad that I don't have a kid like me," I turned to Dr. B. "There was nothing they could do with me. To punish me, every time I would go to the church dances or out with my non-Jewish friends, they would try everything. If they withheld my allowance, I stole from my mom. If they locked me in my room, I crawled out the window. Sometimes I would run away for hours. Once I remember hanging out with some friends beside the river. We had a little rickety shack there, like a clubhouse. My dad came to find me. He grabbed my wrist and started dragging me home. Across the main street from our house was one of these large homes for bad girls, you know, delinquent girls – kind of like a prison, but not really. 'You see that place?' he shook my arm hard, 'the next time you run away, I am going to put you in there. I'm not kidding!' I remember thinking that I would run away again the next day, because I would be better off in that home. I was much more like those bad girls than like the daughter he wanted me to be. These fights went on for years.

"I really was a bad kid. I remember one thing – I used to hang out with these guys, Bobby and Ronnie and all their friends. They were sort of the juvenile delinquents at my high school. One night we were coming home from a party and one of the guys had a car. There were about eight of us piled into the car and I was in the back seat, sitting on Bobby's lap. It was wintertime and we had blankets covering us up. I felt Bobby's hand move up my leg under my skirt. It felt nice. Then I felt it go even higher. All the while, everyone in the car was laughing and rehashing the party. I was quiet because I was concentrating on Bobby's hand. Soon I felt his finger slide under the elastic of my underpants. Really, I wanted him to do that. It really felt good. In the meantime, everyone else was laughing about something that happened at the party. Then his finger slipped inside me. I was so wet I thought his finger would slide all the way out again, but it didn't. I moved a little on his lap. I never wanted that to stop. I really liked how it felt and I didn't care that I was in a car with seven other people. Then he slid several fingers in me and started moving them around. We were covered by a blanket but I think people might have suspected what we were doing. When we finally got to my home and I had to get out of the car, I didn't want to disengage myself. So you see, my dad was right. I really did belong in that home for the delinquent kids. I should have gone there a long time ago."

"Did you ever go out with the Jewish kids?" Dr B. inquired.

"Sure, I tried. Once there was this guy named Frank. I met him at a bar mitzvah dance. He was a good dancer, I was a good dancer, and we loved to dance together. So we started going out sort of, meeting at the bar mitzvah dances. There was one almost every Saturday night in those days and I always got invited because, well, all the Jewish kids got invited. Anyway, once Frank actually asked me out to one of these dances, like a real date. I had never had a real date before. I was really excited. I thought maybe I could be 'normal' after all. My parents seemed very pleased that I was going out with a nice Jewish boy. He arrived to pick me up, wearing his brown suit and red tie, and he was polite to my mom and dad. I had on my blue dress with the crinoline because I loved how it swirled when we jived together. I was actually happy. Frank and I walked together to the synagogue social hall, holding hands in the street as we walked. I felt so proud – and normal. When we got there, we started dancing. I don't think we missed a dance for the first two hours. Then, in mid-twirl, three of the guys tapped Frank on the shoulder and asked him to come out with them for a minute. I never saw him again. I waited for hours, but he was gone. I looked at the other guys who had come back into the room, all smirking and talking among themselves. I couldn't understand what happened. I finally gave up waiting and walked home alone, tears rolling down my cheeks. I quietly snuck into the house – a reverse kind of thing for me 'cause I was usually sneaking out – but I didn't want my parents asking me how the evening went.

Years later, I found out that the guys had taken Frank aside and told him not to hang out with me because I went out with the *goyim*, you know, non-Jewish kids. "She dates *shaygetz*," they told him. They said that if he continued to go out with me or dance with me, they wouldn't hang out with him any more. They told him to leave the dance and he did. Somehow, I never really blamed Frank for this; I mean, he wanted friends too. But I hated those other Jewish guys. And after the Frank episode, I never went out with Jewish guys again until my husband."

Chapter Eighteen

Weeks passed. Most of our original theater group were halfheartedly rehearsing for another play – minus Sid and Ward, whose manic actions and vocalizations were now known throughout the hospital. Maybe it was because of the emerging summer, maybe because of the success of our first play, but our drama group wasn't quite so enthusiastic this time. Lela was not in it because she was planning to return to New York soon. Things were okay with Dr. Brennecke, but I felt we were at a bit of an impasse. I knew that I was approaching a time when I could no longer shy away from the intense inner feelings that were plaguing me and that I would have to talk about them with her in order to progress.

I had wanted to tell her how I felt about my breast, or lack of it; I still thought of it as my deep dark secret and did my best to hide it when showering or getting dressed, even when I had my "arm-to-arm special" shadowing me twenty-four hours a day. All my feelings of being inadequate, physically and mentally, were still plaguing me. Somehow I was unable to calmly talk to Dr. B. about it. That malformed breast was the one thing that tormented me more than anything. It was the symbol, the external manifestation, of the fact that I was so flawed. I didn't want to be a flawed person.

We started talking about the possibility of my going back to school.

"I'm too stupid," I sulked one day, scootching deep into my armchair. I can't do *anything* right and no one understands me anyhow."

The eyebrows went up. Dr. B. was masterful at asking all kinds of questions non-verbally.

"No ones understands me," I repeated, feeling mighty sorry for myself that day.

"Maybe some of your problems come from being too smart," Dr. B. remarked.

"Oh yeah, that's right, me, too smart. That'll be the day."

"It's a possibility that your being intelligent has not worked to your advantage, has led other people to misunderstand you. It's a possibility," she mulled.

Winnipeg, Manitoba; May 1956

I was twelve years old and in ballet school. I hated ballet school and would much rather have been playing basketball. I was the youngest student in Madame Grandpierre's oldest class. Most of the other girls were sixteen, and I was only twelve. I think Madame Grandpierre did not know what to do with me so she just stuck me in the largest class. We were in the Winnipeg Playhouse, getting ready for our annual ballet recital. Each class did one or two pieces, to show off our progress during the year. My class, the oldest class, had all the 'good' dancers, not including me. I would much rather have been with the less good dancers, since that was definitely my category – less good. Maybe she hoped I would just disappear in the sheer numbers of that class.

Carol, the sixteen-year old star of our class, was preening in front of the mirror, putting on extra make-up. I kept pulling up my white tutu, trying to keep my nipples hidden, as the white flimsy material kept slipping down my completely flat chest exposing those little pink buttons to the world. There really was nothing to hold it up.

Magdelaine had just come into the dressing room. The girls were all talking excitedly about being on such a big stage and the word 'modest' was used.

"What does that word 'modest' mean?" I asked. I was only twelve and the rest of them were all in high school.

Carol explained it to me carefully, proud of her new role as teacher. "Do you understand now?" she asked.

"I do," I replied. "Thanks so much for explaining it to me, Carol."

Just then Magdelaine whipped off her clothes and strutted around nude in the dressing room.

"She sure is 'modest' isn't she?" I laughed, proud that I could use my new word in an ironic joke.

All six of the girls began jeering.

"You didn't understand that word at all," Carol said.

"Honestly Ruthie, you are so stupid," said Magdelaine.

"No, no, I did understand. I was making a joke," I protested.

"Sure, sure, I bet."

"Dummy."

"Honestly, I don't know why she is in this class in the first place."

I tried to explain again that I really did understand, but to no avail. I went over to the corner of the dressing room and quietly waited for our performance to begin, ashamed of myself and not really understanding why.

Our recital piece was about to start. Madame Grandpierre had carefully rehearsed us over and over. The Chopin started and we all readied ourselves to enter the stage en pointe, *from the tallest to the shortest, our right arms around the waist of the girl beside us, our left arms curved up over our heads. Carol led, her lithe body* en pointe, *her right arm gracefully leading the way onto the stage. All twelve of us were to be up on our toes. I was last – the youngest and the shortest and now, according to all the others, the stupidest. I was fighting tears, and not really thinking about the dance. I gave the top of my tutu one last desperate tug upwards as I felt Marie, beside me, rise up on her toes. I followed suit. I was the last to enter onto the stage, just before we were to form a circle. As I came forward tippi-toeing onto the proscenium, I tripped over a large chain that was holding the heavy red velvet curtain in place. The chain rattled, I stumbled, Marie stumbled, the girl next to her stumbled, and this continued all the way down the line, through Magdelaine and up to Carol – one big line of stumbling ballet dancers trying to balance on their toes and failing, lurching onto the stage at the Winnipeg Playhouse. I started to laugh. It was funny, really, all the girls up on our toes faltering in our attempts to stay upright. Even if it were my fault, it was still funny. Madame Grandpierre did not think so. That night was the last night I ever wore a tutu or danced ballet.*

Rockville, Maryland; July 1965

I started laughing as I recounted this for Dr. B. "Everyone was *so* serious," I said. "You would think I did the worst thing in the world. I mean, I did feel badly, knocking the line over like that. I was pretty clumsy, tripping over the chains. What made it worse was that the audience burst out laughing. That really made Madame Grandpierre angry. This was supposed to be a serious ballet performance." I grinned. "Ah, the end of my ballet career."

"But Ruth, you see how you were misunderstood by the girls. I think that is something worth thinking about. I suspect you have been misunderstood many times in your life and have been mistaken for being stupid when, in fact, you were actually more intelligent than anyone believed. Think about it."

I did, but somehow, I still felt stupid. I always felt stupid, no matter what happened.

There was a summer party at the Center. It was one of the rare occasions they had alcohol, served in a punch. A dance was held in the main room, but most of us sat about in the sitting room, talking. Lela and I went outside for a few moments.

My standing there with her under the moonlight, realizing that I would not see her when she left the hospital the end of this month, caused a panic to bubble up inside me. Much to my own surprise, I found myself urging, "Lela. Run away with me. Tonight. Please. Let's go right now. We can take Jeff's car."

"Oh, Ruthaiki, I can't run away with you. I'm going home soon."

"Please, Lela, I can't stand not being with you. Let's run away. We can go to Greece. They'll never find us there."

"*Chriso-mu*, don't be silly. We can't do that."

"Lela, I want to be with you, to hold you, to love you."

"What? We don't even know what to do with each other. You want us to get into ridiculous positions and pretend to have sex? I don't even know what two women do!"

"Lela, please, we'll figure it all out. We've been doing okay so far." I was hurt by her last remark, especially since we had been spending so much time lately being physically intimate and romantic with each other, with no problem whatsoever knowing what to do.

She put her hand on my arm. She was gentler now. "Ruthaiki, listen, I am getting out of here in a few weeks. I don't want to jeopardize that. You will be getting out soon. Then we can go to Greece together, just like we planned. *Endaxi*? Okay?"

She raised her eyes. I looked at her thick, dark hair falling over her shoulders and ached for the wanting of her.

"Come," she said, "let's go back inside. There's a party going on." She gently put her right arm around my shoulder and eased me back through the doorway. Almost immediately, she went off to talk with Jefferey.

I looked about the kitchen. Everyone had gone into the other room to dance or talk. I was alone. I was never going to get out of this place. Some big changes had to happen. I felt abandoned and stupid. I could feel my heart pounding in my chest. With no idea as to what I was planning, I grabbed an almost empty bottle of Canadian Club off the counter and ran out the back of the building into the parking lot. Across the parking lot was Dr. Brennecke's new office, where we had been seeing each other the past month. All along the perimeter of the buildings and parking lots were thick bushes. It was dark now, the trees in the woods mere shadows – the buildings, outlines. I crawled into a little space between a building and a bush, just off the parking lot. It was directly across the doorway from Dr. Brennecke's office. I had an appointment with her at 7:00 a.m. I squatted against the building, not fully understanding why the tears were flowing down my face. I felt as though my insides were going to fall out because of the pain in my heart. I couldn't bear to face anyone; I thought they would all know how miserable and deserted I was feeling – and then they would never let me go home. I decided that the smartest thing for me to do would be to hide there in the bushes until the morning and then tell Dr. Brennecke everything, to break the silences I had been locking up inside me. I would sit in a thoughtful quietude all night, as though on a vigil, and in the morning, I would walk in with her. She would not let anything bad happen to me. I drank what little rye was left in the bottle, sniffed and put the empty bottle down beside me. I put my arms around me and felt like a little child. I knew I could not go back to either the Center or the ward until I had talked with Dr. Brennecke.

I sat for a while in the darkness, becoming friends with the foliage. I was looking forward to my vigil, thinking how beautiful the early morning light would look on the trees.

All of a sudden, I heard footsteps running in the parking lot.

"Hey, Alvin, what's up?"

"Hey Derrick, Simkin's escaped."

"Oh, great! Let's go get her! I hope I find her first. Where do you think she might be?"

"Hey, Mrs. Marinides, where do you think she went? We want to grab her!"

I heard other voices, all running around like hounds getting ready for the hunt. Then I heard Lela, "I don't know about *you*, but *I* am looking for a human being."

I almost came out of my hiding place to say, "Here I am, Lela, here I am," but something in the voices of the male aides cautioned me. They were clearly excited by the chase. I pulled myself in closer together and hunched against the building. The safest thing for me to do at this point would be to wait for Dr. B. to come to work in the morning and walk into her office with her.

Lela came running back into the parking lot. "Oh, Jefferey, I thought she might be at our favourite tree, but she wasn't there. She may have gone into the woods. I don't know what to do."

"I'll get in my car, Lela, and drive around. Don't worry, we'll find her."

Just then, the engines of several cars roared into gear and two vehicles sped out of the parking lot with the hunters hollering directions. A third car started to move but stopped, its headlights shinning right at me.

"Oh shit, they've found me. Now what?" The car didn't move. There was sudden silence. My heart was beating clear out of my chest. I was sure they were sneaking up on me from the side. Still the headlights shone on my bush, still no sound except the palpitations of my heart, pounding in my ears. I was certain the beating of my heart could be heard all the way to Main Four. My mouth felt dry. I could feel sweat from my forehead. I just could not handle being roughed up and packed tonight, the night of my vigil. I thought if I could get away for the night, I would be fine. Once I could get to Dr. B. in the morning, I would be safe. I just needed to run into woods and elude them for eight more hours. I could do that. Still silence. Still headlights on me, blinding me to whatever was going on around me. I looked around and could see nothing, just lights shining on me. I was positive they were sneaking up on me, getting ready to grab me, roughing me up before the inevitable cold pack. I couldn't let that happen. I had to do something.

I stood up, grabbing the empty bottle by the neck. I smashed it hard against the wall of the building. I heard the voices yell in unison.

"There she is, grab her!"

"Get her, pack her!"

"Grab her, hold her!"

I stepped out onto the parking lot, still with the lights on me and unable to see anything in front of me. I held the neck of the bottle out, its jagged body clear in the headlights.

"Don't come near me," I cautioned, "or I will kill you." I waved the bottle out in the air. I started moving across the parking lot towards the trees. If I could get to the woods, I would be safe. I knew I could hide there. I looked over to see at least ten men standing huddled together.

"Don't go, she'll kill us."

"I knew she was dangerous."

Something inside of me laughed; me, a child, holding all these men at bay.

Just then Lela burst into the parking lot. As she started walking towards me, she was grabbed from behind by Alvin and Derrick.

"Let go of me, you oafs. Ruthaiki, come here. Put that bottle down. Let me go!" She kicked out behind her. Two more aides came to hold her as well.

"Now, Mrs. Marinides, you can't go over there. She'll hurt you with that thing."

"That's right, Mrs. Marinides, you need to stay here. We can't let you go near her."

"Stay away!" I yelled, brandishing my broken bottle. I was halfway across the parking lot, backing up towards the woods.

Just then I saw Lela kick Alvin in the groin and elbow Derrick in the stomach and pull loose. She ran towards me.

"Give me the bottle. Put that bottle down." She had her hand out toward me.

"Lela, don't come near me. I'll kill you."

"Now, Ruthaiki, you wouldn't do that. Give me the bottle." She came closer, followed by the pack of aides, cautioning her.

"Don't get too close now, Mrs. Marinides, she's dangerous."

Lela brushed back her shoulder as if to brush away these human fleas. Slowly, gently, she came nearer. "Give me the bottle, Ruthaiki. Let me take it from you. Come on, now. Put down the bottle."

Tears were pouring down my face. I could no longer see – not Lela, not the horde beyond her, not my future, not even tomorrow morning. Without feeling anything except the horror of what the future held for me, I started automatically slicing the jagged edges of the bottle up and down my arms, deeper, harder – feeling the release of the blood, not feeling any pain – hacking and slicing, up and down.

Soon Lela had me in her arms, the bottle beside her. I dropped to my knees and the pavement, Lela's arms still around me. She was kneeling on the asphalt, and I was lying in her arms. All the aides gathered around.

"Give me a tie!" Lela commanded. There was no response.

"Would one of you gentlemen please give me a tie. Or something for a bandage. She's losing a lot of blood!"

It seemed as though they were disconnected. They all stood watching as Lela tore the shirt off her back and started wrapping my arms. I felt nothing. I did not feel my wounds on the outside or the inside. I did not feel my body. I watched curiously, from above, as this beautiful woman soaked up my blood on her shirt. I watched impassively as ten men stood around, murmuring among themselves.

I watched as Dr. Evanson walked up.

"I am the doctor on call tonight. Well, well, Miss Simkin, what have we here?"

I felt Lela tighten her hold on me.

"Well, grab her, can't you see she's tried to escape? Don't just stand there, you idiots, grab her legs. Hold her down!"

I felt hands around my ankles. I could not tell if they were holding me tightly or not.

"As for you, Mrs. Marinides, go to your ward at once. We can handle her."

Lela looked up at the face of Dr. Evanson. "I am not leaving her now. Can't you see how upset she is?"

"Please, Dr. Evanson," I muttered, "please let her stay with me."

He smirked. "Will you promise to behave if Mrs. Marinides is with you?"

I nodded my head.

"Very well. Get the van and drive her to the hospital for stitches. Mrs. Marinides can go."

He went over to the side of the parking lot to talk with Alvin and some of the other aides while we waited for the van.

Lela helped me stand up and I leaned into the sweater that someone had put on her. The green van pulled up and I was placed in the back seat between Lela and Alvin. In the front was Derrick, and Dusty, the driver. Dr. Evanson got into his car and led us to the main gate. Just before the gate, he pulled over and we stopped behind him. He came up to the car and leaned in the back window.

"I would like to speak with Mrs. Marinides for a few minutes, to give her instructions about the hospital. Mrs. Marinides, would you step out for a minute, please?"

Lela rolled her eyes, gave me a squeeze and slid out of the van. Just then, six aides came from apparently nowhere and grabbed Lela as Steve slipped into her place. The van squealed out of the main gate, Lela's and my shouts drowned out by the screeching of the tires. I sat still, stunned by the betrayal.

At the hospital, I told Alvin I had to go to the bathroom. He told me he was not allowed to let me out of his sight and he would have to go with me. The image of his large black frame towering over me sitting on the toilet made something inside of me shift. I got up from the toilet, calmly walked out of the bathroom with Alvin right behind me – and then became a wild woman. As though all my adrenaline had been stored for this moment, I was stronger than all of them. I jumped up on a table and pulled over the large lamp. I knocked over the sterile trays. Four large men were chasing after me; I eluded them, laughing at the screams of the nurses. It was my mission to destroy the emergency room at Suburban Hospital, and I set out to do it with aplomb. Finally, with the help of many more hospital staff, they got me on a stretcher where they tied me down. Yet I was not settled enough for the doctor to stitch my arms. Even with the sedative I was given, I still struggled and would not remain quiet.

Then Dr. Brennecke walked in. She came up to me, put her tiny hand on my stomach and said, "Okay Ruthie, you've shown us all how crazy you are. We believe you. Now lie still and let the good doctor sew you up." And then she turned to the aides. "Wait outside for us please."

"But doctor, Dr. Evanson told us…"

"Wait outside. Never mind what Dr. Evanson told you. I am here now." She pulled up a chair and sat beside me. In twenty minutes I was ready to leave.

"I am taking her back. You aides can drive yourselves back in the van."

"But Dr. Brennecke, Dr. Evanson said we were to bring her right back to him."

"She is not his patient now. She is my patient. Don't argue any more. Now go." With that, she put her arm around me and limped out beside me. We got into her old white Cadillac convertible with the top down and drove back to the hospital in silence. She came up to the ward with me and walked me into my room. She would not let anyone else come in. On my pillow was Aristophanes, with a note pinned onto his red collar: *'O Aristophanes s'agapo poli.'* I translated for Dr. Brennecke. It means 'Aristophanes loves me very much.' She smiled. "Get undressed now, Ruthie. Get into bed."

She sat beside my bed and held my hand in silence until I fell asleep.

The next morning, two aides walked me to my hour. Dr. Brennecke dismissed them, although they insisted they had to wait outside for me. She hissed through her pursed mouth when they told her to call them if she needed them. Shaking her head, she led me into her office where we finally talked.

Chapter Nineteen

In August, just over a year after she had arrived, Lela was discharged and was going home to New York. My therapy sessions had become full of tears anticipating my impending loss. Now, it was upon me. I didn't know how I could bear staying behind without Lela.

I had been working very hard with Dr. Brennecke. I felt there was nothing I couldn't discuss with her. I sometimes thought of myself as an obsessive miner, digging away at a vein of feeling here, exposing a lode of guilt there – excavating the pain, freeing it from the darkened mine of repressed emotions.

One day I was sitting in her office raving about my father again.

"He is so mean. How can he be so mean?"

"Tell me more about this," Dr. B. urged.

"One day, I drove out to the lake. I pulled up in front of the cabin and saw that a lot of my relatives were there, my uncles and cousins. I walked in the door."

Falcon Lake, Manitoba; July 1961

"Oh, look, Ruthie's here," my father announced. "Let's play choo choo with her. But I want to be just before her."

My cousin Jerry laughed. "Okay, we'll play choo choo. C'mon."

"But I have to be just before Ruthie. I want to play it with her."

I grinned, confused but very pleased that my father wanted to play with me, whatever that meant.

"I don't know how to play this game, choo choo," I said.

"It doesn't matter. You don't need to know anything. I will show you," my father said.

"Okay," I shrugged, thrilled that my dad was going to show me anything.

I watched as my cousin Jerry trotted into the room, saying "choo choooooo" and picking his wife Carol from a crowd of people, he turned around and went off into another room with Carol trailing behind him. Then the two of them came back, choo choo-ing, and picked Uncle Abe and went off into another room. And then the three of them repeated the choo chooing, and the whole room was chosen one by one, with the choo chooing until there was just my father and I left. Then Barbara, the last person on the line picked my father, and I was left standing alone in the living room, still smiling that my father actually wanted to play with me.

"Choo choo, choo choo," they all sang as they trotted into the living room. My father then took me by the hand and I followed him into the other room. I watched Jerry kiss Carol, Carol kiss Uncle Abe, Uncle Abe kiss the next person and so on and so on until Barbara kissed my father and my father turned to me. I smiled up at him as I turned my face to be kissed, only to have him slap me across the cheek. Everyone burst out laughing, but no one laughed harder than my father. The tears burned my eyes as I ran from the room, their laughter echoing down the hall.

Rockville, Maryland; August 1965

"How could that possibly have been funny?" I asked Dr. Brennecke. "He laughed more than anyone. He only wanted an excuse to hit me. I hate him!"

Dr. Brennecke looked at me with kind eyes. "Sometimes," she said, "people have trouble showing their true emotions. Maybe your father wanted to show you something different but was unable to do that."

"Yeah, right." I grumbled.

"And what about the ping pong game? What was he trying to show me then?"

"What ping pong game?" she asked.

Falcon Lake, Manitoba; August 1961

It was a beautiful day at the lake. I was sitting outside reading my book.

"Hey," my father yelled at me, "how about a game of ping pong?"

"No thanks, dad, I'm reading right now."

"What's the matter, afraid to play the old man?"

"No, I just don't feel like it right now."

"C'mon Ruthie," this from my mother, "play with your father. Show him how good you've become. You never spend any time with him anymore."

"Ooookay." I started to put my book down.

"Wait, give me five minutes, then meet me around the back at the ping pong table."

"Okay dad." I thought maybe he was going to the bathroom.

Five minutes later found me at the ping pong table, along with more than twenty friends and relatives.

"Hey Ruthie," my Uncle Jim shouted at me, "your dad told us all about the big match."

"The big match? What big match?"

"The big match between you two. Your dad asked everybody to come watch."

I shrugged my shoulders and bounced the ball up and down on the red rubber-coated wooden racket.

"Ready?" my dad asked. "Let's go."

I threw the ball across the net for a rally.

"C,mon fatty, hit that ball," my dad spit out.

I returned the ball.

"C'mon, stupid, c'mon fatty, what, you're going to let your old man beat you? C'mon, you fat pig. Play like you mean it."

Tears sprung into my eyes as I tried not to let it show. I couldn't see the ball to return it.

"Ha! Point for me! C'mon stupid. Your old man is beating you."

This verbal barrage lasted the whole game. He did in fact beat me. I could not see the ball for the tears in my eyes and the pain in my heart. And the more he ridiculed me, the more everyone laughed.

Rockville, Maryland; August 1965

"That was so humiliating. I couldn't believe he would do that to me. But especially I couldn't believe that no one would stop him. He just carried on and on." I cried in Dr. B.'s office while she sat quietly beside me, holding my hand.

My work with Dr. Brennecke continued, vacillating between talking about my father, my family, my feelings and Lela, whose absence caused a physical pain throughout my entire being that at times felt absolutely unbearable.

The intense therapy work continued, and Dr. B. and I discussed the possibility of my becoming an out-patient.

"Guess what, Lela!" I said excitedly that night on the telephone. Lela and I had spoken every night since she had left the hospital.

"Dr. B. says maybe I could be an out-patient in November!"

"Oh *chriso-mu*, that's wonderful. That's great news!"

"Yeah, and then we can go to Greece, just like we planned. I can't believe it is all really happening," I gushed.

"How are you, Lela? How are things in New York?"

"Just fine, Ruthaiki. I'm waiting for you. Desmond tried to come into my apartment again today."

"Oh yeah? What did he do this time?" Every day since Lela had been home, Desmond had tried to weasel himself into her apartment, sometimes disguised as a delivery man, sometimes as a building mechanic. Lela would tell me about his latest escapade and we would both laugh. Then we would talk about going to Greece together.

"Today he tried to deliver some bagels to my place. I told him to leave them with the doorman," she giggled. She had sworn never to see Desmond again. Her therapist was delighted with that decision, but not as much as I.

"Well, I guess I'd better go now Lela – Mrs. Decker is starting to give me dirty looks."

"Okay, *chriso-mu*." We both said the Jesus prayer to each other and hung up.

The pain in my heart intensified. I missed her so much it was palpable. She was the first person in my world whom I ever really believed truly loved me. She was my world.

Rockville, Maryland; September 1965

One evening, I was talking to Lela and I could tell that something had changed. I heard it in her voice.

"Lela, what's wrong? Something is wrong."

"Nothing, *chriso-mu*, nothing is wrong." I knew she was lying.

It took three days for her to admit to me that Desmond had finally tricked his way into her apartment and her life and wasn't leaving.

"Lela, what will we do?"

"I'll figure something out, Ruthaiki. *S'agapo.*"

I love you too Lela." Lela began speaking to me again in Greek so Desmond wouldn't understand her.

The day after our last telephone conversation, Dr. Stepford came up to the porch in the middle of the afternoon, followed by Mrs. Lohmer.

"May we see you in your room please, Miss Simkin."

"Oh god, what have I done now?" I wondered, as the three of us walked down the hall.

"Sit down, please," Dr. Stepford motioned to the bed with his hand. "I'm afraid I have some bad news for you. Mrs. Marinides was found dead in her apartment this morning."

I must have collapsed into a dead faint. When I came to, they suggested I stay in my room while Dr. Stepford went to tell the rest of the ward, a suggestion that I refused.

"Please, may I go to the funeral?"

"I'm afraid that's quite impossible," Dr. Stepford responded.

"You don't understand. I must go to the funeral. Otherwise, I'll never believe she's really dead."

"We'll talk about it later," he answered, straightening his shoulders and his tie, getting ready for the unpleasant task before him.

I walked to the sunporch and sat in my rocker while everyone was rounded up for the meeting. Dr. Stepford told them what he had already told me. The staff then had to deal with some of the more upset patients on the ward. I rocked. I rocked and rocked for hours and wouldn't speak with anyone. When people inquired, I just said I was okay. I didn't want to share my love or my loss or my pain with anyone. Soon Dr. B. came to sit with me. We sat in silence into the evening.

The next day, Dr. Brennecke came for me early in the morning. We walked outside where she put the top down on the large old white Cadillac. We drove into the Maryland countryside in silence. The wind whipped at my face, at my hair.

I look about and see the azure sea. I am lying on the deck of our boat. Soon I am caressed by thick, black hair. Lela, leaning over me, places kisses on my face, then lies down beside me. I feel the wind, smell the salty air, my arms envelope her.

"S'agapo, chriso mu," she murmurs. My heart is bursting with happiness.

My heart is bursting with…pain. I look about the Maryland countryside. This is not Greece. This is not the ocean. There is no Lela. Lela is dead. I don't want to comprehend that. No! I won't! I look over at Dr. B. driving carefully yet quickly, both hands on the wheel – her lips pursed, deep in thought. I feel so confused. This is not right.

I sit very still in the car. I want to scream and flail about. I dare not move. I can't bear one more fibre within my being to hurt. I close my eyes. I open my eyes. Trees. Rolling hills. It is quite beautiful. But it is not Greece. Dr. B. is not Lela. Lela died. She really left me. She left me. I thought she loved me, but she left me. She could have waited. She could have called me. She could have come to get me. She could have written me a note. She didn't know she was dying. It was an accident. But she couldn't have really loved me if she died. I stopped the cacophony in my head by turning on the radio. Beethoven's Seventh Symphony poured out. One of Lela's favourites. I started to sing along to the Third Movement.

The words fell out of my mouth, "Le-la's dead. Le-la's dead. What – am I going todo? Ta da. Le-la's dead. Le-la's dead. What – am I going todo? Ta da da da da."

I didn't realize I was crying until I felt the kleenex Dr. B. proffered. I started singing and blowing my nose with the full accompaniment of Beethoven.

"Le-la's dead." Houonk. "Le-la's dead." Houonk. "What – am I going todo?" Sniffle snort.

The whole exercise was so ludicrous I burst out laughing, quickly joined by Dr. B.

Now the wind in my face was coming off the Maryland countryside and not the Aegean Sea and now the pain in my heart was oozing out, escaping through all my pores, infiltrating the car, the seat and Dr. B., who seemed deep in thought, dealing with her own pain. I scrunched deep into the seat and felt as much as I was able. The sobs came again. This time there was no singing or joking. Tears cascaded down my face, silently, quickly. How will I live my life without Lela? How will I fill the void left by her leaving? Why would I want to live anymore? What will I do without her? Who will love me? I felt Dr. B. touch my hand. I looked over at her. She smiled sadly at me. I gripped her hand fiercely as we silently sped through the countryside.

At the end of the day, she stopped at a drive-in and encouraged me to eat something.

"I have to go to the funeral, you know."

"Yes, I know. I'll talk with Dr. Stepford."

And so it was arranged. The hospital agreed to let me go only if Dr. Brennecke and Mrs. Lohmer came with me – at my expense, of course. They had armed Mrs. Lohmer with hypodermic needles in case I "acted out." I remember asking her to show them to me on the plane and giggling at how stupid the whole idea was. I didn't act out. I got better. I was going to live my life.

New York City; September 1965

The funeral was in New York. We flew down from Washington for the day. I had already met some of Lela's family and had been adopted by them as an honorary Greek kid. They all liked me and I them. We went straight to the church where we bumped into Dr. Will, Lela's doctor, who told us he had been walking the streets for hours. We went inside and waited for the funeral to begin. There couldn't have been more than thirty people there in the cavernous church. The time came to go up to the coffin. I wanted to see what was there. There was Lela, all made up and painted in a most unnatural way. But it was clearly still Lela. She didn't have the blue terrycloth robe on, but some other black dress. I believed it now. I believed she was dead. I paused over the coffin long enough to say our Jesus prayer for the last time.

After the funeral, we all went back to the family's hotel rooms, as most everybody was from out of town. There, I finally heard the story of what happened. Apparently the manager of the apartment building got a call from Lela late one night, saying there was a dead man in her apartment. He went up, and there was Desmond, lying dead on the floor. He called the police. Lela was very calm and cooperative. The police called the coroner, who said he would be there in a couple of hours. Lela called her brother Bill, who then spoke with the police, asking them not to leave Lela alone. Lela then told the police she was tired and was going to her room to lie down and to call her when the coroner arrived. When the coroner came, they went into her room to get her and she was dead. Drug overdose, they said.

I have often thought about what really happened and I think I know. Desmond and Lela were drinking, and had already taken some pills. Desmond said, "Lela, do what I want you to do or else I will take all these pills and kill myself."

Lela laughed and said, "Go ahead." So he did. Lela thought he was bluffing. When she realized Desmond really did kill himself, she took a sodium amytal to calm down and then had a drink, a double Johnny Walker Black, and then another sodium amytal when the police came and then another scotch – and then just two more amytals to help her sleep until the coroner came. And then she never woke up. I honestly believe that she didn't know she was going to die. She never would have left me like that. I know that.

When I returned from the funeral, I plummeted into a depression. Dr. B. insisted I have ground privileges. Dr. Stepford and the rest of the doctors went on record disagreeing with Dr. B., but since she was my therapist, I got the privileges. I spent hours each day sitting in the Kiosk at a small table, facing the wall, listening to the juke box play over and over the Beatles' 'Yesterday.'

Betty came up and put her arms around me.

"You're pretty depressed about Lela, aren't you, Ruthie? You must miss her very much."

"No, I'm fine," I smiled sadly at her.

Only to Dr. B. did I confide my profound pain and feeling of betrayal.

Rick and Rachel were out-patients. Lenore was somewhere in DC. Lela was dead. I sat and rocked. Dead. How could she be dead?

One evening, Margaret Bullard came out to sit with me. She placed her basket on the table and, sitting facing me, took out her papers and began to work. Within half an hour, without saying a word, she presented me with two delightful pen sketches of me, signed and dated by her. Wordlessly, she packed up her basket and left.

Two weeks after Lela's death, Dr. B. asked if I'd like to meet Janice, the new music therapist.

"Why? Why should I meet her?"

"Didn't you used to play the piano?"

"Yeah, but not for a long time now."

"Well, why don't you see how you like her. Maybe you can have lessons in the piano room."

This did interest me because the piano room was a tiny cottage of one room with a huge grand piano in it. The piano filled the entire room. Windows on all four walls looked out onto large trees. I loved that room and used to sit there with Neville when he played piano and flute.

"Well, I'll see her, sure."

I liked Janice. She gave me piano lessons nearly every day. I found that I liked Bach a lot and, within a month, was playing hours a day. I loved the solitude of the room and the precision of Bach. Playing for hours a day helped the internal pain. Soon Bach took over a very small part of Lela that was lodged in my heart.

In the evenings, I sat alone in my rocker. Neville had been quite precipitously discharged a few weeks ago. Usually, when someone is going to be discharged, everyone knew about it for weeks, maybe months beforehand. With Neville, no one seemed to know anything. One day, he was leaving. He was returning to his life – to resume being a psychiatrist, his wife and children by his side. I was very puzzled. I thought Neville leveled with me, but I knew nothing about this. I wished him well and kissed him goodbye.

Chapter Twenty

The next few months flew by. All I wanted to do was concentrate on getting out of the hospital. Autumn came and went and still I spent five hours a week with Dr. Brennecke. Most patients had one or two hours a week, but somehow she had arranged for me to come every day.

"I want to go back to school, Dr. B."

"Good. Do you know what you want to study?"

"I want to be a doctor, like you. You know, I thought I was too dumb to be a doctor, that I wouldn't be able to pass the sciences. But then I had all those psychological tests by Dr. Ricoh and she told me that I could pass anything I wanted. She said I was very intelligent. In fact…" I lowered my eyes, paradoxically uneasy about this next bit of information, "she said my IQ was at the genius level. What do you think?"

"Well, I agree. You can take anything you want."

"Yeah, maybe I'm not too dumb. Anyway, I want to try. I really want to get back to school. Could I try to register now?"

"No, but just as soon as you are discharged. Now, why don't we continue our work from yesterday?"

I admired Dr. B. more and more. I found out a bit more about her. She had been a famous orthopedic surgeon, specializing in orthotics for children. She worked a long time in the South. Because she chose to work with black children, she had dearly paid. Her ethics were more than the Klan could tolerate. Her life was threatened many times. Her home was burned down and her animals murdered. She came back to DC, where she opened a pediatric orthopedic hospital and became internationally well-known for her progressive work. At the height of her career, she decided to switch specialties.

In her late fifties, she started her psychiatric residency alongside much younger colleagues. She was ridiculed by many physicians for leaving a specialty like orthopedic surgery, especially when so successful, to become a psychiatrist. It was at this point that she got to know Dr. Evanson, when they were both residents on the same ward for one rotation. She subsequently told me that healing bones was not enough any more and that it did not necessarily help people to become healthy.

I was working on Bach's Invention No. 8 in the piano room, trying to develop more speed. I was concentrating on it and at first did not register the knocking. Finally I realized someone was tapping at the window. It was Ambrose, looking as though he had a juicy piece of news. I got up, stretching my arms and flexing my back, and went outside.

"Hey, Ruthie, have you heard about Neville?

"What about him? Isn't he doing just fine?"

Ambrose laughed. "You thought you knew him. You aren't so smart." He bent over to pick up a piece of string lying on the ground.

"He was in jail, you know. He was arrested and put in jail for running a homosexual whorehouse. What do you think of that?"

I was dumbfounded. Neville in jail was almost inconceivable. He was so straight and so normal. And a homosexual whorehouse! That was stretching my belief. I looked over at Ambrose, who was smirking as he picked some lint off his sweater. Ambrose did not lie.

"And…" drawled Ambrose, "after he was arrested and put into jail, he hung himself. He's dead now." Ambrose smiled that sick smile of his. "Yep, Neville is dead now."

I went back into the piano room, closed the door, and played wildly for the next two hours until my session with Dr. Brennecke began.

Rockville, Maryland; January 1966

I now spent my time either playing the piano, having therapy sessions, or alone. Very occasionally I would play a bridge game. Just after Christmas, Dr. Brennecke had convinced the administration I should be discharged. A lot had happened the last month. I found out that Dr. Evanson had totally lost it, and was now a patient in St. Elizabeth's. I could not find out any more details than that. Strangely enough, I was neither surprised nor moved by this news. Dr. B. told me that she had not approved of his appointment to our hospital because she had worked with him earlier and was concerned about his stability. She had tried to inform the doctors at Chestnut Lodge, but was overruled by the all-male administration. Perhaps my old doctor's new mental patient status helped the administration look favourably upon my discharge. I was told I could start looking for an apartment in the new year,

To my amazement, the first place I went to – Grosvenor Place, where Jefferey's apartment had been – had a vacancy of a one-bedroom apartment. I could not believe my luck. It was on the fourth floor, just perfect for me. I immediately arranged to leave a deposit. Jefferey had since moved to New York, but I still felt the building was a friendly one for me.

Then it was happening. I was going to be discharged and become an out-patient. I would just have to show up at ward rounds once a week and keep all my appointments with my therapist.

Before the big day, I was allowed to spend more and more time in my apartment getting it ready. I would come back to the ward late in the evening and fall into bed, leaving again the next day immediately after my session with Dr. Brennecke. I hated having to come back. I still had not spent a night in my place.

One day I was near the Kiosk talking to some of the new patients when Alvin and Derrick came up to me.

"Hey there, wild woman. How's it going?"

"Yeah, we heard you were leaving us soon. Good luck. But you know, we all thought that you were a lifer." Alvin gave my shoulder a friendly squeeze.

The days prior to my moving out, I spent as little time as possible at Chestnut Lodge. I would just sit on the floor of my as-yet unfurnished apartment and grin, thinking about what the future held for me. I loved not having anyone around me. The very first thing I moved into my new home was a record player and I played music constantly. Waiting for the bus to take me down the Rockville Pike back to the Lodge, I would make up words to classical music. I had worked my way through most of Beethoven's Seventh symphony, continuing with the lyrics I had started in Dr. B.'s car the day after Lela died. The entire symphony was about Lela. It amused me greatly to sing it to myself as I waited for the bus to come. Soon Beethoven's Seventh brought a smile to my face instead of tears. Lela would always be with me. I knew that. I knew that I could never live my life without her. I refused to do that. I could feel her surrounding me and the pain very slowly transformed into a warm loving feeling.

I remember well that Monday morning towards the end of ward rounds, when Dr. Stepford announced, "Well, I am pleased to make an announcement. Today, after rounds, Ruth Simkin will have the status of out-patient. I know that we all wish her well."

Rounds were over. And I was free. Just two years, ten days, and four hours later.

Within eight years, Dr. Brennecke and my parents came to my graduation where an M.D. was added to my name. I was now a physician and now I could write the orders. A whole new set of adventures had begun.

Epilogue

Victoria, BC; 2004

Mrs. Semple was living out her last hour on this earth. I pulled my chair closer to her bed, wrapped my hand around hers, and settled down to wait with her, to bear witness for this life that was ending. The year was 2004 and I was now a specialist in hospice and palliative care medicine, working at the Victoria Hospice. I felt very privileged to be doing this job and loved going to work, even though parts of it were sad. After more than thirty years of being a physician, I had become a good doctor, and felt I was able to help the majority of my patients. If I had time, as I did that day, I liked to sit with my patients, particularly those who were alone as they made their transition. There is nothing like watching a person leave this realm to make one aware of human frailty and mortality. I sank deeper into the chair and began to think about my own life and all the things that had happened to get me to this place.

"We all thought you were a lifer," I remember Alvin saying as I was getting ready to leave Chestnut Lodge. Those words still echo in my mind some forty years later. I recall looking at Alvin and thinking, "A lifer, ha! Not on your life!" – chuckling as I walked across the lawn away from the Kiosk. Little did I realize that the experience of being at Chestnut Lodge would indeed always remain with me for as long as I am alive. As it turned out, I was, in fact, a "lifer" – but in a different way than either of us expected.

I didn't know that I would come to think of the hospital as a training ground for life; that I would understand more than most about the inner workings of people and myself. I didn't realize at that time that my experience at Chestnut Lodge would enable me to square my shoulders and soldier on, to do the impossible in life. Having once done the impossible, it's not that difficult to do it again. And again. And again. And in these ways, and so many more, did I become a "lifer."

I also didn't know then that I would think of Lela almost every day of my life, for decades upon decades after her death – missing her viscerally throughout my entire being – as though part of me was cut away when she died and I was left with the pain of that dismemberment. Her picture sits on my dresser to this day and I usually have a daily chat with her. I imagine her responses and I still hear her deep throaty laugh in my head. Though my heart aches when I hear that laugh, I wouldn't want to live without hearing it.

Several years after my discharge from the hospital, I went to Greece and met all Lela's friends who treated me like family since they had all heard about me from her. I went to her grave and left her two lemons, because she loved lemons and hated fresh flowers. I couldn't buy 'morbidities'.

I continued my Greek lessons with Panaiotis Sapountzsis all through my stay at the hospital and well after I was released. We became good friends, seeing each other often. My Greek had become so proficient that at one point I was offered a job teaching Greek to English diplomats at the State Department. For many reasons I declined, but the pride of my accomplishment stayed with me for years. Taki's family adopted me and I spent many happy weekends at their home in Reston, Virginia, speaking not a word of English for days at a time.

The first thing I did when I moved out was to become 'Ruth' – after all, I was in my twenties and an adult. The second thing I did was try to learn how to behave properly in the "real world," as we patients used to call it. And to get used to time. Living in the mental hospital intensified everything. A day in the hospital was like a week or even a month in the real world – as it is when one goes to camp or lives in an accentuated environment. Time seems compressed and a friendship forged over two weeks of living together can seem to equal one of years in the making.

When I first moved out of the hospital into my apartment in Rockville, I had a lot of adjustments to make. I didn't realize immediately that the intensity of living in a mental hospital changes one's perspective on life. In the hospital it was considered normal to talk about one's fantasies – sexual or other – to talk about one's innermost feelings, whether they be negative towards someone or not. In fact, all these open expressions were encouraged. Not so in "real life." I found out very quickly that most people were embarrassed by my complete honesty and openness. I had to learn how to censor my thoughts and feelings, to stop them from coming out of my mouth.

My dog Peppy came to live with me almost immediately upon my release and that made it easy to meet folks. The dog-walking area of the apartment complex was always full of people and pets and it was not long until Peppy was friends with a little white bichon whose owners were two young women my age. We quickly bonded and I practised my "normal living" with them. I explained to them just a bit about my past, because I had yet to learn to censor myself. After they got over their initial shock, they helped me by explaining what was socially acceptable and what was not.

The third thing I did was attempt to go back to school. Rockville, Maryland, where my apartment was located, was considered a suburb of Washington, DC. There were many universities, colleges and junior colleges in the surrounding area – zillions of them it felt like. I got rejected from every single one. It simply had not occurred to me to lie. When asked what I had been doing the past few years, I answered honestly. I was actually very proud that I managed to emerge from the hospital in a relatively unscathed and functional state.

"How do we know you're not going to have another nervous breakdown?" I was asked.

"But I didn't have a nervous breakdown. I'm fine, really. Please just give me a chance."

No such luck. I went to a junior college and took the only three courses I had not taken before, got A1 on every one of them – and then was re-rejected by all the universities again.

"We don't take mental patients," I was told.

"But I'm not a mental patient," I would argue.

"Well, you were, harrumph, mumble, mumble. Good day." And so it went.

One particular experience remains from attending the junior college. It provided me with one of the more humorous incidents of my life. In a psychology class, the students were asked to describe the four different types of psychoses. Describe them, hell, I had been living with them all for the past two years.

"Hebrewphrenic," a young man ventured. I remembered David the hebephrenic who never spoke. Ever. Not in the two years I was around him. And I don't think he was even Jewish!

Another student had a try: "Catalonia." I remembered the catatonic Marsha, who never moved. She had lain on her bed for so long, the muscles in her feet had atrophied. When the new anti-psychotic drugs became available and she started to recover slightly, she had to have surgery before she could even walk.

"Simple Phrenic," ventured a third student. At this point, it was all I could do to not fall off my chair in hysterical laughter. There were numerous simple schizophrenics in the hospital. In particular, I remembered Andy, whose reality was so different from mine. He was sure he lived on an alien planet and the rest of us were blind for not seeing the obvious.

The students couldn't even manage to mangle paranoia; they had simply forgotten it. How could I ever forget Max or Margaret, two classic paranoid schizophrenics if ever there were any.

That incident in the classroom brought home to me how different my reality was from the average student. And almost half a century later, I still laugh when I recall hebrewphrenic, simple phrenic and catalonia.

One day, after yet another batch of university rejections, I saw an ad in the newspaper for a course beginning in a few weeks for lab technician training. I really wanted to go into medicine, but that was seeming more and more unlikely – at least being a lab tech was somewhat related. The day before I was to report for lab tech training, I was in a therapy session with Dr B. at her home, lamenting the fact that I would never be a doctor and had to settle for this simple job that was not studying medicine. I was hoping the nauseous feeling in my stomach every time I thought of being a lab tech would soon disappear. I really did want to be a doctor.

"I give up. I just give up," I sighed. "I really tried, but the people in admissions are just out of it. I tried to tell them I never had a nervous breakdown, that I am okay, but they all just smiled like they knew something I didn't know and shook their heads. I had to do something, so I signed up for lab tech school." The deep nausea returned. How could I become a doctor if I could not go back to school?

Dr. B. sat silently for a few minutes, deep in thought, then suddenly sat up in her chair and out of the blue asked me, "Do you have any objections to going to a Catholic school, one taught by nuns?"

I looked up at her, puzzled. "Any objections? No! I would go to school anywhere I could. I don't care if nuns are the teachers."

"Just wait here one minute," Dr B. said as she slowly got up, grabbed her cane and limped out of the room. After a few minutes, while I was left to pat Timothy the Rottweiler, she returned with a huge grin on her face.

"I have a good friend who works in the office at Trinity College. It is a small

Catholic university in Washington, DC with an excellent academic reputation. You are to report tomorrow morning at 9 a.m., when you will be interviewed by the Mother Superior. I am not promising anything, you understand, but if the Mother Superior thinks it is the right thing to do, she will let you attend college there. Is that alright?"

"Alright? It's fantastic! Oh, will she care that I'm Jewish?"

"I don't think so. And now, let's continue with our session. Where were we – I believe you were talking about your father…."

That was the only time Dr B. ever interacted within my personal life outside of the psychoanalytically-oriented psychotherapy we continued for the next four years.

I loved Trinity College. I entered as a junior (third year), but within a few months, I switched to being a sophomore (second year), deciding to stay longer and take a degree in chemistry and physics. As an undergraduate at Trinity College, I ended up doing cancer research for the National Institutes of Health. I also excelled in physical chemistry, where, together with my professor, I discovered a constant and published a paper on it, winning an award from the Washington Chemical Society. (A physical constant is a physical quantity that is believed to be both universal in nature and constant in time. There are many physical constants in science, such as the speed of light, or mass of electrons or protons, but my constant was much less significant.)

Another wonderful thing about Trinity College was that I fell in love again – with a nun. After she left the convent, we lived happily ever after for about four years. Her name was Eileen and I thought she was beautiful, both inside and out. She was extremely intelligent – to this day I am still turned on by sharply functioning grey cells! She was tall, about six inches taller than my five-four, and she had long, lush, thick curly brown hair.

One day we were walking through the campus, Eileen still in full nun regalia. A gust of wind blew her veil up off her neck exposing the beautiful head of hair that, as a nun, she was not supposed to have.

"Sister, your hair!" I exclaimed in surprise.

"Yes, isn't it lovely?" she said with a beatific smile. She was marvelous.

She had gone to Catholic schools all her life, then become a nun and lived in the convent for eight years, teaching at Trinity College. That was where we met, me fresh out of the "nuthouse," she just getting ready to leave the convent. That first summer we lived together in my apartment. Then Eileen went off to Berkeley to pursue a PhD. and we had a bi-coastal relationship for a short while. At Berkeley she was the house-mother for a non-denominational

Christian home for undergrads. When I went to visit at Thanksgiving, she told me she had just had an evaluation by the people who ran the house.

"You're doing a great job, Eileen, but we have one criticism."

"Oh, what's that?" asked Eileen.

"It's your language."

"My language? What do you mean?"

"Your language, Eileen. You swear. You use dirty words."

"Dirty words? Swear? What are you talking about?"

"Eileen, you say 'fuck' all the time!"

"Fuck? Oh, is that a dirty word? It sounds so natural when Ruth says it."

The previous summer, every time I had dropped something or stubbed my toe and needed an expletive, I used 'fuck.' Eileen thought it was an expression like 'golly gosh.' She had never heard the word 'fuck' before, and it never occurred to her that I would be swearing. This was in the 1960's when 'fuck' did not have today's common usage – except in mental hospitals and prisons and other such institutions.

After four years together, during some of which we travelled about the world, I wanted to go back to Canada. She wanted to remain in Washington, DC. It was time for us to part. I drove her back to DC to help her get settled. Since she had never lived there alone as an independent woman, I felt responsible for her. I wanted her to have friends with whom she could go for coffee and to movies or talk with. In DC, I took her to many gay bars, hoping she'd find friends to hang out with. I was quickly running out of time as I was due to return to Canada and school. The night before I had to leave, in desperation, I took Eileen to a humongous restaurant/bar where each table had a large number and a telephone. You could call other tables to ask someone to dance, or just to chat. It was a gimmick that seemed to work well. I did not know anyone there, but I was determined to find some friends for Eileen. I saw a table near-by of intelligent-looking (those grey cells again), interesting women engaged in animated conversation. I decided to call them up to introduce them to Eileen – but they didn't pick up their telephone.

"What snobs," I thought as I heard it ringing and ringing, unanswered. "Let's dance, Eileen." I took her hand and led her onto the dance floor. Two women from the rude table got up to dance too – it was then that I saw them signing.

"Oh, I get it. They're deaf." In my arrogance, I, who could barely finger spell and had never even heard of American Sign Language, signed "H" "I" to one of the dancers. She immediately stopped, came over and I laboriously spelled out our names. Her name was Kanny. Eileen could not even finger spell – but she could smile.

I left for Canada the next morning. Eileen and Kanny are still living together, almost forty years after meeting that evening.

Such a romantic story – something I wanted for my life. Fall in love, live 'happily ever after' – perhaps to make room, at times, for the 'unhappily' – but the 'ever after' would be a constant. But the romantic 'ever after' stayed with Eileen and Kanny, and passed me by.

If I thought I had been rejected from a lot of schools before Trinity College, I certainly surpassed it in 1969. I graduated cum laude from Trinity College and was then rejected from twenty-five medical schools in two countries. I'm glad that I had developed a little ego strength along the way.

"Too old." (I was twenty-five).

"Wrong country." (I was a Canadian citizen with a US visa).

"We already have our quota of women."

"Frankly, we're worried about your past history in the mental institution, mental institution, mental institution, mental institution……."

I now knew that being discharged was certainly not the end of my relationship with Chestnut Lodge.

After I graduated from Trinity College, I went to Winnipeg to visit my family. Before I euphemistically "went away," I used to play basketball for the University of Manitoba and so, of course, I ended up in the gym watching a game with all my old cronies, many of whom were now married with families. I was holding Deena's five month old, chubby-cheeked, adorable Amanda, bouncing her on my knee, googling baby talk to her while her mother, who had played forward to my defense, left the gym for a few moments. Amanda and I were both laughing at our bouncing game. When Deena returned to the gym and saw that I was holding her daughter, a look of absolute horror crossed her face as she ran up and grabbed Amanda from my arms and looked accusatorily at the woman who had given this "mental patient" her baby.

"It's not that I don't trust you, Ruthie," she stammered, "but after all, you were in a mental institution." Mental institution, mental institution – the echo continued, as I fought back my tears and the wrenching pain in my heart.

While in Winnipeg, I heard about a new medical school scheduled to open up in Calgary. They were accepting "unusual" students. I moved back to Canada, set up residence in Calgary and applied to the new school. If I didn't get in, I would become a farmer. The only two things I could envisage myself doing were medicine and farming. Since I didn't know anything about either, I applied to the University of Calgary and bought some land.

That first year in Calgary, before the medical school opened, was fun. I took all kinds of courses I hadn't before taken – biochemical genetics, immunology, virology – and thoroughly enjoyed them. The competition for the medical school, opening the following September, was fierce. There were more than twelve hundred applicants for thirty-two places. I got one of them.

The next five years were taken up with medical school. The rest of my life was pretty much put on hold as I studied and studied and studied some more. I was the first person from the University of Calgary Medical School to go into private practice. I became a specialist in family medicine and worked in Calgary as a family physician for the next fifteen years.

My personal life picked up after medical school. I met Maria at a Status of Women Action Committee meeting and we were together almost fifteen years. We were active in politics and the community. Each of us were on many different boards of directors, both health and arts related, as well as being passionately involved in the local, provincial and federal feminist movement. We were financially stable – we took trips to Fiji, cruises in the Caribbean, safaris to Africa.

In the early 1980's, I went to study at the Shanghai College of Traditional Chinese Medicine in Shanghai, China, and got my certification in acupuncture. Later in the 1980's, I went to England to study with Dr. Katarina Dalton, of PMS fame. I was proud of the work I did in medicine, both allopathic and alternative, and the work I did within the community. I was very proud of the home Maria and I made together. I was living in the real world and doing it right.

Maria and I jointly won the 1981 "Woman of the Year" Award in Calgary – we were both nominated individually but I thought it would be "romantic" if we won as a couple. Silly me, because "romantic" was definitely not something to describe the ending of our fifteen year relationship.

After our breakup, I left Calgary, traveled around the world again and then returned home. But it was all different. Maria was now living with a boyfriend. I was happy for her if she was happy, but regretted leaving in the first place. I wandered around my huge mausoleum of a house filled with memories of better times. I had trouble concentrating. I got more and more depressed. I tried to practice medicine but couldn't focus enough to do a good job. I got physically ill, but no one really knew what was wrong with me.

I decided to learn how to make holograms and opened Western Canada's first holography gallery. I became a business person as well as a doctor, but I've always been a better doctor than anything else. After about four months, I got bored. When I looked around for something else, oops, I got depressed again.

I decided to take some time off and go into therapy. That was a bad decision. After a disastrous experience with a psychologist who badly misused me, who would no longer work with me unless I completely severed relationships with my family, something I was not inclined to do, I found myself in Vancouver trying to get back on my feet again. I was extremely depressed at this time and almost non-functional.

I despaired for six months. Then an old friend from Calgary told me about a piece of property for sale on Salt Spring Island. I always did want to get a piece of land on an island and only moved to the city to facilitate therapy – a cosmic joke on me all right. In October, 1992 I came to Salt Spring Island. I saw and I bought – my despair left behind in Vancouver. Ten and a half acres on the ocean, an otter in the bay; a seal leapt out of the water, an eagle flew by. The October sun was so warm I walked about in a sleeveless shirt, and there just happened to be ripe berries and grapes waiting to be popped into my mouth. It was like Disneyland! By November I had moved to the land, where I lived in a small cottage before building my dream house. I was now a farmer.

I became a yuppie farmer for a decade, growing garlic and greens and missing medicine terribly. So I went back to school and became the first person at the University of British Columbia to complete a fellowship in Palliative Care, a relatively new specialty. I then went to the US to write my national boards. After passing them, I became a certified specialist in Hospice and Palliative Care Medicine. I loved hospice work and deemed it a true privilege to be able to practice in that field. I worked at the Hospice in Victoria, BC while living on Salt Spring Island, but I hated commuting. After a few years of rushing for ferries to go to work and rushing for ferries to go back home, I sold my dream house and moved to Victoria. My work as a hospice physician won out over my Disney-like Gulf Island property.

During the time I attended Trinity College, I saw Dr. Brennecke very regularly – initially three times a week, quickly dropping back to two and then one appointment a week. She sat with my very proud parents at my graduation from Trinity College and was quietly thrilled with my medical school graduation. While in medical school, we corresponded by mail and once or twice after graduating as a physician, I flew to Rockville to see her. We would often discuss "doctor things" as both of us enjoyed talking about medical issues together. Then one day I got a phone call from her minister telling me she had had a stroke. I flew out and stayed as long as I was able. She was in the hospital, and I spent my days with her, telling her about my experiences practicing medicine and reading to her. We recalled the time she had visited my parents in Palm Springs, staying for several weeks. My parents could not do enough for her. We all realized that, had it not been for her, I likely would have been written off completely and remained in that hell hole of a hospital. She was one of the most dignified women I had ever met – quietly intelligent and so caring. The fact that she had been administrator of the toughest unit in the hospital spoke reams about her. It was a job not many could have managed, but all the men from Main Three held her in great esteem and protected this diminutive woman who could not even walk without her cane. Her quiet dignity demanded respect.

Soon the stroke and an arduous life took her. I left Rockville, bereft. My friend, my saviour really, was now gone. She could no longer be my back-up plan. I was it. I loved her like my mother. And I miss her still.

Shortly after the death of Dr B., I phoned my father, by now remarried after the death of my mother. He was living in Palm Springs.

"Hi dad, I want to come down next weekend to talk with you. No parties, no barbecues, no nothing – just you and me talking, okay?"

"Okay Ruthie, if that's what you want."

It was. We talked for three days. We sat in his study and I told him everything that had been heavy on my heart.

"You know, dad, you really hurt me that time you played that stupid game choo-choo."

"But Ruthie, it was just a game, everyone was playing it."

"I know, but it was a cruel game and I was very hurt by it."

"I'm sorry you felt that way. Honestly, I didn't mean to hurt you."

"And that ping-pong game. What was that all about?"

"What ping-pong game?"

"You don't remember? You challenged me to a game and then insulted me. You called me fat and stupid. How could you forget that?"

"Oh Ruthie, don't you know how proud I am of you, of all that you accomplished? I don't think you are stupid. I really am so proud of you."

We spoke and cried for three days. I unburdened myself, but I didn't think anything would change other than I would have said what I had to say. But after that weekend, things did change. First I got a call from my dad.

"Hi Ruthie. You know, the other day I was on the golf course, and someone was trying to tell me something and I thought to myself, Ruthie was right, I really don't listen."

I almost dropped the phone. From that time on, for the next five years my father had left in this life, we became best friends. I saw him as often as possible and was with him, along with my family, at his death. Those five years made up for everything. We laughed together, cried together, hugged each other a lot and generally enjoyed and particularly respected each other. It was one of those gifts from life, to have those five years with my dad.

My epilepsy left me as it descended upon me – quietly and without any apparent reason. My last seizure was a quarter of a century ago and I no longer take medication for epilepsy. I seem to be able to stave off seizures. When I get a pre-seizure aura, I concentrate fiercely and it leaves – no seizure. Why I had the seizures, why I no longer do, will likely never be answered.

I have lived with animals every single day since I got out of the hospital. Mostly dogs, but I have also had cats, a pet bunny, a mynah bird and a pet pig, Willy, who lived in the house and wanted me to sing him lullabies so he could fall asleep. But dogs have always been my closest companions. The animals have always been loyal and loving, something most humans, myself included, haven't always been able to master completely. I can't imagine living my life without an animal companion.

Glass still lives with me, pretty much retired due to old age and leakage, but still very much a part of my bathroom décor, sitting proudly on a window ledge between an orange soap fishie and a purple ceramic turtle. And I still have that blue and white striped pajama top from the very first hospital I was in, although it is shredded from decades of wear.

Gradually I realized that when I walked out of that institutional door, I did not leave it behind. That experience is with me every day – not in isolation, but together with the totality of my past. I recently read that the past makes us who we are in the present. I like the person I have become – in spite of my experiences, or maybe because of them.

I know now that I no longer need a therapist, that I have all the tools I need to maintain balance in this insane world. For the most part, I am content with my life and grateful to be living it. I have become an integrated person and have discontinued my non-functional behaviour. I stopped believing in the fallacy that if I didn't do everything perfectly, I would get sent away again. I was sent to the mental institution because I was not the right kind of daughter. I was sent away from the schools because I was not the right kind of student. I was always trying to fit in, to do it right, whatever "it" was – except I never could, or wanted to or knew how. I was always unsure of myself, always questioning myself, always afraid I would be sent away.

That unsettledness was a legacy of the past; one with which I have now come to terms. But even as recently as ten years ago, I felt someone could come at any time and say, "You have to be locked up now." No more. I am solid within myself. I still struggle at times to maintain balance, but overall, I am succeeding. When my depression or self-hatred rear up, I am able to figure out what caused it and deal with it appropriately. I have become friends with my body, although I am no longer fat, a condition that plagued me for decades. I had been in so much physical and emotional pain because of my obesity, it simply did not make sense to continue on like that, so I am now half the size I was before and more than twice as content with myself.

I still want to trust people so badly that I trust everyone openly and willingly, another legacy which often leaves me hurting emotionally. I can't believe that everyone in this world is going to betray me. I am somehow reminded of Anne Frank – she who could think there is always some good in humankind. I guess that's how we survive. If I didn't believe that there was goodness in the world, I couldn't exist. I reframe my experiences again and again so that I can believe there is some sense and logic and love in this world.

Things happen that change our perspective in a split second. The other day I was driving along in the very early morning, top down on the convertible, humming and happy to be living on such a beautiful day. All of a sudden I heard a loud thump. I pulled over and there on the grass of the golf course to my right stood a deer. It stood on three legs, the fourth one broken by my bumper. I will always have sadness that I hit that deer, particularly when I drive by the golf course every day, knowing that a life was lost because of my actions. That's what happens in life – things stay with us, put in a place in our minds that hopefully allows us to function. The sadness will not ever go away completely. And so it is the same with the sadness, with the pain, from my past experiences; they will never leave me completely. I put them away and try not to dwell on them, but at times when I least expect it, the memories well up and flood my being with sadness, anger or confusion. I regain my balance, put the memories in a little place where they won't bother me for a while, and carry on. And so the cycle repeats.

For all the decades that I was a physician, I never forgot my past. I love medicine and I love being a doctor, but being a physician meant one important thing to me in particular: it meant that now I had the power. I had the power and no one, no one, was ever going to lock me up again. Never. And no one ever did.

Acknowledgements

A book does not exist in a vacuum. Many people have helped ease this into existence. Thank you to all my friends and family who have given me so much support and encouragement. I can't name you all, but I do thank you all. In particular, thanks to:

Joan French, the first person to hear parts of this book, who always asked for and seemed to enjoy more bedtime stories;

My uncle, Abe Simkin, who has been by my side from the second I was born and has never failed to believe in me, to support me and to show me nothing but love;

My wonderful siblings, Judi Simkin, Jack and Nanci Simkin, Sam and Carol Simkin and all my nieces and nephews – I could not ask for a more supportive and wonderful family;

My writing group: Mavis Andrews, Mary-Wynne Ashford, Rebeca Dunn-Krahn, Sharon McLeay, and Elana Scraba, whose much appreciated comments, enthusiasm and support urged me forward;

My four-legged friends, particularly Wolfie and Lupie, no longer with us, and the remarkable Reenie, who keeps me company when I write and fills my life with joy;

Carol Ann Sokoloff and Richard Olafson from Ekstasis Editions, the best publishers an author could have, who have made a very difficult process seem easy;

Dvora Levin, whose constant urging and cajoling have finally convinced me that I am, in fact, a writer. Her wonderful listening ear and intelligent comments have been invaluable. Without her, this book never would have come into existence.